UNITED E[
DIVIDED EUROPE

UNITED EUROPE
DIVIDED EUROPE

Edited by
Walter Baier, Eric Canepa
and Eva Himmelstoss

MERLIN PRESS

transform! Yearbook 2015
United Europe
Divided Europe

English edition published in the UK in 2014 by
The Merlin Press
99B Wallis Road
London
E9 5LN
www.merlinpress.co.uk

Editors: Walter Baier, Eric Canepa, Eva Himmelstoss

Managing Editors 2015: Lutz Brangsch, Dominique Crozat, Elisabeth Gauthier, Cornelia Hildebrandt, Kuutti Koski, Bernhard Müller, Sigfrido Ramírez, Barbara Steiner

Editorial Committee: Maxime Benatouil, Lutz Brangsch, Dominique Crozat, Teppo Eskelinen, Elisabeth Gauthier, Adoración Guamán, Cornelia Hildebrandt, Anej Korsika, Kuutti Koski, Vagia Lysikatou, Gregory Mauzé, Bernhard Müller, Roberto Musacchio, Sigfrido Ramírez, Barbara Steiner

Sponsored by the Rosa Luxemburg Foundation with funds from the German Federal Foreign Office

transform! europe ASBL, Square de Meeus 25, 1000 Brussels, Belgium
Partially financed through a subsidy from the European Parliament

Cover Illustration: Sandra Gobet

ISSN 1865-3480

ISBN 978-0-85036-628-0

Printed in the UK by Russell Press, Nottingham

CONTENTS

Preface

Walter Baier, Eric Canepa, Eva Himmelstoss:
        United Europe, Divided Europe   7

Syriza and Europe: An Interview with Alexis Tsipras   9

Essays

Étienne Balibar: Europe – Nations: The Missing People
        and the Crisis of Legitimacy   21
Walter Baier: The 'National Question' and European Integration   35
Elisabeth Gauthier, Joachim Bischoff, Bernhard Müller:
        Right-Wing Extremism and
        Modernised Right-Wing Populism in Europe   49
Frank Deppe: 1945 – 2015: What Does History Tell Us?   64

Divisions in Europe and Challenges for the Left

Steffen Lehndorff: The 'Austeritarian' Integration Dividing Europe   87
Patrice Cohen-Séat: Europe: A Lock and a Key   98
Gabriel Colletis: An Alternative European Industrial Policy?   107
Marc Delepouve: A Left Project for Research in Europe:
        Some Principles and Proposals   118
Lutz Brangsch: The European Union and Its Neighbours   131
Anej Korsika: Some Notes on the Socialist Alternative
        in Post-Yugoslav Space   146

European Elections: A Snapshot of the Balance of Power

Cornelia Hildebrandt: The European Elections: An Analysis	159
Fabien Escalona, Mathieu Vieira: Social Democracy Caught in the European Trap	170
Thilo Janssen: Far Right Parties in the European Parliament	183
Inger Johansen: The Danish People's Party: A Journey to the Centre	191
Luís *Ramiro, Jaime Aja*: The Left in the Storm: The Radical Left and the Elections in Spain	197
Alfonso Gianni: The Italian Vote and the Problem of a New Left Political Entity	209
Jiří Málek: East of the West – The Visegrad Four	215
Krzysztof Pilawski, Holger Politt: Elections in Estonia, Latvia, Lithuania, and Poland: In the Spirit of Neoliberal Economics and Tradition	224
Maxime Benatouil: transform! europe 2014 at a Glance	231
Authors and Editors	241
Members and Observers of transform! europe	246

PREFACE

Europe today is facing a multi-faceted crisis which has struck not only the continent's economy, social systems, its politics, and democracy, but also the legitimacy of European integration and the values it stands for.

The fact that a transnational entity such as the EU is pulled by the centripetal and centrifugal forces of its contradictions is nothing new, and it is not particularly alarming in itself. However, the European crisis, which broke out in 2008, and neoliberal austerity policies have exacerbated contradictions within and between the European states in a way that has caused ruptures of historic proportions.

In this volume we try to examine these ruptures from various perspectives. In the first part, essays by Étienne Balibar, Walter Baier, and a collaborative article by Elisabeth Gauthier, Joachim Bischoff, and Bernhard Müller attempt to draw the connections between newly arising national conflicts, the visible crises in social relations and democracy, and the diminishing appeal of European integration. This set of alarming developments also constitutes the background for growing right-wing populism on an EU scale which – despite some borrowings – greatly differs from traditional fascist movements. The first part of this book will conclude with Frank Deppe's essay 'What Does History Tells Us?', which traces the deep historical roots of the European crisis.

This volume begins, however, with an extensive interview with Alexis Tsipras whose party Syriza (which was founded in 2012) not only represents a realistic alternative to the governing parties in Greece but, in light of its possible accession to power, could set a European precedent and may yet profoundly change Europe's political landscape.

In the second volume of the book Steffen Lehndorff, Patrice Cohen-Séat, Gabriel Colletis, Marc Delepouve, Lutz Brangsch, and Anej Korsika examine individual fault lines in the European construct, austerity policies, the EU's unchanged undemocratic structure, potential European industrial and research policies and, finally, the European Union's relationships with its neighbours, which is becoming increasingly strained.

In the third section we return to the European elections, which were held in the middle of last year. Cornelia Hildebrandt, Fabien Escalona, Mathieu Vieira, and Thilo Janssen attempt a global picture pieced together from the outcomes in all 28 member states. What emerges is a significant increase in the votes of the radical left in Europe but also substantial growth within the radical and populist right, its nationalism infecting the whole right-wing spectrum, as we can see in the European Parliament.

Inger Johansen (Denmark), Luís Ramiro and Jaime Aja (Spain), Alfonso Gianni (Italy), Jiří Málek (Czech Republic), and Holger Politt and Krysztof Pilawski (Estonia, Latvia, Lithuania, and Poland) present some of the most interesting election results.

The volume closes with Maxime Benatouil's report on the activities of the transform! europe network in 2014.

The transform! europe network was established in 2001 during the World Social Forum in Porto Alegre by a small group of intellectuals from six different European countries, representing left research institutions or journals, who wanted to coordinate their research and educational work. Today transform! consists of 27 member organisations and observers from 19 countries.

The network is coordinated by a board of eight members, and its office is located in Vienna. transform! maintains a multilingual website and publishes a continuously growing number of reports, analyses, and discussion papers on issues related to the process of European integration.

In publishing this yearbook, we would like to further expand our contribution to the sociological and political science debates. Just like the biannual journal which transform! published from 2007 to 2013, the yearbook will be simultaneously published in several languages; it now appears in English, French, German, Greek, and Italian. Expanding our audience and broadening the horizon of the experiences reflected in *transform!* are not the only reasons why we publish our journal in several languages. We do not see translation as a mere linguistic challenge but consider it a way to bridge political cultures that find their expression in different languages and in the varied use of seemingly identical political concepts. This kind of political translation is of particular importance when set against the current historical backdrop of the left in Europe, and it focuses on finding unity in diversity by combining different experiences, traditions, and cultures. It is at the heart of transform! europe's work.

We would like to thank all those who have embarked on this adventure with us: our authors, our coordinators for the various language editions, and finally our publishers, especially The Merlin Press.

Walter Baier, Eric Canepa, and Eva Himmelstoss

SYRIZA AND EUROPE

An Interview With Alexis Tsipras

interviewed by Haris Golemis

Haris Golemis: *Just three years ago, Syriza's presence in Greece's political landscape was quite small. Today, Syriza is predicted to be the frontrunner in the next elections – making you the next Prime Minister of Greece. What factors do you believe have led to Syriza's meteoric rise in popularity, and do you believe that similar results are possible in the near future, elsewhere in Europe?*

Alexis Tsipras: The effects of the crisis on Greek society have been truly devastating. It comes as no surprise that there have been major changes in the political scene. Syriza has always offered a detailed analysis of the crisis and the underlying causes. While the mainstream parties led people on – rather brazenly, I might add – we were vehement that austerity would have severe negative consequences and lead to recession; these policies simply weren't sustainable. We supported grassroots initiatives, including major demonstrations and the social solidarity movement. Lastly, our political emphasis has been on uniting the left. This was critical – and it really resonated with people.

The response from the Greek people was immediate – and clear: During the May 2012 elections, Syriza captured 17 per cent of the vote, and during the second round of elections the following month, Syriza's numbers increased to 27 per cent – just three percentage points less than the centre right party. It's important to note that we achieved these numbers despite the mainstream media's relentless fear mongering. While we did our best to address these scare tactics, we weren't able to overcome them to the extent needed to be placed first in the elections. We didn't rest on our laurels after the elections, though. We diligently worked to develop a detailed programme outlining how to exit the crisis, including ending austerity and renegotiating the terms of the debt.

Today, we have a fully comprehensive programme to address the debt. Key aspects include renegotiating the terms with our European partners, along with a detailed plan to spur economic growth, address unemployment, strengthen the welfare state, and provide relief to the members of society hit hardest by the crisis. It is imperative that we implement these changes; austerity and budget cuts are not sustainable and only serve to further destroy social cohesion.

Syriza's rise is not about a 'protest vote' against the mainstream parties responsible for Greece's demise in the wake of the economic crisis. Syriza is winning over voters because it's the only party that offers a viable alternative solution. In the recent European elections, we came in first [in Greece] with a four percentage point lead; since then, we've been polling at even higher numbers, well ahead of the parties in the ruling coalition government. We'll see a major shift in the political landscape soon, but this isn't making us complacent. We remain committed to the work ahead, both on the political and social levels. We're under no illusions about the challenges we'll be facing when we first come to power – a historical first for us, as well as for post-war Europe. We're determined to see this through, with the support of the people, building consensus but not shying away from conflicts when they arise. As Franklin D. Roosevelt said, 'the only thing we have to fear is … fear itself'.

To answer the second part of your question, I'd like to point out that while we witnessed a rather dramatic political shift in Greece, similar shifts have also been occurring elsewhere in southern Europe. United Left and Podemos captured 18 per cent of the vote in Spain in the European elections, very close to the Socialists and the Popular Party whose popularity has since plummeted. These numbers represent an increase of two and a half times from the results of the 2011 national elections. We hope that the United Left and Podemos will have even stronger results in the upcoming 2015 elections. Also, Sinn Fein's success in the European elections was a significant development for Ireland, another country decimated by the Memoranda for bailing out the banks. Italy is showing signs of an uptick for the left, a trend seen in many European countries, including Slovenia.

In the early 1990s, the European social democrats formed an alliance with the right to promote neoliberalism across Europe – something they are now paying dearly for in the wake of the economic crisis. This is why I believe that the left is Europe's only hope for overcoming the crisis. The austerity policies implemented by conservative and social democratic governments have reached their tipping point, as have the fiscal targets assigned by the European Union, which are unachievable for any country. This simply can't continue. If Europe does not 'turn' towards the left – embracing growth, decent work and the welfare state – its other choice will be right-wing extremism and Euroscepticism. The setbacks will have terrible consequences.

The rapid political changes across Europe spurred by the crisis have aided the left, creating new opportunities. The social struggle for decent work and dignity is one of the most critical – and one that the left is deeply committed to. A stronger left increases the chances for major changes in Europe, shifting the balance in favour of labour. Syriza aspires to be the catalyst for these changes, creating a 'domino effect'.

It is important to note that our work doesn't just end with abolishing austerity. Our mission is not simply to carry out the unfinished work of post-war social democracy, but rather to enable the radical transformation of society across Europe, based on socialism and democracy. This is our goal as we seek to form new social alliances that will unite the working and middle classes, the unemployed, the most disadvantaged members of society, intellectuals, and social movements, around a common struggle: the struggle to liberate society from the effects of cutthroat profiteering, and to foster social justice and democracy, an economy that will focus on people's needs, and a welfare state that ensures education, health, and dignity for all. To call a halt to the 'free-market' policies responsible for miring Europe in the economic crisis, the European left must have a feasible and realistic political strategy, in addition to a unifying vision – these go together.

HG: *Your opponents, on both the right and left, claim that your position on abolishing the Memoranda and austerity, and renegotiating the debt will result in one of two possible outcomes since Greece is not a political heavyweight in the EU: You will either have to backtrack, recognising that you can't achieve your goals or you will be forced out of the eurozone and/or European Union. What is your response to such claims?*

AT: First off, I think that we should be more worried about what will happen if Greece does not change course and continues being the guinea pig for the neoliberal policies that have been implemented to supposedly address the crisis. There are many people in this country searching through the trash for food or whose homes no longer have electricity. The elderly are faced with the decision whether to spend their pension money on food *or* medicine – the money they receive isn't enough for both. The real economy is in shambles, and unemployment has skyrocketed. Our young people consider emigrating their first option. And the possibility of being stuck living under these conditions for the foreseeable future is all too real – trapped by austerity and recession, without decent wages or work, without dignity.

We do have another choice, though – one where we can feel pride. The European Social Forum's motto comes to mind: 'If not us, then who? If not now, when?'

Obviously, we don't intend to run the ship into the ground. We are opposed to austerity, and we're not alone in taking this position; there is growing resistance to these policies, not only in Greece, but across Europe. We're prepared for the challenges we'll surely face, and we're carefully preparing for these; we intend to honour our commitments. With the confidence and support of society, we'll be building a future on solid foundations.

Being forced out of the Eurozone is no simple matter – first of all, it's not allowed under the European treaties. A 'voluntary' exit is extremely risky, with dangerous consequences for Greece and for Europe – especially given the fragile nature of the current economic, social, and geopolitical realities. It's in no country's interest to further disrupt the continent's already tenuous balance. Such a risk can be avoided altogether if governments and institutions in the EU accept that Greece and other smaller European countries are equal partners in the EU and that they have a democratic right to elect leftist governments. Given these circumstances, I'm personally optimistic about the developments we can expect.

In order to be fully transparent, we've been clear about our intention to renegotiate the terms of the debt. We will seek to have a large part of the debt waived, and the repayment of the balance subject to a growth clause. You can't repay a debt if you're not allowed to work – this was exactly the logic that was applied to Germany's debts after the Second World War. Without a similar compromise, Greece's economy cannot achieve much needed economic growth. We've also been forthcoming about having public investments excluded from the Stability and Growth Pact (SGP), as well as having national bonds backed by the ECB.

We strongly believe that the issue of the debt has to be dealt with at the European level. Additionally, a 'European New Deal' is necessary, to allow for public investments funded by the ECB. Reparations due to Greece from the Second World War are also on the table. We've alerted our European partners that a left government will seek to recoup these, until now, outstanding funds.

As I said before, I'm optimistic about the developments – even though I'm sure that they won't all come about smoothly. The insistence on strict budgetary discipline by the German government and a few smaller allies will undoubtedly add friction; however, there is a slow but growing dissent across Europe – including those whose dissent would have been unthinkable just a few months ago. For this reason, I believe that Syriza will be able to generate wider support for its political positions.

So, getting back to my initial point – if we chose inaction, we can be certain that we'll be missing a historic opportunity for change; we're committed to using all of the resources at hand, and seeing the matter through to a solution.

HG: *You, along with other members of Syriza, have been in contact with individuals and organisations, including conservative politicians and executives from the private sector, who are not necessarily supporters of the left. You've met with Pope Francis, Wolfgang Schäuble, Mario Draghi, representatives of the International Monetary Fund, and even participated in the Ambrosetti Forum. What are you hoping to gain from these meetings, and how has your message been received?*

AT: Syriza's rise was initially treated as a dangerous development by European leaders, as well as by the Greek political mainstream. There was talk of 'extreme radicals' willing to risk a eurozone exit and widespread political turmoil in Europe, and the 'theory of the two extremes' was used to lump Syriza with far-right and Eurosceptic parties.

This was done to portray Syriza as unfit to negotiate with the European partners, and unfit to run the country, bringing about Greece's certain downfall if elected. Fortunately, this rhetoric has subsided; most people have come to terms with the likely fact that the next Greek government will be a government of the left. And I think this is a positive development.

The international contacts we've made have helped bring about this shift. It's understandable that many people are interested in meeting us, hearing our views, and exchanging ideas, to get a better sense of our goals. And we're interested in learning the same about our contacts, as well.

As we've become better known, this has helped to dispel the myths and rumours that Syriza wants to create mayhem in Europe; we're now viewed as a party that will be a reliable ally – or opponent – with a strategic plan, policy positions, and nuanced views. We are open to meeting with anyone, to discussing our policy positions, and exchanging views. This in no way means we will owe future favours or will make concessions in our programme.

Of course, there has been some grumbling – that a left party should not be meeting representatives from the world of 'capital'. While I understand these sentiments, I believe it's important to be able to defend your views; regardless of whom you speak with, what's key is being able to hold your ground, to express your views, rather than simply saying what the other person wants to hear. Our goal is to show that we can credibly debate the issues, as well as offer a viable alternative to the current political framework. Our discussions, and the way that our views have been received, makes it even more clear to me that meeting with these contacts is absolutely the right thing to do – regardless of whether they hold opposing views.

Our international efforts and the contacts Syriza has made highlight the contradictions and conflicts that exist in Europe, giving us greater insight – something which is exceedingly useful. For example, when Syriza was invited to participate in the Ambrosetti Forum, it was not because the organisers suddenly became fond of our views or because they wanted to coerce us in some way. To be frank, we were invited to help send a message to the German government; our position, that Europe must put an end to austerity and focus instead on growth, was met with applause. Despite this, we were fully aware that we didn't share common views on the issues of decent work and the welfare state with many of those in attendance. However, on the points where we can agree, we intend to make the most of these alliances; we simply don't have the luxury not to. I firmly believe that this is the right course of action.

We are in no way opposed to meeting with individuals where we have strong differences of opinion, like Wolfgang Schäuble. Our goal is not to catch anyone off guard with our views. We believe in being transparent. By holding these kinds of meetings we seek to foster dialogue, which may ultimately aid in the process of future negotiations. The members of the current [Greek] government are the only ones not benefiting from our efforts abroad; they cannot continue with the usual scare tactics, trying to paint Syriza as an unwanted partner in Europe that is bent on bringing ruin to Greece.

I'd like to specifically call attention to my visit with Pope Francis, which was organized by transform!. The Pope has an impressive social [justice] agenda. The fact that this meeting took place is indicative of just how critical Greece's position is considered, both symbolically and literally, given the extremely fragile social balance in Europe. My country has suffered a humanitarian catastrophe that is unprecedented during peacetime, but we are also the country that is closest to reversing the policies that have brought us to this point. This will be significant for all of Europe, and especially for our peoples and societies. I believe that this is what caught the Pope's interest and led to our meeting.

This meeting truly illuminated the problems we face in Greece, given the Pope's global prestige; it helped raise awareness of the situation for people in Europe and beyond. The increase in solidarity positively affects Greece and the Greek people – and Europe, as well. With greater solidarity comes a greater chance for seeing change across all of Europe.

HG: *You've visited a number of countries in the past that no longer subscribe to neoliberalism, such as Venezuela, Brazil, and Argentina. Many of your adversaries consider these visits part of the 'radical' days of Syriza, and that you've since 'changed your tune' and stopped associating with 'bad company' now that the party is on the verge of governing Greece. What are your thoughts on this?*

AT: Latin America has also been subject to the IMF's 'adjustment programmes' – the same ones that we've become subject to in Europe post-2008, from the IMF and others. These programmes were implemented through the use of military force in some cases, with devastating results for society. Today, these countries have cast aside neoliberalism and have developed their economies as they've seen fit, putting emphasis on growth. They have broad support from their citizens despite the challenges they face, as they pursue new methods of wealth distribution and productive reconstruction, universal access to healthcare, education, and social security, and the strengthening of their democratic institutions.

And it certainly seems that the efforts are paying off. This greatly interests the left across Europe, as we intend to challenge neoliberalism on the continent. We can certainly benefit from cooperating with Latin America through the exchange of best practices on key matters, such as our shared views on economic crises, debt, or international trade agreements. The left has been following the developments there for quite some time, long before the consequences of the crisis resulted in the historic opportunities that are now before us.

The supporters of neoliberalism are averse to these kinds of developments that are not in line with their views, and would have us believe that only those who support their doctrines are 'democratic' regardless of the level of coercion or corruption involved; social movements and politicians who don't value markets over people are considered populist. It's time for our adversaries to make peace with the fact that the left is creating an alternative programme for governing in Europe, as well as new alliances.

A close working relationship with our European partners does not preclude us from drawing on certain examples or experiences from Latin America. As we form our political and social strategies, it's important to monitor how developments are unfolding in Latin America.

HG: *Syriza's chance to govern and implement new policies is a matter of great importance to the left, trade unions, and social movements across Europe – and one of great interest to transform!. In what ways can these supporters and progressive European citizens help during the pre-election period and after your much anticipated win?*

AT: This is a really important issue, because the left derives its strength from society.

The dire situation in Greece brought about the opportunity for Syriza to create change. Our efforts will gain momentum when we form our government. We realise there will be many challenges, and the real work will begin once we've been elected. We're not just fighting for change in Greece – ours is a struggle for political change across Europe, a struggle against the current system that allows speculators and the world of capital to hold people hostage. We believe politics and economics should be centred around people's needs, decent work, a thriving welfare state, environmental protections, democracy.

The left's success in Greece could create new opportunities across Europe. The left stands together with the various grassroots movements, and all people – be it in the North or the South – who realise that our common future depends on a democratic and social Europe. We've received, and continue to receive, so many messages of solidarity and peace from across the globe. Solidarity isn't something that's simply an emotional boost – it's also an important factor in the social and political struggle to change things in other countries.

To give you an example from the European elections – our comrades in Italy chose to name their party 'L'Altra Europa con Tsipras'. It's not the name that's significant actually but the message that the party wanted to convey. They explained that they, too, wanted to 'feel Greek', to create momentum for change in Italy, similar to what was happening in Greece. And that boosted momentum for all of us. We both reached the goals we had set out for our respective countries, while sending messages of unity and solidarity.

I truly can't express just how we felt upon seeing the word, 'Syriza' on the walls in Taksim Square during the uprising in Istanbul. We very much rely on the help and support of the left, progressive parties, social movements – of all those who are involved. If we are in fact elected, our government will have the task of putting new policies on the European agenda. To this end, public support from across the European Union, putting pressure on governments, strengthening movements that call for progressive changes, will be our biggest 'allies'.

We don't think of ourselves as existing in a separate sphere – we're a part of the European left, and together with all the parties of the left, we face a common struggle. We're interested in the success of all these parties; our joint successes will be the only way to achieve the results we hope for, both in the medium and long term. Each step taken forward, each small or big victory, in Europe and beyond, is important because our struggles are shared.

A win for Syriza, and the formation of a left government in Greece, will be a first major step for all of us. The assistance and support from other countries will be critical; it will be a message of hope to the Greek people, fortifying people's resolve and determination to take matters into their hands.

In today's highly connected world, every initiative, every show of solidarity, every poster, every message of support that reaches our country from abroad, gives us energy to forge ahead and work toward our goals. The left is here to create change, to foster new social partnerships, to stand up to 'business as usual'. And we will do so, with integrity, with a new approach to international relations, with unity and action across the board.

translated by Maria Choupres

ESSAYS

EUROPE – NATIONS: THE MISSING PEOPLE AND THE CRISIS OF LEGITIMACY

Étienne Balibar

What I would like to discuss here is the possibility of resolving the crisis of Europe in a *European way* – in my opinion this is the only conceivable solution if the crisis is to be truly resolved, given the impossibility of returning to national and therefore nationalistic economic-political systems without deepening the consequences of the crisis. However, a resolution is in no way certain. In my view, the key to the solution lies in a democratic invention at the continental level, that is, a new distribution of power and a new combination of the 'insurrectional' and 'institutional' aspects of democracy (which is what I call a dynamic process of conflict or competition between democratisation and de-democratisation).

Organic crisis

My *first thesis* concerns the notion of an organic crisis. As we know, it involves two ideas: 1) The processes intertwined within the crisis pertain to the economic and political spheres; they also involve an essential moral element, which ranges from the delegitimation of political forms, that is, the loss of their capacity to govern by incorporating the population into the institutional procedures of representation (a phenomenon that is very visible today in Italy but also latently in other European countries), to the crisis of the collective values that guarantee individuals' feelings of identity and their capacity for self-realisation. 2) The idea that the crisis is not part of a so-called 'normal' cycle of disaggregation and regeneration of the institutions and the conditions of social production, both of whose causes and whose remedies are found within the system, but instead is irreversible in nature. This makes impossible, or rather inconceivable, a 'return', even if modified, to previous forms (except in a more or less reactionary nostalgic form). The crisis has in this case reached a point of historic no-return, in which its resolution requires a rupture and the invention of something new, without it necessarily being possible to locate forces capable of creating the social formation able to effect the break (and without it being necessarily possible for these forces to arise together, unified by the same goal).

It seems to me that we are seeing precisely these two aspects in the current crisis of 'European construction'. (I am referring to the functioning of the European Union, its principal institutional form, but I well understand that the European construction, seen from a comprehensive geographic, historical, and geopolitical vantage point, involves a more complex amalgam of 'circles' and of continental 'interdependencies', whose convergence one more or less took for granted but which is being put to the test in the crisis, with its elements proving to be heterogeneous and probably incompatible). This construction has reached a point of no-return because the deterioration of the 'structural' antagonisms among the elements of its 'material constitution', in the context of the global financial crisis erupting in 2008, has struck at Europe's very 'political system', revealing its artificial or anachronistic character. This means not only that this system is truly 'nowhere to be found' between federalism and delegated national sovereignty, but that its typical 'statism without a state' functions only to reinforce the policies and positions of power, which in the end destroy the construction itself.

However, this absolutely does not mean that Europe, as an interdependent system, could 'return' to a pre-federal system of states that are ideally 'sovereign' from the economic, and also the cultural or juridical, point of view, as right-wing and left-wing nationalists continually dream of (naturally with different intentions), oscillating between competition and cooperation in relation to variations of interests and national ideological differences. Not only would this imaginary return be achieved at the cost of catastrophic developments in spheres such as industrial activity, scientific research, and culture, but it would not really be possible without a further destruction of the nations themselves – we can adopt this negative version of Milward's famous thesis, according to which Europe's construction has essentially been a way of preserving and prolonging the capacities of the nation form in Europe. This naturally does not mean that the present forms – government institutions and practices – of the European construction are suited to the resolution of their crisis. On the contrary, we see their destructive effects every day, in contrast to their proclaimed objectives, not only in the form of a monetary norm that makes it practically impossible to draw up a common economic policy for relaunching industrial activity – transforming it according to the new technologies and environmental conditions, thus an economic policy for reversing the phenomena of precarity, mass unemployment, and impoverishment. We also see this under the form of a 'governance' structurally articulated according to minority interests, which is now producing a dramatic level of antagonism between the interests and sensibilities (not to mention the passions) of the masses constituting Europe's population, on national or regional, but also social, bases, such as to render spectral the idea of a community of interests – without which (or without whose prevalence) the very idea of a political construction becomes absurd. We can thus speak of an absolute *double bind*, or of a point of no-return within the no-return itself, and precisely this is what an 'interregnum' is for Gramsci.

Europe's 'contingent necessity'

In my opinion, and this would be my *second thesis*, we would need to relocate all of this 'pathological' phenomenology, as Gramsci said, in a much more complex historical perspective to simultaneously understand its *necessary* aspects (in the historical sense, naturally, that is, those corresponding to long-term global tendencies) and its *contingent* aspects tied to political choices made in Europe in recent decades, but under the pressure of the global tendencies). I venture to say that we have to do here with a paradoxical *contingent necessity*, which naturally only appears a posteriori. It contrasts just as much with the (essentially 'anti-Europeanist') idea that this situation of a deepened crisis without 'immanent' solution was inevitable, or 'genetically' inscribed in the conception of the 'European project', as it does with the idea (supported by the EU's 'official historians') that an implicit teleology exists in Europe that makes crises the privileged means of federalism's progress.

The European project initiated in the post-war years, in the framework of an incipient Cold War, and as a strategy of including western Europe in the competition between 'two (economic-political) systems', was from the beginning of course a capitalist, and in certain respects also imperialist, construction, but it was not neoliberal because neoliberalism did not exist but formed in part as a policy and break with certain organic aspects of European capitalism, which derived from a whole history of social movements and struggles, and from the confrontation with fascism. This organic aspect of European capitalism involves what is generally called the 'social state' (which I have suggested could be more precisely called the 'national-social' state), which the European project wanted to transform but which also made up its essential foundation.

But, on the other hand, as far as the idea is concerned, or rather the quasi-Hegelian myth, of a European construction that always ends by surmounting its crises, in particular resolving the conflicts between national interests through the experimental discovery of the unifying capacity of common economic interests (a sort of 'cunning of (European) reason' quasi theorised under the name of the 'Monnet method', which has become the shibboleth of European federalism, certainly not of the democratic version wished for by Altiero Spinelli but in the technocratic version that today prevails in Brussels), this myth crumbles when it becomes clear that, beyond the level of propaganda, there in fact is no common economic interest; rather, there is an antagonism that leads to potentially explosive phenomena of domination and inequality, since these do not simply involve classes or social groups within each nation but the nations themselves, or significant parts of them. Thus, from the 1950s on, the evolution of the European structure has been marked by significant changes in the relations of social forces, whose development needs to be reconstructed with precision and caution. It would in particular be important to study the coincidence of the turning points in economic policy with the gradual hegemonic evolution of the neoliberal programme, with successive enlargements of the EU's geographic space, and with the transformations of the economy and of geopolitics. This does not mean that the most recent inversion, which has subjected the European structure to the laws of financial capitalism in the context of a *historic acceleration of globalisation* after the end of the division of the world into ideological blocs, is not qualitatively different. We can say that the consequence of this – which was also naturally a conscious objective from the point of view of the EU's ruling class – was the *reversing* of the position of the 'single market in Europe' in relation to the liberalised world market, which has progressively been displaced towards new 'emergent' centres of capital accumulation with dramatic consequences for its political functioning: Instead of representing a capacity for *collective* response (not to mention resistance) to the tendencies of the world market towards unbridled competition between individuals, territories, nations, and social groups distinguished by anthropological differences, etc., the EU has transformed itself into a mechanism for *introducing* this unfettered logic within its frontiers, which could only lead to an acute political and social crisis, even if the financial crisis did not intensify all of its tensions.

With this, we come to what really makes up the core of the questions that I am suggesting are at issue in this analytical part of these theses, that is, the relation between the negotiations still underway in Europe around a 'revolution-restoration' in the Gramscian sense and the aporia of the various negotiations over the 'democratic relegitimation' of the European structure (that is, of European institutions and policies) in the recent period, whether these issue from representatives of the dominant capitalism, from intellectuals with a liberal or liberal-social orientation, like Habermas, or from representatives of a left that sees itself as more radical.

Revolution from above?

The first thing to point out is that the negotiations around a revolution-restoration do exist, or have existed. In my opinion, this has become evident at an exact moment [late in 2011, Eds], that is, when, almost simultaneously, a coordinated move on the part of the European Commission, the European Central Bank, and the German and French heads of government imposed a change of government in Greece and Italy, which though certainly not illegal was exceptional and without parliamentary support (and also blocked popular consultations), in order to implement the 'structural reforms' – austerity measures transforming social legislation in exchange for loans or European guarantees to save public budgets and bring down debt. With the IMF's intervention, this was accompanied in Greece, Portugal, and Ireland by internal neocolonial phenomena, with de facto limitations of national sovereignty through legislation and the forced liberalisation of the national sectors of the economy.

It is then that people began to speak, referring to the 'Troika' or to the European Commission as a 'commissary' dictatorship or 'revolution from above'. Habermas himself has begun to develop the notion of an 'executive post-democratic federalism', a characterisation which implies that we are in fact at the beginning of a turning point towards a new type of political regime, at the European level. According to him, this decisively contaminates the functioning of national political institutions, because the interaction of the two levels, executive-supranational and parliamentary-representative, has become irreversible, devoid of democratic legitimacy in the name of urgency and efficiency but destined to acquire a definitive value unless the parliamentary-representative aspect of the European institutions is immediately strengthened in the context of a federalism of a new type. I agree with this description with some changes of terminology, but I think that at the level of interpretation, or, if you will, of the definition of a new 'material constitution', either there are still difficult problems to resolve, or the successive episodes have complicated things more than clarified them. In the first place, there is a basic difficulty regarding the role and form of the institution that appears as the key representative of the European system of power in the last instance, which is neither the Commission, nor the Council of Ministers, nor, even less, the Parliament; rather, it is the European Central Bank (ECB). This function, both of imposing rules and of intervention in emergency situations, can be fulfilled by the Bank precisely because its statutes confer an 'independence' on it in relation to the other centres of power, removing it from all direct popular control. This is truly a radical political innovation because it displaces the locus of sovereignty in relation to modern states and at the same time introduces a type of legitimacy different from those considered by political science. This is partly due to the unexpected effects of the 'ordoliberal' ideology of German origin that has underpinned the institution of the single currency and the new articulation of politics and economy in the current phase of the domination of finance capital, in which the authority of the states (including the most powerful of them) is to be conditioned by their access to financial markets and international credit.

But can we really see the ECB today in Europe as a 'sovereign of a new type', even in an incipient way? Yes, in a certain sense, because a collapse of the single currency can be avoided only with the introduction of a certain degree of harmonised, or centralised, economic governance, beyond the simple disciplining of public expenditures, and because only the ECB can manage and impose this orientation, functioning, so to speak, as a 'constituent power' of European unity. But no, on the other hand, because precisely at this point contradictions internal to the new distribution of powers appear, which tend to transform the conflict between 'Commission' and 'states' into a conflict between 'bank' and 'states'. From this point of view it will be especially interesting to follow the development of tensions between Berlin and Frankfurt, that is, the two centres of power that European public opinion (above all in the countries and classes victimised by forced austerity) tends to see as aspects of a single hegemonic power, if not a new German imperialism, in Europe. (There is of course no doubt that there is a hegemony, but a sole system of power dominated by Berlin is another matter. I think that among other contradictions to be examined it is more likely that we can point to a duality of power whose models need to be sought within the old problem of the eagle's two heads, and not in new characteristics, given the substitution of the religious apparatus by that of finance). If we add to this the fact that in a continent with a long historical tradition of representative democracy (with elements of social democracy), it will be very difficult to have financial authority pass from a situation of *potestas indirecta* to that of *potestas directa*, one can perhaps better understand that the result of the 'revolution from above' has up to now been to *delegitimise* Europe's 'pseudo-federal' structure and reinforce nationalisms, which lead into a blind alley.

It is precisely at this point that the negotiations emerge, the models of the 'democratic relegitimation' of federal Europe discussed by politicians and ideologues conscious of the preceding impasse. They need to be examined not only in an isolated way but also comparatively because they range from one extreme to the other of the political-ideological spectrum and because their common premise is their recognition that, at least in the modern epoch, and also in circumstances that could be seen as exceptional rather than as the realisation of a latent 'state of exception', every form of the legitimation of a political power, even of technocratic 'governance', has to include a factor of popular consensus. Naturally, however, starting from this premise, the various strategies are completely divergent, and in my opinion they have up to now proved to be equally inadequate, impotent, and aporetic. They essentially involve *three models*: the 'conservative' one represented by those (like Minister Schäuble) who want to add to Europe's technocratic structure some symbolic elements of popular legitimacy (for example the election of a European president through universal transnational suffrage); the liberal-social model of those who (like Habermas and others) want to give Europe a democratic 'constitution' in the formal sense (above all insisting on the creation of effective parliamentarism at the European level, with the double representation of single citizens and of nations or, better, of national adherences; or, finally, the 'radical' model of those who have maintained that the European construction can be legitimated only if it shows itself to be *more advanced* in relation to the national states as regards democratic forms or procedures. I would say on this last point that such an idea, as beautiful as it may be, is still located, at least formally, within the representation of a linear progress, of a history of democracy composed of retards or regressions and of advances. It does not truly take account of the crisis nor of the need for a break, or in other terms it seeks a relationship between legitimacy and democracy without starting from today's dominant phenomenon, that is, a combination of de-legitimation and of de-democratisation.

Society without political capacity

The phenomenon that needs to be addressed is in fact not a simple *lack of the people*, or of the *demos*, as has long been said in discussions on the possible creation of a new political structure – political in the strong sense – at the European level, whether or not it is called a 'federation' – but I do not see a possible alternative term, as long as we accept that the history of the federation form remains open, and that the task of Europe in this sense is not so much to apply an extant model as it is to invent a new one. What emerges from this fifty-year history, which has come to an end with the current crisis and which shows the aporia or impossibility of resolving the crisis at an institutional level, is rather a *dissolution of the 'demos'* in Europe, that is, of the 'community of citizens' and of the capacity to act in the political sphere and to control power or institute counter-powers. Or, if I can once again venture a paradoxical, almost oxymoronic, expression, what is involved here is the *preventive* dissolution of the 'demos' in Europe, actually of the preventive dissolution of a *virtual*, a potential, 'demos'. This means that in the last fifty years in Europe, if we put aside the model, the fantastic image, of a 'supernation' endowed with a single collective identity of the ethnic type, what has really been created is a 'European society', naturally to different degrees and under the influence of tendencies from below, including phenomena of the transnationalisation of culture and ways of life but above all of processes of normalisation imposed from above, by the normalising activity of the European Commission, by the homogenisation of juridical forms, and by the homogenisation of educational systems. But this society in formation, even if incomplete (though 'incomplete society' is a terminological contradiction), has really been prevented from acquiring the appropriate *political capacity*, that is, of representing itself as the bearer of common interests independent of the conjunctural decisions of the powers. And this has been the case also due to the fact that Europe's political superstructure has been conceived as a technocratic power, not depoliticised but elevated above ideological and social conflicts and political alternatives, and it has been maintained in this fictional position by the nationalism of the dominant classes and of the popular classes themselves. Thus a sort of conspiracy of the extremes or of mutually opposed interests is due, on the one hand, to the defence of the corporative privileges of the political class but above all to the wish to avoid on the supranational level that class conflict, that confrontation with the mass of citizens as the bearers of demands and rights, in fact rights of resistance, which for the bourgeoisie was the permanent problem of a democratised state form (here I am following some very apt ideas of Carlo Galli's in his book *Il disagio della democrazia*). However, this conspiracy of opposed interests is also due, on the other hand, to a nationalism from below, whose objective bases are mainly found in the fact that social security, social rights, thus the recognition of a form of social citizenship, have been the results of 'national-popular' struggles inside the national state and guaranteed by national constitutions. Nevertheless, the moment is approaching at which society's political capacity, and thus the capacity of popular politics, only really exists as a spectre, as a nightmare, at the national level and has not been able to take shape at a transnational level or has been impeded from doing so, which produces dramatic effects if, at the same time, society's standard of living and its working and educational conditions, above all those of the new generations, are dismantled by the economic transformations, by the new precarity.

The *third thesis* regards the relation between *legitimacy* and *democracy*. Legitimacy in the realistic sense is the authority of a government, a system of laws and norms that command the obedience or following of the majority, or which, if they are not obeyed, have the capacity to sanction disobedience. This obviously means that the legitimacy of a political system or project is not necessarily 'democratic', even if (particularly in modern times) it needs a popular element as I have said above. Therefore, in an absolute sense, the idea of an EU whose legitimacy (that is, capacity to govern) would be based on a combination of efficiency ('output legitimacy') and emergency (the 'defence' of European identity within a dangerous globalisation) is not unthinkable. But this does not mean that it is practicable if precisely its non-democratic character incites rebellion, disobedience, or results in apathy when the mobilisation of all would be required. However, there is another difficulty from the other side: If democracy achieves a certain degree of adequate radicality (which means if it is not just a name given to a technocratic-oligarchic system) it becomes essentially 'paradoxical' (as far as it is 'illegitimate domination' in Weber's sense) because it 'paradoxically' implies that power should not be legitimated if it cannot be, at the same time, contested, and in fact it is. Therefore democracy would be a regime in which at most obedience and disobedience of powers would both be possible, in varying proportions. In this sense, democracy can be an objective *per se*, as the regime of liberty, or as a means for transforming the social system, but it does not guarantee legitimacy and cannot guarantee it a priori. The paradox, as we know, is resolved in the ancient forms, studied by Machiavelli, through the tribune of the plebs, and in the modern social state by the fact that social conflicts, or rather class conflicts, make up an organic part of the material constitution of the state – which is naturally not automatic as we know that the historic price was blood and tragedy. Nevertheless, the idea that emerges from this is that democratic legitimation for Europe certainly makes sense but cannot result solely from the introduction of forms of parliamentary representation, even if these are absolutely necessary, as I agree; rather, it is the parliamentary forms of legitimation that need a *surplus of politics* to be legitimate themselves. One sees the difficulty of the situation: At most the political structure of the European Union would begin to legitimise itself if powerful social movements would recognise it *while strongly contesting it*, forcing it to negotiate and find compromises, not only between nations and states but between the governors and the governed.

Democracy between progress and regression

The *fourth thesis* has to do with the very mode, essentialist or dynamic and dialectical, of thinking of and using the notion of democracy, returning thus to the problem of the missing 'demos' and of its production. As Rancière fittingly holds, democratisation is not a 'political regime', which could be defined by a type of constitution or of institution (even if, in given historical conditions, it of course needs institutions and can be formalised in a constitution that can function as protection against anti-democratic movements and as a barrier to more advanced democratic 'evolutions'). What exists, therefore, is not *democracy* but rather the *democratisation* of extant institutions (above all state institutions but also civil ones in general) as a process without a pre-established end (which does not mean that it does not have goals). If we then combine the results of the preceding theses, we see that the *demos* as a reality or political power cannot historically be the effect of democracy, which is more or less fully realised depending on how intense the processes of democratisation are. However, we need to add an additional element here that is clearly, if not brutally, illustrated by the current situation (certainly in Europe but also more generally in the world), namely that such processes are always conflictual, resulting from an unstable equilibrium between tendencies of *democratisation* and tendencies of *de-democratisation* (Charles Tilly). Either one or the other can win; there really is no middle way. Therefore the forms of democratic invention always depend on the modes of a de-democratisation that are underway or are possible.

But these things are very complicated because the forms of de-democratisation underway, in Europe and elsewhere, are very complicated. They produce aggregate effects of depoliticisation or the collective *disempowerment* of citizens, of the general transformation of active citizenship into passive citizenship, which in the end is subordination rather than citizenship. The very broad category, but also the vaguest, that of *neoliberalism*, is certainly inadequate; rather, it would be an epistemological obstacle to analysing this complexity, from the forms of the privatisation of the public sphere to the reversal of relations of government between the juridical powers and the economic or corporate powers (which for this reason become themselves political in the strong sense), passing through the anthropological mutation of communication and social 'sympathy' through the electronic networks.

Fifth thesis: the relation between *political democracy* and *social democracy*. Here there is need of great length; therefore I will be very brief. My idea is that this relation (more or less denied by 'liberal' tradition) has always been essential but that present circumstances confer on it an unprecedented importance.

This is because the notion of a morphological distinction between 'state', or the political sphere, and 'civil society', including the economic sphere, no longer has any meaning. A fusion of political power and of economic power of a new type is being produced, which has its sometimes very severe internal conflicts, as I suggested, recalling the limits of the possibility of considering the ECB as a sovereign even though it behaves like the director of continental policy; but they are not conflicts between the economic and the political in the traditional sense. Rather, what is involved here are conflicts that have to do with the distribution of power in the absolute and the choice between opposing policies, especially in the economic sphere, with enormous social consequences. In a certain sense, with the combination of 'privatisation of the state' and 'governance' we are at opposite poles from Gramsci's 'enlarged state', but on the other hand we can find a new sphere of interpretation for it, one that is contemporary and still more constrictive than the notion of 'expansive democracy', which originates with Gramsci. In this setting, the problem of the invention of democracy is not only that of finding a formula for 'social democracy' beyond the liberal state outside of society; it is not only that of opening a path of democratisation *beyond the (national) social state*, but of finding practical alternatives – in the sphere of society and of institutions, from the municipal to the transnational, in fact global, level – to financial 'governance', which naturally presents itself as liberation and modernisation, but which, penetrating every social relation from public services to the choice of governors and representatives of the community, operates a systematic de-democratisation.

And with this I arrive at what really makes up the most important programmatic point, but also the most difficult to my way of thinking. It involves plurality, or I would better say *multiplicity*, the intrinsically multiple, therefore heterogeneous, character of the processes of democratisation in so far as they involve resistance and alternatives to the effective or virtual tendencies of de-democratisation. This is true of all history but naturally is suggested in a particularly convincing way by what is happening now. However, I would not like to recommence here the old discussion of the existence or non-existence of *forms of democracy* that are different or mutually opposed, of whether they are in fact different 'regimes', but called by a single name by dint of a tradition that functions, in fact, more like a symptom of an unresolved problem than like a framework of analysis (and which generates, in particular, the discussion on the presence or absence of the *demos* in democracy, that is, in the institutions of its symbolic power; I am referring here once again to the above-cited book by Galli). I would like to do almost the opposite, that is, leave the problematic of the regimes to move on decisively to the problematic of the processes, and I want to sustain the idea that only in a utopian discourse can the *diverse modes of democratisation* be reduced to a single type. But I also want to put forward the idea that between these modes there is not only a difference but also articulation and reciprocal necessity. This seems very important to me precisely at this moment because, on the one hand, seeing as I think that the observable modes of de-democratisation in the current crisis of the European Union are many and not reducible to one type, I consequently think that the ideal programme of a democratic party for Europe (or a party for a democratic Europe) could not limit itself to a single demand or to imagining a single mode of democratisation of society and the state. And, on the other hand, it is precisely this polymorphism, this strategic mobility and plurality of combined objectives, which I believe I see in the language of the movements that are the most radical and at the same time the most responsible, which have emerged as a response to the social, moral, and political crisis, such as the Spanish *indignados* movement in particular, demanding effective control of parliamentary work and the elimination of corruption at the same time as they are experimenting with creative forms of self-organisation of struggles and of life, against the backdrop of an enormous revolt against the human destruction represented by mass unemployment.

If there is a sense to this we of course have to try not to construct a typology of democratic forms but to indicate loci, factors, and above all what I called twenty years ago *construction sites of democracy* and which I would today prefer to call *factors or movements of democratisation* that go back to diverse forms of collective organisation and action but which naturally always have to do with the distribution of power, with the problem of what the Anglo-Saxons (especially the feminists at the beginning) have called *empowerment*, which is not very different from Spinoza's 'capacity to act' in the sphere of power and against domination. I would say that three modes of the democratisation of the exercise of institutional and also social power can be seen, all three being political, each of them permanently moving between opposite poles, whether in the form of progress or of regression but also perhaps of a mediation between contrasting possibilities.

The first of these modes naturally concerns the institution of *representation*. There is no politics, beyond the state itself, without representation, not only because – as Gramsci observes no differently from Max Weber on this point – there is no politics without the distinction between the governed and the governors (which does not necessarily mean distribution of these roles in an exclusive and permanent way between different groups, even if a class society always tends to impose this rule), but also because a certain mode of representation is what makes *deliberation* possible, that is, the exercise of the collective faculty of political *judgement*. But representation, as we can observe in history, with its constitutional and insurrectional factors can largely oscillate between the contrasting poles of the *authorisation* of the governed, lacking control after an election which can also be very democratic (Hobbesian representation, let us say) and *permanent control* over the representatives, either indirect, like the 'imperative mandate' of the Jacobins, or the permanent observation by public opinion by means of communicative power. When, as is the case today, not only representation hypocritically tends towards an authorisation that presents itself as the deterioration of popular control because in reality this has been substituted by the occult control of capitalist *lobbies* and by legal or illegal corruption it is probably desirable to move decisively towards a re-establishment of effective forms of popular control, that is, of the obligation of the political class to give an accounting in order to resist de-democratisation. However, in general it is also probably true that the democratisation of representation, or of representative democracy itself, in order to produce what Nadia Urbinati describes as a combination of representativity and advocacy, can only seek a contingent equilibrium between the two poles of authorisation and of control, neither of which is democratic in its extreme version. This goes in a different way for the two other modes of democratisation, which I believe I can identify, that is, a) *democratisation as the development of civil conflict* (in the Machiavellian sense), between the two apparently incompatible poles – both however in reality being forms of political practice e.g. division, choice, 'party-ism' – of 'social war' and of mere constitutional 'pluralism'; and b) *democratisation as the self-government* of citizens (between the pole of 'participating' institutions, which can become a cooptation, an instrumentalisation of active citizenship, and 'communism' or of the autonomy that can also become acosmism or anarchism, that is an exit from the common society). I do not believe that in fact any of these modes has ever existed in an isolated way in practice because it was the struggles – the social conflicts that could also be violent – that imposed an enlarged and effective or substantial representation, while struggles, the conflicts, that formed the substance of the process of democratisation of modern states (not only their passion, as many admit, but also their *social intelligence*, as Gramsci showed) have always combined factors of more or less democratic representation towards the outside and internally (which were called 'organisation') with factors of self-government. Therefore, if 'communism' has never really existed in universal history as a mode of production or isolated social formation, it really has existed as sociability in the struggles without which there would have been no democratic conquest, just as today the more or less communal and self-managed forms of communication that are resisting the empire of prefabricated mercantile communication are essential in order to invent practices of conflict and resistance at the local or transnational level, and thus at the European level. And for this reason it seems important to me to indicate how certain present-day movements of re-democratisation of society and of *active citizenship* ('acts of citizenship' according to Isin) are located between these diverse modes or are trying to combine them (as in the case of the Spanish *indignados*).

And I believe I can also interpret in this sense, though in a prospective way, Sandro Mezzadra's recent proposal, in which he sees in the current crisis of the European construction (which subjects the peoples of the continent to a drastic alternative of regression and of invention of the new, according to the Gramscian model of the *interregnum*) the possibility of a 'constituent moment'.

I maintain the idea of the *democratic revolution* as a strategic factor; that is, I would call for *structural reforms* opposed to those which today are required by 'Community' institutions: parliamentarism with the power of control and decision-making at the European level, legitimacy of conflict, fiscal reform, etc. Thus I would like to go beyond the dualisms of socialist tradition: reform or revolution, war of manoeuvre or of position, and initiative from below or from above.

translated by Eric Canepa

THE 'NATIONAL QUESTION' AND EUROPEAN INTEGRATION

Walter Baier

To rescue for their people the thousands of German men and women who annually succumb to the murderous effects of capitalist exploitation: This constitutes the national conquest aspired to by the working class. It is not the territorial principle but social policy that represents the means of this national conquest ....

Otto Bauer, 1906

Europe is experiencing radical change. The civil war in Ukraine shows just how quickly events can take a dramatic and negative turn. That issues of domestic and foreign policy are to blame for this outburst of violence is just as true as the fact that this conflict is one between national communities, the origin of which dates back many centuries.

However, this is not the only example of the new relevance of national questions in Europe. Who would have expected that almost half of the Scottish population would vote for Scottish independence from the United Kingdom or that Catalans would hold a referendum on seceding from the Spanish state?

While at the end of the last century the dissolution of multi-national states such as Yugoslavia and the Soviet Union was understood as part of a catching-up process, which sharply contrasted with the peaceful integration of the European Union, it is now the European West which is experiencing disintegrative tendencies.

At the end of the last century, Eric Hobsbawm, doyen of left historiography, counted 42 regionalist movements in Western Europe.[1] Today we have to acknowledge that the crisis and austerity policies have not only fuelled nationalist resentments between the member states of the European Union but have destabilised existing states along national fault lines.

The proposition that the single market and the currency union have led Europe to abandon the concept of nations and enter a post-nationalist era has proved to be utopian and wrong. If there are no supranational democratic counterbalances to the transnationalisation of capital, the social disintegration this transnationalisation causes is expressed in a crisis of national relations. This and only this is what the ubiquitous term 'crisis of European integration' means. Only a policy change in the states and the European institutions can prevent any further expansion and deepening of this crisis. For the time being, however, this is not in the offing, which is why the left has to brace itself for a long debate on nationalism.

The current nationalist wave in Europe had a predecessor at the end of the twentieth century when immigrants seeking jobs, along with refugees from the global South, led to the formation of new national minorities, some of which, dispersed over several countries, have a larger European population than some individual European states.

The presence of national minorities, however, generally contradicts the nationalist idea, connected to the concept of the nation state, that every nation forms its own state and every state is populated by only one nation.

European reality has never corresponded to this idea, which had become hegemonic in the nineteenth century, because European states were home to an increasing number of nations and national minorities. This incongruity of states and nations thus provided a permanent cause of European conflicts and wars.

Since 1945, some of the national relationships as well as the situation of many (but certainly not all) indigenous minorities have improved. This is an achievement of the consolidation of the social state as well as European integration. However, as compensation for this, as it were, the new national minorities from Kurdistan, Turkey, sub-Saharan Africa, or Asia were asked to culturally assimilate, which corresponds to an outdated concept of social coexistence and creates the possibility of reactivated nationalist turmoil. This is exactly what we are experiencing in the war on terror declared by George W. Bush in 2001, which has taken on the character of a global cultural struggle.

In this way, the classical setting of the old conflicts is recreated, and it is used by nationalist populists as a sphere where they can project their conception of social and political conflicts.

Conversely, the new minorities are expressing themselves with increased self-confidence today. This was seen in the demonstrations of tens of thousands of people of Turkish background in Germany and Austria, both in favour of and against Turkey's President Erdoğan. These demonstrations were more than just a domestic conflict imported from Turkey; they also expressed the national identity of the resident Turkish populations.

The same can be said of the protests of Muslim youth all over Europe against the Israeli invasion of the Gaza Strip. The emergence of anti-Semitic resentment is of course unacceptable, and the state has to combat it by utilising the laws that apply to all people who live in the state in question. However, the youth rebellions in the suburbs did not only relate to Israel and Palestine but also to the social and cultural disintegration of a major group of young people living in the EU. It is not enough to simply use police repression against them.

The conflicts we are experiencing today and, more importantly, can expect in the future, show that the social coexistence of people with different cultural backgrounds does not work spontaneously, but needs political regulation.

The national relationships in Europe are all the more complex because there is a coincidence of growing interstate nationalism and national disintegration with the existence of supranational national minorities. The political regulation of these increasingly complex and difficult relations lies beyond the capacities of individual states; the appropriate dimension for dealing with this is European integration. This means, however, that a democratic conception of the coexistence of nations and national minorities in Europe, which represent a social reality, is a key element of a democratic programme for European integration.

Nationalism and social disintegration

The European Union has resolved neither the contradictions within societies nor those between states and nations, but it has moved them from the battlefields to the conference rooms in Brussels. This represents a step forward for civilisation, and we cannot allow it to be reversed by newly incited nationalism.

It is easy to condemn European nationalisms by looking at the suffering and chaos they have caused. It is harder, though, to identify their social origins and the political mistakes which have led to their victories. Answers can be found, as the Hungarian-Austrian economist and social historian Karl Polanyi put it, in the market economy, on the one hand, which has produced mass unemployment and general misery instead of being functional and, on the other hand, in political measures which have further exacerbated social contradictions instead of mitigating them.

Barely a century later, the memory of these effects of European nationalisms has faded, and millions of people are observing that states, as well as Europe as a whole, are failing to protect them from unemployment, from losing their homes, and from being excluded from social security systems. The inhabitants of Europe, who are still enjoying relatively comfortable living conditions, are told that the victims of the crisis are themselves to blame for their dire situation and that they are living off everybody's tax money now. Is it, therefore, really surprising that Euroscepticism and nationalism are sprouting up everywhere?

Here the left faces a twofold challenge. It has to uncompromisingly oppose populist nationalism, because never in history have discord between peoples and xenophobia helped in solving social problems. But the social problems caused by government policy, which millions of Europeans are forced to face, are real. That is why the left has to intransigently oppose the policies enacted in the member states in the name of Europe – policies responsible for the current misery. They have allowed nationalist and right-wing extremist groups to flourish.

How can we face this challenge?

The majority of European citizens are neither anti-European nor nationalist, but the results of the European elections show that their approval of European integration is not irreversible. The window of opportunity for peace in Europe on a solid economic and political foundation can also close again. For now, the siege mentality haunting pro-European forces is no help. Something else is necessary: to acknowledge the fundamental fact, which drove European reconstruction, that Europe can only be unified if it is a social Europe.

The radical left's strategic dilemma

The strategies of radical left-wing parties to deal with European policy are still diverse. Most parties' attitude can be described as Eurosceptical, but not anti-European. Only in the Scandinavian countries, whose accession to the EU coincided with the implementation of neoliberalism, are there radical left parties for which opposition to the EU 'in its present form' is their main identity marker, which they use especially to dissociate themselves from the social democrats, writes Luke March, a British political scientist working in party research. However, according to him it is an open question whether right or left-wing parties benefit more from a strong opposition to the EU. Even though right and left EU criticism are diametrically opposed to one another in content and motivation, it is hard to establish empirically whether the voters really notice the difference. On the one hand, March continues, there are indications that high EU-hostility in the population is likely to be associated with higher electoral success for [radical left parties]'.[2] If this is true, simplistic EU criticism could, in the long term, have a boomerang effect for the left. This is not principally about electoral politics. In view of the crisis, the left has to ask itself what role Europe should play in a concept for a transformation of capitalist societies.

The Greek political scientist Gerassimos Moschonas sees the left facing the strategic dilemma that the treaties and the institutional composition of the EU work against the radical left. In his view, Europeanisation has deprived the left's traditional goal – conquering the state through revolution or by parliamentary means – of its meaning. 'In the European system there is no Winter Palace to occupy or surround [...], and there is no strategy of coordination of the national lefts [...], nor a common social base ready to be mobilised around the same strategic objectives.'[3] In a system which is governed on several levels, he concludes, the strategy of seizing power cannot find a target.

For Moschonas, if the radical left acts rationally, it must play on the European level. But in doing so it will make a frustrating discovery: The operating principles specific for Europe based on unanimity or qualified majorities in the different institutions work conservatively and technocratically, just like multi-level governance, and are closed to change.

The two central links of this chain 'can be called "grand coalition" and "reform"'.[4] However, they are both the opposite of radical. Moschonas' recommendation of adopting a clear pro-European strategy implies for him a 'de-radicalisation' of the radical left. Leftists who advocate an anti-EU strategy would agree.

Does this mean we have to choose between Europeanisation and radicalism? Also, must the radical point of view really be attached to the defence of national sovereignty?

If we want to change the balance of power we have to identify intermediate steps and transitions. This is nothing new. For the specifically European path, as described by Moschonas and defined by compromises and coalition-building, Gramsci used his famous concept of the 'war of position', which he proposed as the rational substitute for the failed 1920s communist strategy of armed uprising.

In a political war of position it is never useful to adopt the opponent's either-or position. This is also true of the juxtaposition of European *federalism* and *souverainism*. This dichotomy, however, is abstract because the implied question of the appropriate division of labour between the different political decision-making levels completely depends on the context of social problems at the heart of the specific conflict. This is why most left parties refuse to take a side in this dichotomy. In his work on European politics of the radical left, Richard Dunphy also rejects 'as too simplistic the tendency to divide the world into rival and mutually exclusive camps of "Eurosceptics" and "pro-Europeans'".[5]

Differences of opinion became clearly visible in the debate on the Treaty Establishing a Constitution for Europe in 2005. There, most parties agreed that the EU should prioritise a social-state orientation but made different proposals for its political-institutional future. This strategic disagreement still constitutes one of the limitations of left politics in Europe, even though the debate on European integration has continued for several decades now.

Europe and the radical left

One of the most prominent buildings of the European Parliament in Brussels bears the name of the Communist resistance fighter Altiero Spinelli. In 1941, during his time in the prison camp on Ventotene island, he, together with two fellow prisoners, wrote the *Ventotene Manifesto*, in which he proclaimed the revolutionary establishment of a federal Europe founded on socialism.

The *Manifesto* was intended as a platform for a broad socialist and pro-European movement and reflected the convictions of many anti-fascists who 'became Europeans' through the suffering they shared in prisons and camps. The *Manifesto of the Democratic Socialists of the Former Buchenwald Concentration Camp* is a similar document. Its first and foremost goal was 'to achieve a European community of states in collaboration with all countries led by socialist governments, which guarantees order and prosperity by introducing a common European economy on our long-suffering continent'.[6]

In 1976 the Italian Communist Party sent Spinelli – who, by then was no longer a member of the party – as an independent representative to the European Parliament where he was elected deputy chairman of the Communists and Allies Group. In the early 1980s a draft for a European constitution, which originated with Spinelli, led to the Single European Act (SEA). At SEA's core, however, was not the democratisation of the EC – much to the disappointment of Spinelli and the left – but the implementation of the common market.

Because of the Cold War and the division of Europe, it is hardly known today – not even within the left – that the idea of a united Europe goes back to the left. But the Cold War has been over for a quarter of a century now, and it does not make sense to interpret today's world from its perspective.

In the debate on European unity, however, we can go back even further in the tradition of the radical left. As early as the beginning of the twentieth century, all of the great personalities of the left – Kautsky, Luxemburg, Lenin, Trotsky, and Bauer – spoke about the idea of a 'United States of Europe'.

The points of view they expressed in the debate were controversial and often polemical, but they shared the common belief that the contradictions which allegedly pitted the European peoples against one another were an expression of social problems that they faced internally. According to the socialist view, if these are social contradictions which emerge in the form of the national question, then nationalism has to be countered above all by social-policy measures. This is also what the passage quoted from Otto Bauer at the beginning of this essay expresses, and it constitutes a major contribution of socialism to the reconstruction of European societies.

The EU is on a collision course with the social state – and no effort by an intellectually enlightened minority to teach the lower classes political correctness will be able to change this. Daniel Cohn-Bendit's and Guy Verhofstadt's *Manifesto for Europe* serves as a typical example. 'Be proud of being a European'; 'do not fear what scares us, but fear fear itself'; 'do not ask what Europe can mean to you, but what you can mean to Europe',[7] is what the authors call out to 26 million unemployed people in Europe, as though the EU were a crazy sect and the authors its gurus. Just as with other gurus, this is above all about money and control. They write, 'in the Eurozone, more than in any other currency union, discipline is absolutely essential',[8] and luckily 'automatic sanctions have been introduced now' for members who do not comply with this discipline, 'because today there are only three member states – Finland, Estonia, and Luxembourg – which actually implement the strict standards of the Eurozone'.[9]

However, instead of applauding the 'automatic sanctions', would it not make much more sense to ask what the point of standards is that have led to excessive unemployment and cuts in social services, and can only be adhered to by three out of 28 states?

NATION – PROJECT AND DESTINY?

The critique of nationalism was already an important issue 25 years ago, when nationalism was aimed against immigrants arriving in Europe at the time. Two monographs, which are still worth reading today, on nation and nationalism were published at the time - Étienne Balibar and Immanuel Wallerstein's *Race, Nation, Class: Ambiguous Identities* and Hobsbawm's *Nations and Nationalism Since 1780 - Programme, Myth, Reality.*

Balibar's[10] essay followed the post-structuralist discourse which was very common in social sciences at the time. His thesis was that nations are mainly intellectual structures, which under certain circumstances achieve institutional reality in the form of states.

According to Balibar, national identity rests on a twofold illusion: firstly, that the generations which have succeeded one another in one territory have passed on an unalterable essence to each other; and secondly, that the members of a national community are the results of a predestined development, the only one possible. According to Balibar, project and destiny are the two symmetrical figures of the illusion of national identity.[11]

And, I would add, it does not matter whether the disastrous coupling of project and destiny results from ethnic descent, as in the traditional right's understanding, or from cultural identification and/or difference, as in the new right's understanding.

Dissolving this illusion, above all the 'symbolic difference between "us" and the "foreigners"'[12] created by the nation and the state was what Balibar focused on. He was reacting to a political dilemma which not only the left in France faced. While the conservative section of the left felt that the social rights acquired through the nation state must be defended even against the newly arrived immigrants, the other part developed a morally motivated, post-national discourse in order to assert the universal validity of individual human rights for the immigrants arriving in our societies. Balibar must be given credit in this debate for having defended human rights, their universal character, and therefore also immigrants.

Still, social state or human rights – could this represent an acceptable dichotomy for the left? In order to resolve this contradiction, we need a different perspective.

The left has never looked at the social state only from the standpoint of individual civil rights, but has seen it as a collective achievement, which has limited the negative impacts and risks of the market economy. As a left project, and already under capitalism, the social state was meant to implement elements of the emancipation of the working class – the people who are in one way or another dependent on the labour market.

However, this has always been hard-fought ground, in which any achievement was subsequently challenged by every technological or economic change. Whenever the working class' representatives confined themselves to defending achievements and did not call for the further development and universalisation of the social state in relation to gender equality and immigrants, they even called the achievements into question.

Moreover, solidary relations in a state do not require only equal economic and social rights. Democracy only works if different ways of life are recognised through collective laws and their practice accepted; this includes the right to use one's native language in public or when interacting with the state, the right to education in one's native language, to the free practice of religion, and finally to the autonomous administration of cultural matters. The concept of nationality to which these rights refer has nothing to do with an illusory identity but involves practical everyday needs. Their consensual solution constitutes the precondition for social coexistence and democracy in multinational societies.

From a social policy as well as a democratic perspective this confronts the labour movement and the left with new questions.

Just like Balibar, Eric Hobsbawm assumed the illusory character of most national narratives, which tend to equate two very different phenomena: a group or collective consciousness and the development of a specific form of state, the 'nation state' which is allegedly based on this consciousness.[13]

Unlike Balibar, for Hobsbawm, a British historian with Austrian roots, it made sense to proceed in his book from what he calls 'the important and underestimated debates among the Marxists of the Second International on what they called the "national question"', namely the debates between Kautsky, Luxemburg, Otto Bauer, and Lenin.[14]

What can we learn from classical Marxism with regards to the politics of nationalities? First of all, we can learn that nations – in whatever way they may be constructed – form a part of social reality from which they cannot be removed or 'deconstructed'. Nations exist and a post-national era – if at all realistic – is a distant utopia which is of no use for today's politics. Are we really living in an era of 'post-nationalism', just as, for example, the Austrian writer Robert Menasse maintains? 'The nations are dead, but they are the only ones who don't know it',[15] he said in a recent lecture. Such a statement, however, cannot be demonstrated empirically. Even in Austria with its wide open economy, 60 per cent of the economic output is consumed within the country's borders, and the state takes half of the domestic product in order to fund its expenses and redistribute wealth. From the point of view of the total national accounting, the 'nation state' as a social and tax state thus remains an important fact and a challenge for democratisation.

The critique of nationalism cannot consist in the denial of the existence of nations. What it does have to confront is the claim that every modern nation has to coincide with a state. This is impracticable. No state can be inhabited only by the members of one nation, which also means that the right to self-determination by no means always implies the founding of a state. The killing that takes place in the name of nationalism is connected to these misconceptions.

One of the great cultural achievements of socialism is that it has removed the national question from the realm of destiny. The nation does not determine the collective destiny of the people.

Socialism and nation

The right to self-determination supported by socialists primarily meant that people should have the right to determine their fate in the framework of nations. They considered as secondary and variable the particular state forms, and other conditions, in which this self-determination occurred. Therefore, the controversies among socialists did not mainly relate to the principle of self-determination, but to the way in which it could be implemented so as not to obscure their programmatic goals whose character was social as opposed to national.

In this context it is interesting to come back to Bauer's special concept of what he calls 'national-cultural autonomy'. Very often it is assumed that this involves territorial self-determination for the different nations coexisting in Austria-Hungary. However, this was really the relatively easily solved part, as the successful example of the autonomous region of South Tyrol shows today. If Bauer's idea were limited to this, however, he would have missed the main problem which kept blocking state reform in Austria-Hungary. The problem was not solely the coexistence of nine nations, but the fact that they were intermixed. According to Bauer, 'the mixing of nations is something no form of national delimitation, however carefully it is carried out, will be able to get rid of'.[16] To the territorial principle – either *ius sanguinis* in Germany or *ius soli* in France[17] – the Austro-Marxists counterposed a different principle, the *personal principle*, which does not organise the nations in territorial entities, but in 'pure associations of persons',[18] entities which everybody, irrespective of their place of birth or residence, could be part of.

According to Bauer, in the framework of a common democratic state, however, 'it is not the case that Germans are allotted power in one territory and Czechs in another territory, but nations – wherever they live – should form separate entities, which independently administer their own national concerns. This way, in one and the same city two or more nations would be able to establish their own national self-administration and national educational institutions – just as Catholics, Protestants, and Jews manage their religious affairs in one city, alongside each other.'[19]

Bauer and Renner were aware of the revolutionary character of their 'new socialist principle of nationalities policy'. According to Bauer, this national-cultural autonomy could become the blueprint for an 'innovative social structure', a 'state of states', into which individual national communities are incorporated.[20]

In terms of civilisation, there could be considerable progress if national problems relating to national-cultural autonomy and the personal principle were negotiated not in the form of drawing state borders, but in terms of the political and cultural rights of persons within states. The dissolution of multinational Yugoslavia serves as an example of the tragic alternative. Not only did it trigger a terrible war between the republics, which separated from one other; it also led to hatred, murder, and rape even in the most remote regions and settlements, where the different ethnicities had lived peacefully in a common state for decades.

Multinationalism is the common reality of European states today. In light of the growing problems, what level could be more suitable than that of European integration to craft the institutional framework for the civilised solution of these problems?

Moreover, Bauer, who had dedicated his study to the resolution of the complicated problem of nationality in Austria-Hungary, concluded by saying that the 'United States of Europe' constitute the 'final goal of a movement', which 'the nations have long since initiated and which will be greatly accelerated by forces that are already becoming visible'.[21]

A new blueprint for integration

Today, the left is facing a similar challenge at the European level. Just as in Bauer's time it is clear that rampant nationalism can be countered only if Europe is redefined as a social integration concept. Social policy provides the key for integration.

If the left, however, wants to prevent national conflicts from once again becoming the projection of social contradictions and therefore an obstacle to the social struggles necessary for their resolution, it needs an independent and concrete programme for the democratic integration of Europe. It has to be based on real conditions, that is, the continued existence of nations, and not on the assumption that they are disappearing. Therefore, we should not imagine a united Europe as a large 'post-national' unitary state which reproduces the model of a national state on a larger scale.

Instead, we should construct a well thought-out balance of self-determination, subsidiarity, and autonomy, which regulates the relations between existing democracies in a new way and provides methods for resolving the growing number of domestic and inter-state national conflicts that prove to be intractable on the basis of the nation state concept.

But how can a democratic Europe be institutionalised?

Starting from the necessity of a social and environmental reconstruction of Europe, what we need is a European Union which defines new social and ecological priorities. For this it has to provide the necessary instruments and policies in the form of banking oversight, redistribution policy, European public services, and European transfer payments. Also necessary are a substantial increase of the Community budget and the introduction of new financial instruments ('Eurobonds').

However, a strengthened and reprogrammed European Union also needs new legitimacy resting on the sovereignty of the European peoples.

No taxation without representation! Europe needs a concise and coherent Basic Law which defines a common legal space in which there is division of powers between the different levels and institutions on the basis of subsidiarity. This requires European citizenship based on equal rights for all people living in the Union and a uniform, proportional electoral law for the European Parliament.

Europe must be a space of parliamentary democracy. In such a democracy the national parliaments and the European Parliament are not pitted against one another as rivals, but must become allies in defending, reclaiming, and extending their rights and stand up against the prerogatives of non-elected executive bodies – such as the European Central Bank, the European Court of Justice and the European Commission – which on both the state and the European levels are accumulating power in an unregulated way. EU treaties such as the Stability and Growth Pact, which legitimise non-elected bodies assuming legislative functions, must be abrogated.

The European Parliament must have the right to freely decide on the European budget, to pass European laws, and elect the European Commission as its executive body. It has to be given full responsibility for fiscal and monetary policy at the European level and exercise control over the European Central Bank.

In order to confront nationalism, it is necessary to recognise that the European Union is a multinational region made up mostly of multinational states whose borders are open. In such an area, national rights are by the same token personal and collective rights, and every individual has the right to join or not to join a national community of her or his choice, in order to exercise her or his cultural, national, and religious rights in a common juridical framework.

We will still need political representation of the states, nations, and national minorities. It is not so important whether such an institution develops from the European Council or from a possibly newly created second chamber of the European Parliament, but it is important that the principle of checks and balances between these institutions and the European Union is recognised. We could imagine the EU's renewal as a Commonwealth of European Nations which is based on voluntariness, democracy, and subsidiarity.

Such a Europe will only be an option worth striving for if it defines itself as a project of peace and good neighbourliness. Alongside its commitment to non-military conflict resolution, its Basic Law must declare the EU's fundamental openness towards all states of the region that want to commit themselves to its principles.

★ ★ ★

Instead of integration, however, Europe is facing the threat of comprehensive social and political disintegration. Such situations have been seen several times in history.

In 1918, Rosa Luxemburg wrote indignantly in her (then unpublished) essay 'Fragment on War, the National Question, and Revolution' about burgeoning nationalism in the dissolving multi-ethnic states: 'From all sides nations and semi-nations who had never formed independent body politics, feel a powerful urge to form a state [...]' 'Mouldered corpses from hundred-year-old graves, filled with new spring fever – today is Walpurgis Night on the nationalist Bald Mountain'.[22]

Luxemburg could be wrong when she wrote about the development of the European system of states. But she was right about one thing: twenty years later, conflicting national ambitions and the Great Depression of 1929 had tied the Gordian Knot in European politics, which the Nazis wanted to cut through with the sword of a world war.

Europe is still far from such a scenario. However, the dangers are now visible, and there is urgent need of solutions to the two most important problems in Europe: the multiple crises which still have not been overcome and the lack of real democracy, which characterises all sectors of society and political institutions.

In these struggles, the left in Europe will either stand the test or go down with Europe.

translated by Veronoika Peterseil

Literature

Balibar, Étienne and Immanuel Wallerstein, *Race, Nation, Class: Ambiguous Identities*, London and New York: Verso, 1991.

Bauer, Otto, *Die Nationalitätenfrage und die Sozialdemokratie* [The Nationalities Question and Social Democracy], Vienna: Verlag der Wiener Volksbuchhandlung, 1924.

Cohn-Bendit, Daniel and Guy Verhofstadt, *Für Europa! Ein Manifest* [For Europe! Manifesto for a Postnational Revolution in Europe], Munich: Carl Hanser Verlag, 2012.

Dunphy, Richard, *Contesting Capitalism? Left Parties and European Integration*, Manchester and New York: Manchester University Press, 2004.

Hobsbawm, Eric, *Nations and Nationalisms Since 1780: Programme, Myth, Reality*, Cambridge and New York: Cambridge University Press, 1991.

Luxemburg, Rosa, 'Fragment über Krieg, nationale Frage und Revolution' [Fragment on War, the National Question, and Revolution], *Gesammelte Werke* vol. 5, Berlin: Dietz Verlag, 1918.

Manifesto of the Democratic Socialists of the Former Buchenwald Concentration Camp (1945), <http://www.tenhumbergreinhard.de/taeter-und-mitlaeufer/dokumente/manifest-der-demokratischen-sozialisten.html> (accessed: 20 October 2014).

March, Luke, *Radical Left Parties in Europe*, London: Routledge, 2011.

Moschonas, Gerassimos, 'The European Union and the Dilemmas of the Radical Left', *transform!* 9/2011, <http://www.transform-network.net/en/journal/issue-092011/news/detail/Journal/the-european-union-and-the-dilemmas-of-the-radical-left.html> (accessed: 20 October 2014).

Murmelter, Gerhard, 'Die Nationalstaaten sind tot' [The Nation States Are Dead], *salto-magazin* 2014, <http://www.salto.bz/article/05072014/die-nationalstaaten-sind-tot> (accessed: 20 October 2014).

Notes

1 Eric Hobsbawm, *Nations and Nationalisms Since 1780: Programme, Myth, Reality*, Cambridge and New York: Cambridge University Press, 1991.
2 See Luke March, *Radical Left Parties in Europe*, London: Routledge, 2011, p. 187.
3 Gerassimos Moschonas, 'The European Union and the Dilemmas of the Radical Left', *transform!* 9/2011.
4 See Moschonas, 'The European Union'.
5 See Richard Dunphy, *Contesting Capitalism? Left Parties and European Integration*, Manchester and New York: Manchester University Press, 2004, p. 7.
6 See the *Manifesto of the Democratic Socialists of the Former Buchenwald Concentration Camp* (1945).
7 See Daniel Cohn-Bendit and Guy Verhofstadt, *Für Europa! Ein Manifest*, Munich: Carl Hanser Verlag, 2012, pp. 55, 60, 62, 64.
8 Cohn-Bendit and Verhofstadt, *Für Europa!*, p. 24.
9 Cohn-Bendit and Verhofstadt, *Für Europa!*, p. 25.
10 See Étienne Balibar and Immanuel Wallerstein, *Race, Nation, Class: Ambiguous Identities*, London and New York: Verso, 1991 (1990), pp. 107 ff.
11 Balibar, *Race, Nation, Class*, p. 107.
12 Balibar, *Race, Nation, Class*, p. 116.
13 Hobsbawm, *Nations and Nationalisms*.
14 See Hobsbawm, *Nations and Nationalisms*, p. 2.
15 Gerhard Murmelter, 'Die Nationalstaaten sind tot', *salto-magazin* 2014.
16 See Otto Bauer, *Die Nationalitätenfrage und die Sozialdemokratie*, Vienna: Verlag der Wiener Volksbuchhandlung, 1924, p. 328.
17 Ius sanguinis, 'right of blood', that is, the right to nationality based on parentage; ius soli, 'right of the soil', that is, the right to nationality based on place of birth.
18 Bauer, *Die Nationalitätenfrage*, p. 353.
19 Bauer, *Die Nationalitätenfrage*, p. 354.
20 Bauer, *Die Nationalitätenfrage*, p. 519.
21 Bauer, *Die Nationalitätenfrage*, p. 520.
22 Rosa Luxemburg, 'Fragment über Krieg, nationale Frage und Revolution', *Gesammelte Werke* vol. 5, Berlin: Dietz Verlag, 1918, pp. 367ff.

RIGHT-WING EXTREMISM AND MODERNISED RIGHT-WING POPULISM IN EUROPE[1]

Joachim Bischoff, Elisabeth Gauthier, and Bernhard Müller

The right's recent success[2]

The results of the 2014 European Parliament (EP) elections point to a shift to the right in the political spectrum – albeit to varying degrees in different countries. In France, Denmark, and Great Britain in particular, but also in Austria, Sweden, and Finland, as well as Hungary and Greece, a number of political parties that position themselves to the right of the conservative-nationalist parties have gained seats in the European Parliament.

In France, the Front National (FN) became the strongest political force with 25 per cent; in Denmark, the Danish People's Party (DF) ranked first, receiving 26.6 per cent of the vote, and in Great Britain the UK Independence Party (UKIP) came in first. In Austria, the Freedom Party (FPÖ) won 20.5 per cent of the vote and in Hungary FIDESZ had a runaway victory with 51.5 per cent. Several parties such as Golden Dawn in Greece and Jobbik in Hungary should be classified as neo-fascist or neo-Nazi. There are thus considerable differences within the political right and extreme right.[3]

This rightward trend was also evident in the national elections held after the European Parliament elections. In Germany, the Alternative for Germany (AfD) has been further consolidated in recent regional elections. In Sweden, the Sweden Democrats managed to substantially increase their share of the vote.

The Sweden Democrats and the end of the Swedish welfare state

In Sweden, the coalition of centre-right parties led by the conservative Fredrik Reinfeldt was voted out of office in an election with a high turnout of 83.3 per cent. While the Social Democrats fell short of reaching their declared goal of 35 per cent (they received 31 per cent; in 2010 their share was 30.7 per cent), it now falls to them to form a government. The coalition of Social Democrats and Greens, however, won only 158 out of 348 seats; they are thus 17 seats short of an absolute majority and must rely on 21 deputies of the Left party (Vänster Partiet) which attained 6 per cent at the elections. Reinfeldt's centre-right alliance managed to win only 142 seats; the right-wing populist Sweden Democrats won 49 seats.

The Sweden Democrats, under their party leader Jimmie Åkesson, more than doubled (12.9 per cent) their share of the vote (in 2010 they received 5.7 per cent), becoming the third strongest force; they therefore have the capacity to block government decisions.

The trends in Sweden are illustrative of the developments in a large number of European societies that are economically well-off and politically advanced. After many years of a tolerant immigration policy, the centre-right coalition made the issue of immigration the heart of its election campaign. Prime Minister Reinfeldt reasoned that due to the great number of unstable regions in the world, Sweden faces an unprecedented influx of refugees and that the consequent costs would render both tax cuts and increased investments impossible for the next legislative period.

Exception no more: right-wing populism in the 'troubled paradise'

In contrast to other European countries, Germany has not seen a successful manifestation of right-wing populism and right-wing extremism in the form of a political party in recent years. It was only for the 2014 European Parliament (EP) elections that an electorally significant right-wing populist party, the Alternative for Germany (AfD), was established; other right-wing extremist parties, such as the NPD, have remained rather insignificant by comparison. However, the electoral potential for a right-wing populist force has been foreseeable for some years.

Up to now, the crystallising of this potential into a political party has failed because of the fragmented nature of the extreme right. The establishment of the AfD has changed all this. Within a very short period (since May/June 2013) a mainly right-wing group of populists has received significant support. After failing to enter the Bundestag by a narrow margin (with 4.7 per cent of the vote) in autumn of 2013, the party managed to win 7.0 per cent of the votes in the EP elections (which had a significantly lower turnout). The regional elections in Saxony, Brandenburg, and Thuringia showed that the AfD had succeeded in its strategy of consolidation, and it is now represented in these regional parliaments with more than 10 per cent of the vote.

As a morally conservative, national liberal, and right-wing populist party the AfD represents a part of the political spectrum which has been articulating itself in Europe for many years now, through the British UKIP, Austria's FPÖ and Alliance for the Future of Austria (BZÖ), Italy's Lega Nord, the Scandinavian parties True Finns, Denmark's DF, the Sweden Democrats, through the Swiss People's Party (SVP), Geert Wilders' Party for Freedom in the Netherlands (PVV), as well as France's FN.

The AfD puts fiscal consolidation at the core of its programme. The party campaigns for a return to the structure of a national state (including a German currency and citizenship), regardless of how European neighbouring countries deal with their massive crises. 'The idea of a peaceful Europe is crumbling under the pressure of the restructuring programmes that are forced upon the countries in crisis. Never before has the EU been so at odds with itself as it is today. This is why the AfD is campaigning for a planned and organised withdrawal from the single currency zone.'[4]

Its programme includes other demands typical of a right-wing populist party: Immigration is acceptable, as long as immigrants have no access to social security and rights. 'The AfD strongly opposes access for immigrants to the German social security system. Social security may be granted to immigrants exclusively in accordance with German legislation without any interference by the EU.' This radicalised attitude, a precursor of which was the CSU's demand for a car toll for foreigners, generates material commonly found in right-wing populist programmes. The AfD has not yet become a consolidated organisation. It is characterised by three political tendencies and milieus: a radical free-market tendency, a national-conservative tendency, and a milieu clearly akin to right-wing populism. The AfD succeeded in instantly gaining an average 10 per cent of the vote in the regions of Saxony, Brandenburg, and Thuringia by presenting itself as a protest party espousing nationalist EU-scepticism, thinly-veiled xenophobia, and a populist critique of the political class. In its election programme, the AfD plays on numerous resentments and attitudes in the population. Massive geopolitical turmoil, as well as internal 'threats' due to the erosion of social justice, the increasing number of immigrants, and disenchantment with politics, is creating a hotbed for right-wing populist attitudes in Germany.

Reasons for the (new) popularity of right-wing populism

Thus, Sweden and Germany have seen a new development of right-wing populist and right-wing extremist political parties and movements, which has characterised other European countries for some time.[5] The recent success of these parties has been very varied. Many have succeeded in establishing themselves as permanent players in the political system, capable of shaping its development.

In the political debate – including among the different tendencies of the left – the reasons for the success of right-wing and right-wing populist parties mostly remain hazy. The main case we would make is that in the course of the profound crisis which has seized European countries and the EU as a whole, political systems have also plunged into serious crisis. The ruling elites have proved incapable of dealing with the collapse of traditional bourgeois civil society and its economic dynamic. At the same time, the widespread criticism of the system is not spontaneously generating progressive options. Profound disillusion, growing insecurity, and the feeling that politics is no longer able to deliver solutions affect the whole traditional political spectrum, including the political left.

Thus, neoliberalism's obvious defeat and the shock it caused do not lead to new dynamics for left political organisations, but create a space adroitly used by modernised right-wing populist and right-wing extremist groups in many countries. The mixture they have devised of criticism of capitalism, condemnation of the political system, and nationalism – an unambiguously right-wing populist position – has been very successful. Today, these parties intend to come to power and realise a profound transformation of the existing power relations. This means that we are no longer facing mere opposition groups, but protagonists who are posing the question of cultural and political hegemony.

Very often in theoretical and political debate citizens of the 'classe populaire' are made responsible for the rightward shift. The problem with this explanation is that members of this social stratum have voted continuously less often in recent years. Instead, it is the middle stratum's fear of downward mobility which best explains the shift.

There is no end in sight of the transformation of the political architecture and of the political arena. The further development of the crisis will lead to further intensification of contradictions on the economic and political terrains. Talk of a lost decade is justified, especially in Southern Europe. Spain, Portugal, and Greece have experienced a massive downturn, and predictions of a quick economic recovery are not very convincing. Social injustice, a driving force of the crisis, was in turn aggravated by it. It is not surprising that the crisis has left deep traces on the political architecture of almost every EU state. One result in some countries, especially those of the South, is the strengthening of left forces. In many cases, however, it has been the Eurosceptical parties of the right which have managed to seize on and reinforce the resentful attitude towards the political establishment in times of massive economic difficulties, high unemployment rates, and radical austerity measures.

The right-wing populist parties have scored successes in their various countries by stressing three political issues: a) profound contempt for the existing political classes or elite; b) rejection of the European Union and the anti-crisis policies it has pursued up to now; and c) the demand to seal off the national social security systems from immigrants and refugees. Marine Le Pen's statement for the Front National may serve as an example:

> The EU is a catastrophe; it is an anti-democratic monster. I want to prevent it from getting fatter, continuing to breathe, touching everything with its paws and reaching to all corners of our legislation with its tentacles. We have lost millions of lives in our glorious history in order to stay a free country. And yet today we simply let our right to self-determination be stolen from us in this way.[6]

In EU member states, a consistent section of the population harbours a markedly right-wing resentment. Its extent and the political forms of expression and organisation vary according to the country. People's everyday consciousness varies depending on how a country has been hit by the crisis, the neoliberal austerity policies implemented, and the degree of aloofness of the political elites. With the increased flux of refugees and immigrants, right-wing parties can appropriately adapt themselves to win greater political influence.

Developments such as those in Sweden and France show that – against the background of clear and dramatic social conflicts – right-wing parties are emerging from their social isolation. The 'de-demonisation' strategies of their party leaderships are working because by this very process the problems themselves are exacerbated. For example, the FN's strategy of 'normalisation' and 'de-demonisation' is successful because the ruling elites are proffering solutions neither materially nor in their social communications strategies. Right-wing and right-wing populist parties are listened to and gain support when the elite's problem-solving capacity is waning and when traditional parties, representative organs, and government institutions have lost touch with citizens. Overall, two developments are noticeable: a) the transformation of a few nationalist and extremist parties of the right into modernised radical right-wing populist parties; and b) the growing importance of such parties in national and European elections.

Financial globalisation and the EU: the deepening social gap and growing fears of the loss of social status

At the dawn of the twenty-first century, all European societies are experiencing social tensions due to accelerated neoliberal restructuring processes. More people are anxious and dissatisfied with their professional existence. In particular, the insecurity among the 'middle class'[7] is turning into a crisis of democracy and consequently of the party system and the democratic decision-making process.

In the left, too, it is widely accepted that the explanatory key for the growing right-wing potential is the direct impact of the crisis on right-wing voters – for example in the case of unemployment. In reality, however, the causes of fear do not directly translate into right-wing mentalities and attitudes in those most affected.

There is a latent right extremism problem in a section of the petite bourgeoisie and of wage-dependent employees. For example, investigations of the social base of the right-wing electoral potential in different countries show that ordinary unskilled workers, skilled workers, the unemployed and certified craftsmen, the self-employed and farmers, people with a low net household income, as well as those questioned who have a very basic education and people who categorise themselves as workers have an above-average tendency to vote for right-wing parties in comparison to people with a middle or secondary school diploma.

In the Greek parliamentary elections of June 2012,[8] 29 per cent of Golden Dawn voters wanted to express their desperation and protest, 27 per cent their attitude towards immigrants and border protection, 14 per cent their approval for the election programme and 13 per cent their patriotic attitude and anxiety about the future of Greece. The proportion of voters who are precarious and/or unskilled workers was above average (24.5 per cent), as was the percentage of unemployed voters (23.5 per cent) and business owners (20.3 per cent). Voters who do not face direct and harsh competition in the labour market, such as civil servants (4.7 per cent), women working at home as home keepers (3.6 per cent), university students (3.6 per cent), and pensioners from the private and public sector were significantly less likely to vote for Golden Dawn.[9]

Various studies have shown different attitudes towards these issues. In a survey of 6,000 participants in France in which social status and political attitude was investigated,[10] it was shown that territorial isolation (living in the urban periphery) and a high level of social insecurity (especially employees of SMEs) correlate with a stronger tendency to vote for the FN. The perception of how democracy is working is also a clear differentiator: 83 per cent of FN voters, 72 per cent of non-voters, and 66 per cent of Front de Gauche voters think that the democratic system is not working. By contrast, only 56 per cent of UMP voters, 48 per cent of Green voters, and 29 per cent of Socialist Party voters share this opinion. Broken down by social position, this outlook is shared by 81 per cent of the unemployed, 78 per cent of people living in the urban periphery, 74 per cent of people with low incomes, and 72 per cent of people who live in households with less than €1,200 monthly at their disposal. A study conducted over a few decades[11] shows that in the group of workers strongly affected by de-industrialisation, de-skilling, and precarisation, those who lean towards the political right become radicalised, whereas those who lean towards the political left tend to join the non-voters.

Due to growing economic and social pressure on the middle strata, and the resultant social fears, prejudiced right-wing attitudes are increasingly found amongst people who live in relatively stable, even well-off, households. This significantly expands the social basis for right-wing populism.

Racism – anti-Semitism – Islamophobia

In terms of right-wing attitudes and mentalities we are confronted with a syndrome consisting of many different sources of resentment.

Right-wing attitudes are – albeit with differences – to be found in all European countries. This was confirmed in a study carried out by the German Institute for Interdisciplinary Research on Conflict and Violence (IKG) in the framework of the project Group-Focused Enmity in Europe[12] (survey period 2008):

- 50.4 per cent of Europeans in part or fully agree that there are too many immigrants in their respective countries. This statement shows an overall and blind rejection of immigrants.
- 24.4 per cent agree that 'Jews are too influential in their countries'. This statement shows a traditional aspect of anti-Semitism reflecting anti-Semitic conspiracy myths.
- 54.4 per cent of Europeans believe that Islam is a religion of intolerance. This belief shows that many people perceive Islam as something negative (and have a negative attitude towards Muslims as well).
- Almost a third (31.3 per cent) of Europeans somewhat or fully agree that there is a 'natural hierarchy between blacks and whites'. This implies that they agree with a very open and direct form of racism which legitimises an ethnic hierarchy because of alleged natural differences.

- The majority of Europeans (60.2 per cent) support traditional gender roles. By demanding that 'women should take their role as wives and mothers more seriously' they support, amongst other things, economic inequality between the genders.
- 42.6 per cent reject equal rights for gay and lesbian people and consider homosexuality 'immoral'.

In 2014 in Germany, people's approval of right-wing extremist statements has decreased significantly in comparison with earlier studies. Researchers attribute this to the relatively positive economic conditions in Germany, which feature economic growth and a stable labour market. However, there are some important exceptions: asylum seekers, Muslims, as well as Roma and Sinti, are experiencing much greater stigmatisation. Contempt for asylum seekers is very widespread amongst survey participants from the new eastern states of Germany (84.7 per cent) and the old states of Germany (73.5 per cent). More than half of the German participants also harbour resentment against Roma and Sinti and almost half of them reject Muslims. 'People continue to be susceptible to the ideology of inequality.'[13]

Anti-Semitism continues to constitute a noticeable and consistent element. In comparison with earlier eras, however, its role, though important, is subordinate. According to a German study conducted on right-wing extremism by the Leipzig research group Research Team on Right-Wing Extremism,[14] 5.1 per cent of participants in the survey can be classified as decidedly anti-Semitic. 11.6 per cent take the view that 'Jews are too influential today'. The resentments are connected and constitute a syndrome.

Generally, Euroscepticism is linked to elevated results in our right-wing extremism questionnaire. Regarding the questions on Islamophobia, contempt for Roma and Sinti, as well as asylum seekers, we are noticing significant trends: 64.1% of the participants who have a positive attitude towards the EU do not feel like strangers in their own countries because of the presence of Muslims. However, only 33.3% of those who have a negative attitude towards the EU reject the idea that they are strangers in their own countries.[15]

A recent study in France shows that xenophobia is on the increase again. 66 per cent of the participants in the survey said that there were too many foreigners in France, and 59 per cent said that immigrants did not make 'enough of an effort to integrate', which is 4 per cent more than the result in 2013. Despite a slight decrease in the number of people rejecting Islam compared to the previous year, 63 per cent of French citizens thought that it was 'incompatible with French values' (compared to 74 per cent in 2013).[16]

Also, in the United Kingdom the results of a study from 2010[17] are clear; prejudices against foreigners, a sceptical and distant general stance towards immigrants, and a xenophobic attitude are not rare phenomena but are widespread amongst the population. In Great Britain, 49 per cent of participants felt that the wages of the native population were falling due to immigration. 67 per cent have the position that immigration mainly constitutes a problem for the country.

In Eastern Europe the failed European integration strategy, as well as the increased manifestations of the crisis and the lack of prospects make for all kinds of tensions. According to the specific context and historic traditions, Sinti and Roma, Jews, national minorities, and other societal groups, including homosexuals, are often subjected to attacks. Nationalisms (e.g. Greater Hungary, Greater Romania, etc.) are often resuscitated during disputes with neighbouring countries or the EU.

Election turnout and criticising democracy

Today's continuous changes in economic structures and social relations, with the resultant change in individual and family living conditions, appear as particularly destabilising factors which are inscrutable, a threat to peoples' identities, and also almost impossible to influence through politics.

Disenchantment with EU policies is particularly obvious when looking at the EP elections. Right-wing populist parties are strongly Eurosceptical and anti-EU. In particular, they criticise the growing internationalisation and centralisation of political decision-making processes in Europe, the single currency, an excessive bureaucracy, as well as the disconnection of political processes from peoples' everyday realities. The shape of this rejection differs from country to country. According to the individual context, either nationalistic or welfare-chauvinist aspects (as for example in the Flemish right) are emphasised. Overall, the positions of right-wing populist parties remain rather vague. They consist mainly of strong dissociation from current policies and aim at giving the impression that they would provide relatively non-bureaucratic and quick responses to people's needs and demands. This is also the reason for the widespread vagueness of political contents, which can even be contradictory, all with a view to ingratiating the parties with the voters.

The crisis and the associated euro crisis provide the right-wing populist parties with an unusually high degree of coherence (by their standards)[18] by enabling them to present themselves as both anti-systemic forces and parties taking concrete action. At the same time, it is true that 'the issue of national preference divides the employees in the face of the bosses while the discourse of nationalist opposition to globalisation exonerates the "French" bosses who are nevertheless responsible for, and the real protagonists of, liberalist globalisation'.[19]

The strong polarisation and boundaries drawn between an allegedly homogenous community and disruptive outside influences can be directed vertically against the political class, or the 'establishment', or it can be directed horizontally against influences which are disrupting society at its centre or in its lower strata.

There are growing doubts about politics' capacity to solve problems. For a substantial number of citizens, politics is no longer able to manage and moderate the accelerated transformations of the capitalist system. The high wages received by parliamentarians and functionaries reinforce the impression that these representatives are far removed from people's everyday realities.

> From the population's point of view there is considerable dissatisfaction with the current state of democracy. [...] More than 75 per cent state the opinion that – contrary to the realm of politics – in the economy decisions are taken rather quickly. For more than 80 per cent this means that the economy dictates the decisions, and not politics. [...] About 90 per cent say that political elites disregard democracy and are only interested in pursuing their own interests. [...] There is widespread scepticism about democracy, as about 90 per cent of the population do not think that the democratic parties are up to the task of solving difficult problems.[20]

The mistrust of functionaries and politicians is symptomatic of the extent of unsolved problems, as well as the idea that the political elites, whatever their political colour, accomplish nothing and are mainly looking to their own private interests. The issue is no longer monitoring the political class; the mood has changed. Everybody expects the worst of parties and politicians, elections are primarily used as a means of protest, and political involvement is declining. Thus, in many countries a dangerous cocktail is being mixed, in which nationalist and radical right-wing parties are increasingly anchored in societies in the framework of an (impending) implosion of political systems.[21]

New developments on the right

At the beginning of the twenty-first century, we are not only dealing with an altered right-wing mentality, but also with a new form of the right on the political stage. The right-wing political spectrum in Europe is based on a social milieu, concentrating on the middle strata, which may be defined as ranging from right-wing populist to radical right wing. In recent years it has become obvious in European countries that increased prosperity affects only the richest one per cent of society while real income is at best stagnant for the middle and low-income strata, which means social differences are increasing. For the sectors of the population who take part in political decision-making processes, it is important that their own wealth does not diminish – independently of whether others get a smaller or larger share of the total economic wealth. The pessimistic attitude towards change, the disillusion with the political class, and the middle stratum's loss of hope are the main reasons for the shift of the political coordinates to the right.

This rightward shift with shrinking electoral turnouts is connected to the emergence of new types of right-wing populist parties. Sometimes they strongly dissociate themselves from the traditional right-wing extremist parties. The right-wing extremist parties with an openly racist and nationalist orientation, for example NPD, Jobbik, or Golden Dawn, can only represent a small part of the new protest spectrum or they must transform themselves.[22]

Characteristics of modern right-wing populism are its frontal assaults on the structures of society's decision-making processes and the political class, as well as the promise to remove social conflicts by a culture-based valorisation of the family and the nation, and so to stabilise the living conditions of the 'ordinary folks'. In contrast to historic fascism, which drew its legitimacy from the nation's racially based superiority, the nationalism (or regionalism, for instance in the case of the Lega Nord) of the new right is built on another theoretical foundation.

> Instead of nationalist claims of superiority, the ideology of the new populist right puts forth the concept of ethnic and cultural particularism which recognises the basic right of all people and races to be different. This reinterpretation, which marks the main difference with classic right-wing extremism, associates itself with what at first seems a quite modern concept of cultural and political autonomy. [...] The anti-liberal flipside of relativism only becomes evident when looking at the domestic consequences for a country. [...] The actual thrust of its neo-right-wing demands lies in its [...] rejection of any kind of ethnic, mental and cultural mixture (and its idealisation).[23]

As a reaction to the success of right-wing populist parties and movements, the traditional centre-right parties have adopted large parts of the right-wing parties' programmes (particularly in the areas of domestic security, immigration, and asylum-seeking) and therefore partially pulled the rug out from under their feet. Right-wing populists have thus indirectly caused a significant shift of the whole political spectrum towards the right and accelerated the development towards an authoritarian capitalism with massive limitations on social and civil rights. This rightward shift, especially in the bourgeois camp, however, only goes as far as is needed to temporarily damage an unwelcome competitor, because the underlying social problems and mentalities are not eliminated by this strategy, but are exacerbated and extended by it.

In many European countries, the populist and nationalist extreme right is gaining momentum due to the radicalisation of the right-wing electorate. And at the same time, the left is losing support in a context of crisis, austerity, the dismantlement of democracy, and the delegitimation of politics. Dealing with these tendencies poses a challenge to the whole of society, especially the trade unions, cultural protagonists, and social and political movements.[24]

The left in Europe is thus faced with the question of how to put a stop to the offensive of the nationalist, populist, and extremist right. Slogans like 'no pasarán' or calls for creating an antifascist front only reflect widespread helplessness. The challenge for the left is a lot more complex. The left, it is true, must take a firm stand against nationalist, xenophobic, and racist tendencies wherever and whenever they appear. What is decisive, however, is whether it is possible not only to organise resistance against the dynamic of the radical right but also to find new and creative answers to the question of whether politics can achieve anything positive. In this respect, all the left's societal forces are facing a very complex challenge.

If the left wants to create a new political momentum, it has to counteract the demobilisation of its potential voters (particularly those most affected by the crisis) with a new ambitiousness and therefore develop a strategy for overcoming unleashed capitalism.

A debate on the question of Europe is an essential element of a left counteroffensive. The left must show that between the current neoliberal orientation and the anti-European orientation of the nationalist and right-wing radical forces there is an alternative that will pave the way for new developments in individual countries and in Europe.

translated by Veronika Peterseil

Literature

Camus, Jean Yves, *50 nuances de droite. Typologie des radicalités politiques en Europe* [50 Shades of Right: Types of Political Radicalisms in Europe], Paris: Jean Jaurès Foundation, 2014.

Castel, Robert, 'Zerfall der Lohnarbeitsgesellschaft' [The Decomposition of the Wage Labour Society], Pierre Bourdieu (ed.), *Lohn der Angst. Flexibilisierung und Kriminalisierung in der 'neuen Arbeitsgesellschaft'* [Wage of Fear: Flexibilisation and Criminalisation in the New 'Work Society'], *Liber Internationales Jahrbuch für Literatur und Kultur* vol. 3 (1999–2000), 2001, pp. 14–20.

Decker, Frank, *Der neue Rechtspopulismus* [New Right-Wing Populism], Opladen: Leske und Budrich Verlag, 2004 (second revised edition).

Decker, Oliver, Johannes Kiess, and Elmar Brähler, (2014), *Die stabilisierte Mitte. Rechtsextreme Einstellung in Deutschland* [The Stabilised Centre: Right-Wing Extremist Attitudes in Germany], Leipzig: Universität Leipzig, 2014, <http://www.uni-leipzig.de/~kredo/Mitte_Leipzig_Internet.pdf>.

Deutsche Gewerkschaftsbund, *Mut zu Deutschland. Für ein Europa der Vielfalt – Programm der Alternative für Deutschland (AfD) für die Wahl zum Europäischen Parlament am 25. Mai 2014* [Standing up for Germany: The Case for European Diversity – Programme of the Alternative for Germany (AfD) for the European Parliament Elections on 25 May 2014].

Gauthier, Elisabeth, 'Cartographie des Droites extrêmes et nationalistes en Europe' [A Geography of the Extreme and Nationalist Right-Wing Forces in Europe], in *Les Extrêmes Droites en Europe, en France et en Nord/Pas de Calais* [The Extreme Right in Europe, in France and in Nord/Pas-de-Calais], *Revue Espaces Marx*, 34 (2014).

Harris Interactive, 'Dix leçons inédites sur la séquence électorale 2014' [Ten Unprecedented Lessons from the 2014 Electoral Cycle], 11 July 2014, <http://www.harrisinteractive.fr/news/2014/11072014b.asp>.

Häusler, Alexander and Rainer Roeser, 'Rechtspopulismus in Europa und die rechtspopulistische Lücke in Deutschland' [Right-Wing Populism in Europe and the Right-Wing Populist Gap in Germany], 2014, <http://www.mobit.org/Material/Rechtspopulismus_08_2014.pdf>.

Heitmeyer, Wilhelm, 'Feindselige Normalität' [Hostile Normality], *Die Zeit* 51/2003.

Kraus, Kristina and Peter Preisendörfer, 'Fremdenfeindlichkeit im internationalen Vergleich westlicher Länder' [Comparing The International Situation of Xenophobia in Western Countries], *Gesellschaft – Wirtschaft – Politik* 1/2013, pp. 59-67.

Le Pen, Marine, 'Achtung Frau Merkel' [Watch Out, Mrs Merkel], Interview in *Der Spiegel*, 23 June 2014.

Michalat, Guy and Michel Simon, 'Les attitudes politico-idéologiques selon le parti dont on se sent le plus proche : zoom sur les sympathisants du FN' [Political-Ideological Attitudes According To The Party We Feel Closest To: FN Supporters in the Spotlight], *Les Extrêmes Droites en Europe, en France et en Nord/Pas de Calais, Revue Espaces Marx*, 34 (2014).

Monzat, René, 'Les racines intellectuelles de l'extrême droite française contemporaine', [The Intellectual Roots of the Contemporary French Extreme Right], *Les Extrêmes Droites en Europe, en France et en Nord/Pas de Calais, Revue Espaces Marx*, 34 (2014).

Müller, Bernhard, *Die Erosion der gesellschaftlichen Mitte. Mythen über die Mittelschicht,*

Zerklüftung der Lohnarbeit, Prekarisierung und Armut, Abstiegsängste [The Erosion of the Societal Centre: Myths About the Middle Class, the Cleavages of Wage Labour, Precarity and Poverty, and Fears of Downward Mobility], Hamburg: VSA-Verlag, 2013.

Peukert, Detlev J.K. and Frank Bajohr, *Rechtsradikalismus in Deutschland* [Right-Wing Radicalism in Germany], Hamburg: Ergebnisse, 1990.

Psarras, Dimitris, *La montée du parti d'extrême droite Aube dorée en Grèce* [The Rise of the Right-Wing Extremist Golden Dawn in Greece], Rosa Luxemburg Foundation Pamphlet, 2013.

Psarras, Dimitris (2013b), interviewed by Michael Löwy and Eleni Varikas, 'The Greek Neo-Nazis of Golden Dawn – No Pasaran?', *The Bullet*, <http://www.socialistproject.ca/bullet/870.php>.

Werner, Alban, 'Eine "great moving right show": Was der Rechtsruck bei den Europawahlen 2014 bedeutet', *Sozialismus* 9/2014.

Zick, Andreas, 'Wir dürfen unsere Toleranz nicht überschätzen' [We Should Not Overestimate Our Tolerance], Interview *Tagesspiegel*, 21 May 2014.

Zick, Andreas and Beate Küpper, *Antisemitische Mentalitäten: Bericht über Ergebnisse des Forschungsprojektes Gruppenbezogene Menschenfeindlichkeit in Deutschland und Europa – Expertise für den Expertenkreis Antisemitismus, Berlin, Stand 2011* [Antisemitic Mentalities: Report on the Results of the Research Project 'Group-Focused Enmity in Europe' – Experts Report for the Expert Group on Antisemitism, Berlin, State of Research 2011], Bielefeld: Fakultät für Erziehungswissenschaft – Institut für interdisziplinäre Konflikt- und Gewaltforschung, 2011.

Notes

1. This contribution is an abbreviated version of a soon-to-be-published comprehensive report on issues of right-wing extremism and modernised right-wing populism. The report will contain a detailed bibliography.
2. On the differences between right-wing extremist and right-wing populist parties see Alexander Häusler and Rainer Roeser, 'Rechtspopulismus in Europa und die rechtspopulistische Lücke in Deutschland' 2014, <http://www.mobit.org/Material/Rechtspopulismus_08_2014.pdf>, p. 10.
3. See Jean-Yves Camus, *50 nuances de droite. Typologie des radicalités politiques en Europe*, Paris: Jean Jaurès Foundation, 2014.
4. See Deutsche Gewerkschaftsbund, *Mut zu Deutschland. Für ein Europa der Vielfalt – Programm der Alternative für Deutschland (AfD) für die Wahl zum Europäischen Parlament am 25. Mai 2014*.
5. See Häusler and Roeser, 'Rechtspopulismus in Europa', p. 10.
6. Marine Le Pen, 'Achtung Frau Merkel', Interview in *Der Spiegel*, 23 June 2014.
7. On the economic and social background see Bernhard Müller, *Die Erosion der gesellschaftlichen Mitte. Mythen über die Mittelschicht, Zerklüftung der Lohnarbeit, Prekarisierung und Armut, Abstiegsängste*, Hamburg: VSA-Verlag, 2013. The AfD sees itself unequivocally as part of the social centre: 'Today, it is in fact the bourgeois centre which is paradoxically the actual revolutionary social class. Of course, the final goal of this revolution is not the classless society, but the

reestablishment of the social market economy and of people's sovereignty against lobbyism' (Marc Jongen, deputy spokesperson of AfD Baden Württemberg, in *Cicero*, 22 January 2014).

8 Dimitris Psarras, *La montée du parti d'extrême droite Aube dorée en Grèce*, Rosa Luxemburg Foundation Pamphlet, 2013.

9 Dimitris Psarras, interviewed by Michael Löwy and Eleni Varikas, 'The Greek Neo-Nazis of Golden Dawn – No Pasaran?', *The Bullet*, <http://www.socialistproject.ca/bullet/870.php>.

10 Harris Interactive, 'Dix leçons inédites sur la séquence électorale 2014', 11 July 2014, <http://www.harrisinteractive.fr/news/2014/11072014b.asp>.

11 Guy Michalat and Michel Simon, 'Les attitudes politico-idéologiques selon le parti dont on se sent le plus proche : zoom sur les sympathisants du FN', *Les Extrêmes Droites en Europe, en France et en Nord/Pas de Calais*, *Revue Espaces Marx*, 34 (2014).

12 Andreas Zick and Beate Küpper, *Antisemitische Mentalitäten: Bericht über Ergebnisse des Forschungsprojektes Gruppenbezogene Menschenfeindlichkeit in Deutschland und Europa – Expertise für den Expertenkreis Antisemitismus, Berlin, Stand 2011*, Bielefeld: Fakultät für Erziehungswissenschaft – Institut für interdisziplinäre Konflikt- und Gewaltforschung, 2011.

13 Zick and Küpper, *Antisemitische Mentalitäten*, p. 65.

14 See Oliver Decker, Johannes Kiess, and Elmar Brähler, *Die stabilisierte Mitte. Rechtsextreme Einstellung in Deutschland*, Leipzig: Universität Leipzig, 2014, <http://www.uni-leipzig.de/~kredo/Mitte_Leipzig_Internet.pdf>.

15 Decker, Kiess, and Brähler, *Die stabilisierte Mitte*, pp. 55 ff.

16 Ipsos.com 23 January 2014, quoted in: *EuropeNews* 23 January 2014, http://europenews.dk/de/node/76264.

17 German Marshall Fund (2010). Study evaluated in Kristina Kraus and Peter Preisendörfer, 'Fremdenfeindlichkeit im internationalen Vergleich westlicher Länder', *Gesellschaft – Wirtschaft – Politik* 1/2013 .

18 Alban Werner, 'Eine "great moving right show": Was der Rechtsruck bei den Europawahlen 2014 bedeutet', *Sozialismus* 9/2014.

19 René Monzat, 'Les racines intellectuelles de l'extrême droite française contemporaine', *Les Extrêmes Droites en Europe, en France et en Nord/Pas de Calais, Revue Espaces Marx*, 34 (2014), p. 31.

20 Wilhelm Heitmeyer, 'Feindselige Normalität' *Die Zeit* 51/2003.

21 Elisabeth Gauthier, 'Cartographie des Droites extrêmes et nationalistes en Europe', in *Les Extrêmes Droites en Europe, en France et en Nord/Pas de Calais, Revue Espaces Marx*, 34 (2014).

22 In the European Parliament parties of the radical right are divided into several groups. For further information see the article by Thilo Janssen in this volume.

23 Frank Decker, *Der neue Rechtspopulismus*, Opladen: Leske und Budrich Verlag, 2004 pp. 31ff.

24 See proposals for the struggle against right-wing extremism in Europe – Alter Summit Conference Budapest April 2014 http://www.altersummit.eu/accueil/article/theses-on-the-struggle-against?lang=en.

1945–2015:
WHAT DOES HISTORY TELLS US?

Frank Deppe

I

Preparing for the year 2014 gave historians a lot of work to do. The centenary of the outbreak of the First World War in August 1914 called forth many books on the character, origins, and consequences of this explosion of violence when the 'lamps were going out all over Europe'. The war put an end to a long period of peace and dynamic capitalist growth in Europe and opened the age of total war and internal crisis. It had destroyed millions of lives – ten million soldiers and seven million civilians dead and twenty million casualties. It also destroyed the optimism which had underpinned the bourgeois philosophy of reason since the Enlightenment. It ended with the breakdown of huge empires, which in the nineteenth century had still dominated world history: Russia's czarist empire, the Ottoman Empire, and the Austrian Habsburg Empire. Proletarian revolutions at the end of the war – following the example of the Russian October Revolution – opened a new age of class struggle and system confrontation between the Soviet Union and the leading capitalist states. The wave of reactionary counterrevolutions against socialism and communism culminated in Germany's fascist terrorist regime after 1933, which successfully prepared a new war to make good the defeat of German imperialism in 1918. The self-destruction and decline of Europe – including the British Empire – continued until the end of the Second World War. The USA, which had begun its rise to world power at the end of the nineteenth century, was one of the winners of the First World War. In the years until its entry into the Second World War (against Japan and Germany) in 1941 its economic and financial dominance within the capitalist world had steadily grown.

The 'Age of Catastrophe' (Eric Hobsbawm), which lasted from 1914 to 1945, characterised the first half of the twentieth century as an epoch of wars, revolutions, and economic crisis – an epoch which raised the aspirations of socialists all over the world. The overcoming of capitalism and bourgeois class society and the end of colonialism and imperialism all seemed to be realistic goals; victory over counter-revolution seemed possible. The future might belong to socialism – such was the mood. Yet the horror of crimes committed in this period not only agonised the survivors of the concentration camps and of the Holocaust but also the victims of the urban bombings in Europe and the explosion of the atomic bombs over Hiroshima and Nagasaki. In addition, the future of socialism was burdened by the crimes of Stalinism.

Politicians commemorating this centenary of the ancient killing fields always emphasise the fact that former enemies became allies and friends after 1945 and remain so today. The brutal lessons of the two wars were, so they say, converted into the politics of European and Atlantic integration. However, in reality it was the pressure of the Cold War and US dominance that pushed forward Western European integration projects following the Marshal Plan. At the beginning of the twenty-first century the European Union (EU) was celebrated by its leaders as an extremely successful project to integrate the economic and political potential of the member states into a powerful empire on the way to global power – a particular kind of empire (so they claim) characterised by economic welfare and the peaceful management of interstate and international relations, an empire which might encourage other regions of the world still dominated by war and poverty to follow the European model.

Especially in Germany, however, public references to 1914 reveal a new dimension reflecting new conflicts and power structures of the international order of the early twenty-first century; that is, Germany claims economic and political leadership of the EU. The German government has declared the end of a period of restraint in foreign and security policy, which was a reaction to the crimes committed by Germany in the two world wars resulting in restrictions on German foreign policy imposed by the Allies after 1945. In 2014 two bestsellers on 1914 dominated public debate in Germany. Christopher Clark's *The Sleepwalkers* and Herfried Münkler's *The Great War* both suggest that Germany cannot be blamed for the outbreak of the war in 1914, with all its consequences lasting until 1945. They conclude that German policy today should no longer be restricted through Germany's acceptance of guilt. In the end, this change is to some extent a natural result of reality itself, which seems to be falling back into the pre-history of inter-imperialist rivalry in the run-up to the First World War. Journalists deplore that the 'ghosts of war' have returned by way of the Near East and North

Africa to Ukraine where a new power confrontation between 'Putin's Russia' and 'the West' or NATO is bringing the world to the brink of another Great War. The 'hot breath of history' is blowing again through Europe.

II

At the end of the war in May 1945 – in East Asia in August – widespread hope was expressed all over the world that a new, a better world could now be built upon the ruins of war – a new world of peace, social justice, democracy, and liberty. On 26 June 1945 in San Francisco the founding Charter of the United Nations was signed by representatives of 51 states, including the United States and the Soviet Union. Its preamble declared:

WE THE PEOPLES OF THE UNITED NATIONS DETERMINED
- to save succeeding generations from the scourge of war, which twice in our lifetime has brought untold sorrow to mankind, and
- to reaffirm faith in fundamental human rights, in the dignity and worth of the human person, in the equal rights of men and women and of nations large and small, and
- to establish conditions under which justice and respect for the obligations arising from treaties and other sources of international law can be maintained, and
- to promote social progress and better standards of life in larger freedom [...]

In December 1948 the General Assembly of the United Nations ratified the General Declaration of Human Rights. It affirmed classical human rights, referring in Article 1 to the tradition of the 1789 French Revolution ('Liberté, Égalité, Fraternité') and added articles in which social rights – including the right to work, to social security, and to health and education – were seen as universal. Together with the conflict resolution mechanism invested in the Security Council, and other instruments of intervention, these declarations constituted a frame of reference for the building of a better world beyond imperialist rivalries, beyond the excessive power politics of national states, beyond colonial exploitation and discrimination, and beyond fascist and racist ideologies open to violence and war based upon different concepts of inequality between people.[1] As these declarations were signed by the governments of the United States and the Soviet Union, the leaders of the capitalist West and the socialist East, they offered at least a historical possibility that the new world of peace and social justice might be built within the frame of a global Anti-Hitler-Coalition around the United States and the Soviet Union, which had worked successfully since 1941 to bring down fascism and German and Japanese imperialism.

III

Yet, this 'open window' in history articulated neither Hegel's *Weltgeist* nor any objective laws of progress governing the history of humanity. History is always made by social actors and forces; thus the situation in 1945 articulated a global relationship of class forces which was the result of class struggles within states and of the war between states. While the First World War had been a clash between imperialist states, the Second World War was, at least according to the politics and ideology of German fascism – a war on three fronts, to restore the power of German imperialism against its imperial rivals in the West, and to destroy socialism and communism not only at home but also through a war against the Soviet Union. Finally the extinction of the Jews in Europe ('the holocaust') was the project of a race war combined with economic motives directed towards the expropriation of Jews in Germany and in the occupied states and the opening of 'lebensraum' for German colonists in Eastern Europe.

The declarations and programmes for reconstruction after the war in the spirit of antifascism, democracy, social justice, and peace reflected the reality that the communist state in the East and the socialist and communist working-class movements in the West – its parties and trade unions – had, often in coalition with bourgeois democratic forces, contributed to the victory over fascism. The first post-war governments in Western Europe – even in the occupied zones of Germany – were coalition governments supported by socialist or communist parties. The biggest of them sent their presidents into government: Maurice Thorez in France, Minister of Charles de Gaulle, and Palmiro Togliatti in Italy, member of the government of General Badoglio who in 1944 had led the coup against Mussolini. The constitutions of the immediate post-war period reflected this strong influence of the left; besides the declarations of human rights and the establishment of representative democracy they granted basic social rights as well as elements of economic democracy (workers' councils and co-determination in industry). Parliaments in different countries passed laws by which the steel and mining industries, but also large parts of the financial sector, were socialised; elements of the welfare state including public health and pension systems were introduced and expanded during the following years. Never before or since has socialism been as strong in the world. The Chinese revolution was approaching victory in 1949; anticolonial movements (for instance in India, Vietnam, Indonesia,

Malaysia, and Korea) had not only weakened the old colonial metropolis in Europe, especially Great Britain, France, and the Netherlands, but also anticipated the collapse of the colonialist system.

IV

This 'spring of hope' did not last very long. The window of opportunity was closed with the transition to the Cold War, which at least since 1948 was separating the old allies of the Anti-Hitler-Coalition, internationally and nationally. The 'Iron Curtain' separated the two camps, each led by a super-power: the US in the West and the Soviet Union in the East. The First and the Second Worlds covered the northern half of the globe. The Third World, the periphery in the South, was characterised by struggles for national independence against colonialism and imperialism and for socioeconomic development, however over-determined by the underlying frontlines in world power and politics: capitalism against state socialism. The systems were antagonistic. Private property and representative democracy in the West, state property and 'dictatorship of the proletariat', or 'socialist democracy', in the East were the basic elements defining ideological warfare: 'freedom and democracy' against 'socialism and anti-imperialism'. Permanent ideological warfare between the systems stabilised power within each of them by legitimising measures of suppression or the persecution of inner opposition.

Communists in the capitalist states, who did not renounce their solidarity with the Soviet Union, were banned and made illegal or severely discriminated against and controlled by secret services. Equally isolated during the climax of tensions between the blocs were independent socialists, in Western Europe for instance, who did not adapt to the climate of confrontation and who opposed the politics of the Cold War and NATO (accepted by the majority of social democrats) and practiced solidarity with the Third World movements. They supported policies of disarmament and détente by opening talks with representatives of the socialist countries in the East, which were initiated in the 1960s. Until then, public opinion had been characterised by the overwhelming presence of anticommunism denouncing communism (and socialism) as aggressive and totalitarian, as regimes of poverty and suppression of the masses. Especially in Germany – where the Iron Curtain divided the Federal Republic and the German Democratic Republic, and also divided Berlin where the wall was constructed by the GDR in August of 1961 – anti-communism was a kind of state doctrine that put pressure on social democracy and the political, trade-union, cultural, and academic left, criminalising the Communist Party.

In Germany, post-war anti-communism built a bridge between fascist ideology, supported until 1945 by large parts of the population, and the new ideology of 'Americanism'. Time and again the confrontation between the systems approached the brink of real war. Waves of mass protest in the GDR (1953), Hungary and Poland (1956), and Czechoslovakia (1968) provoked calls in the West for interventions; in Berlin (1961) and Cuba (1962) tanks and missiles were directed against each other. In the imperialist wars in the Third World (especially in Vietnam in the 1960s and '70s) both superpowers and their allies were engaged in supplying the adversaries with weapons and political support (until in Vietnam the US intervened directly, practicing a particularly brutal form of warfare). Within the systems, such crises bringing them to the edge of hot war strengthened the positions of the ruling regimes, although there were massive protests at home, for instance in France against the war in Algeria in the 1950s as well as in the US against its war in Vietnam.

This 'Third World War' – with huge numbers of victims at the periphery – was mainly determined by the logic of atomic armament, which threatened any aggressor with total destruction. The super powers controlled the strategic weapons based on long-distance missiles; the armament race produced ever more effective systems of destruction and defence, raising the costs of the military sector. 'Warfare capitalism' – especially in the US – was undergirded by a 'military-industrial-scientific-complex' dominating not only the economy but also state apparatuses and the institutions of science and technology. In the Soviet Union, the military sector – with its high-technology departments (missiles, space technology, and computers) – was strictly separated from an economy with low productivity. Military investment by the state, enforced by the arms race between the super powers withdrew resources fundamental for the modernisation of the economy and the improvement of the living standards of citizens. The arms race pushed forward by the West was part of the general warfare to bring down the Soviet Union and socialism. In the 1980s – under Ronald Reagan as US President and Mikhail Gorbachev as General Secretary of the CPSU – this strategy scored its ultimate success.

The Cold War ended in 1991 with the collapse of the Soviet Union and the 'system of socialist states' in Eastern Europe. Yet history did not follow a straight and uniform line. In the 1960s and '70s the power structure of world politics as well as the internal relationship of social and political forces within the developed capitalist countries was challenged by new social movements and class struggles. Internationally, the victories of anticolonial and anti-imperialist struggles (in Algeria, Cuba, Angola, Mozambique,

Ethiopia, and Vietnam), the formation of a bloc of non-aligned countries in the United Nations, many of them with a socialist orientation, and the relative stabilisation of the socialist countries around the Soviet Union, which extended its military position (China instead fell into the chaos of the Cultural Revolution), indicated a slight shift in the global power relations in favour of the socialist bloc. The internal situation of the developed capitalist countries was characterised by first signs of decline within the post-war economic 'Golden Age', at the same time revealing social contradictions within these countries (for instance poverty in the US mostly based in the black community).

The cultural revolution which started in the late 1950s, with Rock'n Roll and then the Beatles, extended to universities and other institutions of education and culture at the end of the 1960s, producing a new generation of young intellectuals now fighting for institutional transformations within the educational and cultural system. Some of them were inspired by Che Guevara, Mao, and Third World Revolution. Although this wave of ultra-radical protest collapsed after a few years, considerable sections of the younger generations were engaged during the 1970s in left parties, trade unions, and the new social movements. At the same time, Western Europe was shaken by a wave of working-class strikes (and not only in France, Italy, and Britain). Trade unions grew stronger, even in the area of political issues, for example enlarging workers control and economic democracy and reform in the education and social policy systems. The political system shifted to the left. Social democratic and communist parties (especially in France and Italy) increased membership and votes in general elections; they formed alliances oriented towards left governments. In Portugal after 1974 the left wing of the army was in the forefront of a revolution which not only brought down the regime of Salazar but was dedicated to socialist goals supported by a strong communist party. In Chile, Salvador Allende and a coalition of parties proclaimed a new road to parliamentary socialism until it was crushed by General Pinochet's military coup in September 1973. In Greece, Portugal, and Spain the left played a leading role in the overthrow of fascist and authoritarian regimes; 'Eurocommunism' in Italy, France, and Spain presented itself as an ideology independent of Soviet leadership and as a programme for transforming developed capitalist societies in the West by enlarging democracy. The social movements of the 1970s raised new political issues for the left: the ecological and the gender questions and a new concept of political self-determination beyond the traditional arenas of party and parliamentary politics. The Green parties which grew out of these movements of the 1970s originally joined the bloc of progressive forces engaged in direct democracy, criticising the American Empire, the model of industrial capitalism, and the politics of neocolonialism. They were later integrated into governments and became part of the political class.

'1968' even spread to socialist countries of Central Europe – in Poland and especially in Czechoslovakia large movements of workers and students opened a radical transformation within the governing communist party itself, which broke with Stalinist traditions and began to accept democracy within the party and within society. The military intervention of Warsaw Pact troupes crushed this experiment in socialist democracy, which was perhaps the last opportunity for a reform of the communist systems in the tradition of 1917 from within. Ten years later, the crisis in Poland was the overture to the final breakdown of state socialism. From now on, the decline of the economy together with discontent among growing parts of the population with political control from above, low standards of consumption, and restrictions of personal freedom could not be stopped. In Yugoslavia and the Soviet Union nationalist tendencies were an expression of these contradictions.

Still, international peace policy continued, following the first steps of détente and negotiations between the US and the Soviet Union after the Cuban crisis in 1962.

Europe – and especially Germany after Willy Brandt and social democracy came into government in 1966 and in 1969 – in the 1970s was the centre of negotiations and treaties on the German Question (including the recognition of the GDR) and on Security, Peace, and Cooperation in Europe. Between 1973 and 1975 in Helsinki nearly thirty European countries – together with the US, Canada, and the Soviet Union – came to an agreement that included the following principles: the inviolability of the existing borders, peaceful regulation of conflicts, non-interference in the internal affairs of other states, and respect for human rights and basic liberties. The Helsinki Conference and its results were an alternative to the aggressive politics of the Cold War aimed at the defeat of the enemy. Still today, it may teach us how rational politics – on the basis of severely contradictory positions and interests – may reduce the danger of war and nuclear armaments. At the same time it may open the way for internal social and political reforms which are not dictated by the climate of mutual threat and ideological warfare.

V

Ever since the early 1970s the dynamic forces of economic growth within the developed capitalist countries of the West have been exhausting themselves; the explosion of oil prices after 1972 was only one factor determining reduced growth rates. Economic stagnation and inflation were characteristics of the Western economies. At the same time, unemployment was continuously growing. The end of the 'Golden Age' was in the air. With the end of the Bretton Woods system, which had since 1944 fixed global currency rates of exchange (in the West) under the leadership of the US dollar and the Fed, the US in 1973 pursued national-interest policies connected to the stability of the US dollar and the attractiveness of the American financial markets. Conservative and liberal political forces, which were afraid of class struggle and of a further shift to the left, from now on opted for a fundamental change in economic and social policies at home. Situated within the ideological 'counter-revolution' against Keynesian policies, which was led by the 'Chicago Boys' around Milton Friedman and oriented to Friedrich Hayek, politicians like Margaret Thatcher and Ronald Reagan waged a battle against the working class and the left, but also against state intervention policies. Neoliberal political economy 'proposes that human well-being can best be advanced by liberating individual entrepreneurial freedoms and skills within an institutional framework characterized by strong private property rights, free markets, and free trade. The role of the state is to create and preserve an institutional framework to such practises'.[2] Socialism, the welfare state, and militant trade unions were blamed for economic crisis, state debt, and unemployment. Neoliberalism propagated a programme of liberalisation and deregulation: privatisation of public enterprises and social security, reduction of social benefits, flexibility of the labour market (in order to create a large cheap labour force, recruited among women and immigrants), and the reduction of wages by weakening the unions. Internal class war was complemented by returning to the language of the Cold War in international politics and preparing a new round of nuclear armament.

Once elected to government the neoliberals went to work implementing this programme step by step. In the 1990s it was extended as economic 'shock therapy' to the former socialist economies of Eastern Europe. China, however, since 1978, after the death of Mao, followed policies of 'modernisation' under Deng Xiaoping, which led the country towards state capitalism and opened it to the world market. Thus, three dramatic developments occurred at the end of the twentieth century anticipating major challenges of the twenty-first century: a) the rapid advancement of China – governed by a communist party – to an economic and political world power within 25 years, b) the failure of military dictatorships and of the politics of the 'Washington Consensus' in Latin America and a shift to the left in many countries, opening the road to a 'socialism of the twenty-first century', and finally c) the wave of religious and political fundamentalism which – since the Iranian Revolution in 1978 – has pervaded the Islamic word from North Africa to the Near East and even to Pakistan, Afghanistan, Indonesia, and the Philippines, even spreading to the immigrant communities within the developed countries of Western Europe.

Through the end of the century the politics and ideology of neoliberalism proved extremely successful in North America and Europe. The political left and the trade unions, which had been so strong in the 1970s, fell into deep crisis. The communist movements and parties all over the world were severely hit by the final crisis of the Soviet Union and its allies. The biggest communist party in the West, the Italian Communist Party of Gramsci and Togliatti, which had grown much stronger in the 1970s, disappeared at the beginning of the 1990s; the French Communist Party had been in steady decline since the late 1970s. Social democracy adapted to the hegemony of neoliberal ideology and politics; New Labour under Tony Blair, and later the German SPD under Chancellor Gerhard Schröder, implemented radical reforms in the spirit of global financial capitalism and free-market-policies, deconstructing the welfare state, weakening the unions, and creating a large sector of cheap and precarious labour. The transfer of industries, especially to East Asia, reduced industrial labour in the traditional centres of capitalism. Resistance from the ranks of the working class remained quite weak. The industrial working class, which was still the backbone of trade union power in the 1970s, was hit by processes of deindustrialisation and rising productivity as a consequence of the microelectronic revolution in communication and production. At the same time new sectors of the working class – without experience in class struggle and trade-union organisation – expanded within the service sector and especially in the areas of low-paid, part-time, and precarious work. The declining core sectors of the white male national working classes were confronted with rising numbers of female workers in the service and care sector as well as of immigrants (of colour) and refugees who provided cheap labour (below the national standards for wages and social security resulting from long trade-union struggles) and claimed benefits from the national welfare states. Racist conflicts growing out of this constellation further weakened the traditional power of the national working classes and their organisations.

VI

Between 1989 and 1991, the Cold War and systemic confrontation led by the two superpowers had come to an end. Francis Fukuyama, a US neoconservative intellectual, proclaimed the 'end of history'. The West – private property, free markets, and representative democracy, together with

NATO – had triumphed over socialism. States and political and social actors were entering a new period of history characterised by the predominance of the global capitalist economy and its contradictions as well as the policies of the big powers, as they established a new world order according to their specific interests. The US, as the remaining superpower, now claimed world leadership – economically, militarily, and ideologically. If necessary, the US would accept the role of the world's policeman, of a 'good imperialist', in order to neutralise or repress those who might disturb or threaten this order. At the same time, starting in the 1980s, the EU moved forward. The Common Market, the Economic and Monetary Union with the introduction of the common currency (the euro in 18 member states) and the establishment of the European Central Bank, and enlargement to the former socialist countries of Eastern and Southeastern Europe were the most important steps of a complete restructuring of European integration now dominated by the logic of free markets, competition, and neoliberal policies within the member states. In 2000 the EU's Lisbon Summit proudly proclaimed that the EU was on its way to become the most powerful economic region of the world. The Treaty of Lisbon aimed at adapting the institutions and the decision-making processes within the EU to the enlargement of the Union, but also opened the way for a common foreign and military policy which was regarded as necessary in order for the EU to become a powerful global actor, as a new kind of multinational empire.

The world economy of the 1990s was driven forward by financial markets and by the integration of rapidly industrialising countries in East Asia (at first the so-called 'Asian Tiger' states, then the People's Republic of China) into the capitalist world market. At the same time, the global financial markets were dominated and regulated by the 'Dollar-Wall-Street-Regime',[3] accompanied by American military dominance. With the 'Volcker shock' in 1979 the Fed had increased interest rates to establish a permanent anti-inflation parameter which would guarantee that the US dollar, backed by US Treasury Bonds, would provide a reliable anchor for international finance.[4] From the 1980s on, financial crisis and instability – provoked by national debts, unstable rates of exchange, and speculative bubbles – has shaken many countries and regions and has been combined with sudden collapses of the stock markets, currency rates, the growth rates of industrial production, and the GDP: in Mexico, Russia, Turkey, Argentina, and East Asia (1996/97). In the so-called 'dot.com crisis' of 2002, which started in the US, new markets of high-technology investments, which had inspired the boom of the US stock markets at the end of the 1990s, crashed and brought down the world economy. Finally, these instabilities converged in the big crisis of 2008 when in the US financial markets broke down, the crisis spread throughout the world, and economic growth rates fell. Massive state intervention was needed to prevent a catastrophe in the financial sectors and the labour markets. Crisis management proved quite successful in some countries (like Germany with its strong export-oriented industries). In others the economy is characterised by stagnation. Crisis management at least prevented an explosion of unemployment as in the crisis following 1929. The power of the financial sector has been restored and new speculative bubbles (most notably in the real estate sector and the stock markets) have built up. Other countries of the EU, especially in Southern Europe, were severely hit by the financial and economic crisis after 2008 and then by the consequences of the authoritarian crisis management within the EU, which was imposed throughout the EU by the new leadership of Germany. Mass poverty and unemployment, increased state debt, and continued negative growth rates are the burdens of the so-called 'crisis countries'. The global economy since 2007 has been on a path of stagnation and deflation. However, the BRICS countries (headed by China) continue to be locomotives of the world economy, although they too have entered a period of declining growth rates.

The climax of neoliberal hegemony was reached about the turn of the century in 2000, although of course with diverse trajectories in different countries. On the one hand, financial instability and the dismantling of the welfare state created new forms of social insecurity. The privatisation of social risks involving age and health created widespread uncertainty and anxiety about the future (not only of older people, but chiefly of the youth). Unemployment is still high, and flexible and precarious work is on the increase, not only in the lower segments of the labour market but also in employment sectors reserved for the academic middle classes. On the other hand, people began to be conscious of the continuously growing polarisation between the incomes and the wealth of the rich (and the superrich) and of the lower classes, including the lower segments of the middle classes, which were confronted with a steady tendency towards economic decline and the expropriation of expectations, security, and rights. 'Winner-Take-All-Politics which make the rich richer and turns its back on the middle class'[5] increasingly violated peoples' common sense of social justice and the just distribution of income and wealth, as well as of the role of a democratic state.

As neoliberalism destroys social cohesion, the crisis of democracy proceeds.[6] The crisis in representation is expressed by the falling rates of electoral participation and of party and union membership, especially among the lower classes and youth. Opinion polls confirm the negative image people have of most politicians. New forms of a radical right-wing and antidemocratic political populism, which attacks the 'old political system' and its representatives, scored impressive results in recent elections at the European and the national and regional levels. In the US the Republican Party (including the Tea Party movement) shifted sharply towards the extreme right. The reputation of the political class among ordinary people and youth is rapidly eroding as scandals, corruption, and lies seem to be natural attributes of a political life and culture dominated by big money, big party and government power, and mass media as instruments of mass manipulation. 'Post-democracy' (Colin Crouch) or 'democracy without demos' (Peter Mair) describe this tendency to hollow out democratic institutions. Economic and financial elites are increasingly exerting direct influence on processes of political decision-making in the state apparatuses. The authoritarian tendencies in the capitalist world are reinforced not only by right-wing or openly fascist protagonists but also by the implementation of austerity policies which restrict the constitutional rights of parliaments and force governments to accept the dictatorship of the European Central Bank and 'Troika', which executes austerity policies from outside. 'Market democracy' – neoliberalism's ideal – subjugates democratic politics (which are based on peoples' sovereignty and choice) to the laws and rules of the market, which means the rules of competition and the interests and power of the upper class.

However, increasing dissatisfaction with the economy and democracy has not yet led to a general uprising or a rebirth of the left. It is only in Latin America that left governments were elected after the failure of the military dictatorships of the 1970s and the neoliberal policies of the 1980s. The working class in the developed capitalist countries of the West remains quite passive, while in China and other Asian countries the number of industrial strikes is increasing. Right-wing populism – based on national 'welfare chauvinism' and hostility to foreign immigrants and Muslims – is marching on. Even the crisis produced modest results after 2008 in terms of popular unrest. Nevertheless, there are new tendencies to left-wing popular resistance and protest. Only in a few countries is the political left nearing a majority sufficient for governing – for example, in Greece with Syriza. Trade unions which have lost members and power in recent decades are still tied up in defensive positions seeking cooperation with capital and the state. Still, the number of strikes – even of general strikes – in Europe has significantly increased during the last few years. In 2011, however, a wave of democratic and social movements passed through North Africa and the Arab world ('Arabellion') and subsequently reached Europe (for example, the 'Indignados' in Spain), the United States (with 'Occupy'), Turkey, Brazil, and other places. 'It's kicking off everywhere', was the joyous announcement greeting a new 'period of social unrest' or even of 'global revolution'.[7] Though these movements had very different roots in their national history and religious culture (in the first place, Islamic fundamentalism) they articulated a radical critique not only of their political regimes, or of corrupt systems of representative democracy, but also of financial capitalism and neoliberal policies, which produce and preserve massive poverty and the division between rich and poor. Young people with academic degrees were in the frontline of these movements protesting against high rates of unemployment among young people and young academics in many countries. In some countries regimes were brought down; in Egypt, the most important centre of the Arabellion, the military counter-revolution restored the old regime. In the Islamic world the influence of an extremely radical fundamentalism, attacking secular regimes oriented towards the West, grew even stronger in various civil wars (Libya, Syria, and Iraq). In Europe and the US these movements criticised social inequality and financial capitalism's hollowing out of democracy ('we are the 99 per cent'). But their honeymoon did not last very long – protest could not be expanded over time and sustained everywhere. The fire of protest is nevertheless flaring up in many countries and regions of the 'one world of capital', though of course shaped by national and regional traditions and cultures. This recent wave of protest might be regarded as an early symptom of future large movements that question the ideology and the power of regimes sustaining global capitalism.

VII

After the demise of the Soviet Union US policies were aimed at assuring and expanding the status of 'Number One' in the world economy and in world politics. Bill Clinton and George W. Bush embarked on several wars: to destroy Yugoslavia, to bring down Saddam Hussein in Iraq, to conquer the Taliban in Afghanistan, to eliminate the regime of Gadaffi in Libya, and later of Assad in Syria. After the 'Nine-Eleven' terror attacks in 2001, George W. Bush declared war on terrorism throughout the world. His successor Barack Obama has continued this war with many direct US military operations, for instance in Africa, and by using the new military technology of drones. These wars did not lead to clear victories; they illustrated the limits of US world dominance in many respects. In Afghanistan, the US army and its allies were eventually forced to leave the country; they had lost the battle. The 'liberated' countries (like Iraq and Libya) here descended into chaos, civil war, and mass poverty and produced new generations of terrorists who viewed the West and the US as their main enemy. The fate of millions of refugees en route to Europe and North America documents the barbaric character of the present world order. Many of them – among them many children – are killed and drowned in the process. Once they reach their destination country they are forced to live in inhuman conditions and are confronted with the native population's racism. The conflicts in the Islamic world, especially the ongoing war between Israel and the Palestinians, have not been resolved. On the contrary, the brutal war against the people living in Gaza and Israel's landgrabbing policies have radicalised the enemies of the West and the US.

On the other side, military spending has put the US economy and national budget under pressure. Increasingly, the contradictions between US global policies and the country's domestic situation are seen as symptoms of US decline. Extreme wealth, very high incomes, and the biggest military budget in the world contrast with mass poverty, public and private debt, the decay of cities and whole regions, the rise of criminality, moral decline, and the ongoing discrimination against black people and immigrants. World poverty is still concentrated in the South of the globe, although economic development in East Asia has reduced global poverty rates during the past twenty years. At the same time, this development has created huge cities, industrial complexes, automobile traffic, etc. Pollution and emissions have worsened the ecological crisis and climate change. The world's megacities, and the whole of the developed countries in the West, have become centres where the antagonisms of global capitalism are concentrated. Their business centres demonstrate the wealth and power of financial capital; their slums or ghettos collect the losers of globalisation and neoliberalism. 'The future of human solidarity depends upon a militant refusal of the new urban poor to accept their terminal marginality within global capitalism'.[8]

The limits of US world dominance reflect the outlines of a new world order. Despite decline, the 'American Empire' is still the most powerful empire in the world. Since the beginning of the millennium, however, new structures in the distribution of world power are emerging. New empires are in the making. In East Asia, China is on the way to becoming a great power alongside India. Japan, with US support, is being freed of the military restrictions which the US imposed on it after the war. Russia, which in the 1990s fell into a deep political, economic, and moral crisis, has slowly recovered under the presidency of Vladimir Putin. Alliances within the BRICS countries and closer relationships with China have strengthened the international position of Russia. Putin is criticising the West for the enlargement of NATO to include former components of the USSR. NATO (and the EU) have continuously tried to integrate Georgia und Ukraine. In both cases Russian policies reacted, even with military intervention, to the expansion of NATO and the West to its borders.

In Europe, the EU, since the late 1980s, has been on a path of constructing a multinational empire united by a common market, a common monetary policy, and by more and more common responsibilities of the Union in security policies and foreign affairs. The EU was severely hit by the crisis after 2008, which is still shaking large parts of member states. Crisis management within the EU has so far prevented its breakdown but has also deepened the social and political differences within it. At the same time, it has enabled the rise of Germany, the economically dominant power up to now, to political leadership within the Union. The dominant sectors of the ruling classes within the EU are quite conscious of the risks presented by the crisis. Their common goal is still to build the EU as a powerful global player in the twenty-first century alongside the other great power blocs. 'Embedded' German leadership might speed up this process, which is still hampered by many contradictions and countertendencies. In the poorer parts of Europe, where austerity policies have pushed millions into poverty, Germany and its chancellor Angela Merkel are not very popular. In the big neighbouring countries, German power and its rise to leadership is still regarded uneasily, with feelings stirred up by memories of the twentieth century's two world wars.

A different sort of empire-building can be associated with the BRICS countries as well as with the much weaker alliances between Latin American countries with a socialist orientation (ALBA). Still, even these new interstate relationships in the twenty-first century have already reduced the economic influence and the political power of the West, especially of the US. They are thus part of the transformations occurring in the global structure of economic and military power and the incentives of national governments or the EU and NATO to translate them into policies. The project of a transatlantic free trade area (Transatlantic Trade and Investment Partnership, or TTIP) is an answer to these ongoing changes within the distribution of power in the world. Former US Secretary of State Hilary Clinton, who is in favour of this treaty, described it as the 'Economic NATO', as the reinforcement of the alliance of declining centres of the North Atlantic West, which has dominated the world since 1500, against the rising empires in the East.

Imperialist policies are oriented to preserving and improving the external conditions of an internal regime. The old and new empires are capitalist empires dependent on profits realised by open doors to the world markets, the protection of investment, safe routes for transports and energy supply, and by stable political constellations on the borders of the empire. Military power has always been used to guarantee these conditions. Ever more competition and conflicts between these old empires and the new empires in the making slowly come to the surface as the main lines of conflict of international politics, and they overdetermine local or regional conflicts, for instance in the Near East. In the Far East, the US is trying to build alliances between Japan, India, Vietnam, and other countries against the growing power of China. Quite peripheral conflicts about small islands immediately turn into aggressive nationalist campaigns and confrontations between governments, which react by increasing their military budgets. In the Near East, the wars in Iraq and Syria of course have specific causes. In Syria, civil war was the consequence of the uprising of large parts of the population against the dictatorship of Assad and his family and against the miserable conditions of their lives. These movements, however, were used to justify military interventions by the West, with Turkey and some Arab states, which had an interest in weakening the Assad regime as a regional strong power allied with Iran, Russia, and China and supporting Hezbollah in Lebanon and Israel. The conflict around Ukraine, which came to a head starting in late 2013, is an example of the new types of geopolitical conflicts and wars which are, on the one hand, nationally rooted in the misery of large parts of the population and the anger against corrupt political regimes. On the other hand, the movement which led to the fall of the Yanukovych regime was directly oriented towards anti-Russian policies and towards EU and NATO membership and against the interest of large parts of the Russian population in Eastern and Southern Ukraine. The West intervened massively to support this orientation. Russia and President Putin, together with the Russians in the Ukraine, reacted by supporting the founders of the 'people's republics' in the Donetsk region and the Crimean referendum for membership within the Russian Federation. When the Ukrainian army initiated a war against these 'peoples' republics', war had in effect come back to this part of Europe. It restored the aggressive language and culture of the Cold War by constructing the new enemy, which was now Putin. It is bringing together the allies within NATO and the EU against the common enemy, allowing Germany to lift the restrictions on its military interventions and weapons' exports, which had been imposed by the victors of the Second World War as well as by German self-restraint in the decades following the war. Inter-imperial rivalry – but between old and new imperial power blocs (which can no longer be on the national state level but are dependent upon one or more powerful national states) – will be a characteristic of the twenty-first century.

VIII

'Never again war!', 'Never again Fascism!' These were the slogans after 1945, inspired by the bloody experience of the first half of the twentieth century. For seventy years Europe did not return to war, and fascism did not have a chance in politics (though the regimes in Spain and Portugal until the early 1970s stood in the tradition of European fascism and yet were supported by the US, NATO, and Western European governments). At the same time, outside the First and the Second Worlds, there were wars against anticolonial and anti-imperialist movements and civil wars, which as a whole killed about 12.5 million people, most of them in Africa and Asia. Even higher was the number of those who died from hunger and epidemics due to lack of hygienic conditions and medical treatment. So, the world as a whole was far from living in peace. In the north, peace was guaranteed by atomic weapons capable of destroying mankind several times over. This was the crazy logic of the Cold War and of global class struggle. As we approach the seventieth anniversary of May 1945, many parts of the world are experiencing war, civil war, terrorism, and the activities of criminal gangs as part of their daily experience of violence and the lack of human rights and constitutional stability. Fascism or right-wing populism, nationalism, and racism are ideological and political answers to a world which is going out of joint. Three majors forces are responsible for the conflicts within the present world: a) the dynamics of capitalist growth, producing social instability and new social antagonisms, mass poverty as the sources of migration, and the continuous destruction of the environment and nature including the potential catastrophes of climate change; b) geopolitical conflicts and power politics between the old and new empires; c) religious fundamentalism which has declared war on the Western world and its culture. At the same time the weakness of working-class politics and of socialist strategies and programmes is a characteristic feature of the present crisis.

Coming up with a left answer to these conflicts and risks is not an easy task. The parties and unions of the working-class movements in the old centres of capitalism have been weakened by the manifold defeats they suffered in the last quarter of the twentieth century. Still, even small left parties are important voices in parliaments and the media; strong unions are necessary instruments in confronting the logic of precarious wage labour and the expropriation of social rights in the struggle for alternative policies oriented towards redistribution of income and wealth, the strengthening of working-class purchasing power, and in moving towards ecological transformation. New social movements – in the areas of ecology, gender equality, urban gentrification, and the critique of capitalist globalisation and global financial capitalism – still play an important role as indispensable elements of a 'bloc' of social, political, and cultural forces able to challenge and, in the end, transform the existing rule of financial capitalism and neoliberal policies. This left bloc is also necessary to oppose the policies of reconstructing the Cold War frontlines and militarising foreign policy. It must fight for conflict resolution through negotiations, by strengthening democracy and popular forces and by strengthening the authority of international organisations dedicated to conflict resolution and peace-keeping activities. To be sure, in different parts of the world the left is confronted with specific tasks rooted in the history, political culture, and class relations of different countries and regions. Be that as it may, Eric Hobsbawm, at the end of his seminal *The Age of Extremes*, which appeared in 1994, was able to identify the general orientation: 'We live in a world captured, uprooted and transformed by the titanic economic and techno-scientific process of the development of capitalism, which has dominated the past two or three centuries [...]. The future cannot be a continuation of the past, and there are signs, both externally and, as it were, internally, that we have reached a point of historic crisis [...]. Our world risks both explosion and implosion. It must change.'[9]

The early socialist and communist working-class movements of the nineteenth and early twentieth centuries were quite optimistic about the transformation from capitalism to socialism. The catastrophes of the past century (including the seventy years between 1945 and 2015) have taught the left that progress is not an iron law of history carried out by the working class. In the past seventy years progress was made by socialist policies that reduced poverty, expanded public education, and built the welfare state and stable democratic constitutions. Progress was also made by the victories of anticolonial movements, by great efforts to build non-capitalist economies and societies after the victories of socialist revolutions, and finally by military interventions against fascism. In Europe, peace and progress in social democracy was a result of countervailing powers acting against the dynamic forces of unrestrained capitalism. Capitalism was 'civilised' internationally by the existence of socialist countries; at home Western capitalism and its political representatives – after the catastrophes of the capitalist economy and bourgeois society in the first half of the twentieth century – were forced to accept 'class-compromise' policies. Progress was made by these policies of 'embedded capitalism': full employment for a period, welfare state institutions, a large public sector, and peace policies. Strong left parties and unions were elements of these politics, which characterised the development of Western Europe until the mid-1970s. However, any progress in these areas was a result of intensive struggles between capitalist (conservative and liberal) class forces and democratic and class movements from below. Today the left is still confronted with the consequence of the neoliberal policies of 'dis-embedding' the capitalist economy and the financial sectors from democratic and social controls. This 'dis-embedding' eventually opened the way for the return of the dangers of war, cultural barbarism, and antidemocratic political ideologies and movements. The left now must be part of larger initiatives and alliances to 're-embed', that is, 'civilise' capitalism at home and in international politics. Within these alliances the left connects the politics of 'civilisation' with the perspective of general welfare, social justice, ecological balance, democratic self-government, and peace beyond capitalism and imperial policies.

This essay draws on the author's recent books (see under Literature).

Literature

Davis, Mike, *Planet of Slums*, London and New York: Verso, 2006.

Deppe, Frank, *Politisches Denken im 20. Jahrhundert* [Political Thought in the Twentieth Century], five volumes, Hamburg: VSA-Verlag, 1999–2011.

Deppe, Frank, *Autoritärer Kapitalismus: Demokratie auf dem Prüfstand* [Authoritarian Capitalism: Democracy on Trial], Hamburg: VSA-Verlag, 2013.

Deppe, Frank, *Imperialer Realismus? Deutsche Außenpolitik: Führungsmacht in 'neuer Verantwortung'* [Imperialism Realism? German Foreign Policy: A Leading Power 'With New Responsibility'], Hamburg: VSA-Verlag, 2014.

Gowan, Peter, *The Global Gamble: Washington's Faustian Bid for World Dominance*, London and New York: Verso, 1999.

Hacker, Jacob S. and Pierson, Paul, *Winner-Take-All-Politics*. New York: Simon & Schuster, 2011.

Harvey, David, *A Brief History of Neoliberalism*, Oxford: Oxford University Press, 2005.

Hobsbawm, Eric, *The Age of Extremes: The Short Twentieth Century, 1914– 1991*, London: Michael Joseph, 1994.

Mason, Paul, *Why It's Still Kicking Off Everywhere: The New Global Revolutions*, London and New York: Verso, 2013.

Packer, George, *The Unwinding. An Inner History of the New America*, New York: Farrar, Straus and Giroux, 2013.

Panitch, Leo and Gindin, Sam, *The Making of Global Capitalism. The Political Economy of American Empire*, London and New York: Verso, 2012.

Notes

1. One of the authors of the 1948 declaration was the French diplomat Stephane Hessel (1917–2013), who – at the age of 93 – published a manifesto entitled 'Indigniez-vous'. It was addressed to young people in the European Union. He compared the social reality of 2010 (high unemployment, poverty, declining hopes for the future for young people, etc.) with the United Nations' 1948 programme and called for resistance against neoliberal policies. The 'Indignados' movement in Spain was a direct response to Hessel's manifesto.
2. David Harvey, *A Brief History of Neoliberalism*, Oxford: Oxford University Press, 2005, p. 2.
3. Peter Gowan, *The Global Gamble: Washington's Faustian Bid for World Dominance*, London and New York: Verso, 1999, pp. 19–38.
4. See Leo Panitch and Sam Gindin, *The Making of Global Capitalism. The Political Economy of American Empire*, London and New York: Verso, 2012, pp. 163 ff.
5. Jacob S. Hacker and Paul Pierson, *Winner-Take-All-Politics*. New York: Simon & Schuster, 2011.
6. For the USA, see George Packer, *The Unwinding. An Inner History of the New America*, New York: Farrar, Straus and Giroux, 2013.
7. Paul Mason, *Why It's Still Kicking Off Everywhere: The New Global Revolutions*, London and New York: Verso, 2013.
8. Mike Davis, *Planet of Slums*, London and New York: Verso, 2006, p. 202.
9. Eric Hobsbawm, *The Age of Extremes: The Short Twentieth Century, 1914–1991*, London: Michael Joseph, 1994, p. 584.

DIVISIONS IN EUROPE AND CHALLENGES FOR THE LEFT

THE 'AUSTERITARIAN' INTEGRATION DIVIDING EUROPE

Steffen Lehndorff

Unwelcome developments at the EU level and economic imbalances within the EU and the euro area are often at the centre of critical analyses of the European crisis. There are popular and also justified fears that these problems might cause the collapse of the currency union. However, these discussions within the left often ignore the role the economy and politics must play at the individual national level as part of a process of reorientation. This is also the message of a forthcoming book entitled *Divisive Integration*, which argues that the chronic EU crisis can only be overcome with a change of policy in some countries, which in turn trigger political reactions in other countries and disruptions at the EU level. One thing is certain: as things stand it will not be possible to effect policy changes without the support and approval of the European institutions.[1]

In order to fully understand this challenge, a logical first step would be to consider the economic and social problems of individual countries.

The continental drift

The book includes analyses of ten countries, which gives the overall impression of a continent steadily drifting apart. The obsessive cutting of public expenses and labour costs that has become the key element of a new EU governance obstructs the pathway to the necessary reorientation of socio-economic models in member states. This observation is especially important because with our criticism of the existing 'structural reforms' being pushed through by the 'austeritarian regime'[2] we do not mean to encourage the belief that reforms are not necessary; they are, especially in those countries most badly affected by the crisis. In fact, the country analyses demonstrate that each country is suffering its own individual illness which made it prone to the crisis. The universal medication prescribed to these countries, however, has nothing to do with their individual illnesses.

The following summary focuses on the analyses of four of the so-called 'crisis countries', as well as on Germany, which is often presented as a model.[3]

After the first phase of the slump, that is, the 2008/2009 global financial and economic crisis, Greece was, of all EU countries, the one which experienced the most dramatic crash. Maria Karamessini describes the 'punitive character' of the financial aid provided to her country and the consequences of the shock treatment which has put in motion a 'spiral of austerity-recession-austerity'. She emphasises the lack of economic perspective this approach reflects; austerity measures and privatisation deprive the state of the instruments necessary for creating policies that stimulate growth. 'Growth will thus depend on the incentives provided to foreign multinational capital and the most internationalized fractions of Greek capital.' It is, however, the impoverished working class which is intended to be the greatest incentive. The working class – people deprived of their rights – constitutes a huge group of people willing to accept jobs under any condition in the face of mass unemployment.

In contrast to Greece, Italy is traditionally a strong manufacturer of internationally competitive industrial products. However, this asset never included the southern parts of the country, and an insidious crisis had been slowly taking hold of the country's manufacturing sector long before 2008. Annamaria Simonazzi explains the 'Italian illness' by pointing to a mix of 'tax evasion, tax elusion and tax cuts' which complicates infrastructural development and the expansion of social services, as does the inefficient and clientelist character of the public administration sector. According to Simonazzi, the existing tax and social policies, as well as policies of deregulating the labour market, foster a 'perverse redistribution'. These policies are intended to create flexibility (though to an inadequate degree in her view) by introducing social insecurity. In conclusion, Simonazzi blames this on the complete absence of industrial policies and a 'political stalemate, with a divided majority held together only by the desire to remain in office'. For her, there are no grounds for optimism.

In comparison with the rest of Southern Europe, Spain has experienced the most extensive capitalist modernisation process of the past thirty years. Josep Banyuls and Albert Recio describe the economic and social dynamics which were defined by a balance between the contradictory elements of the neoliberal basis of economic policies and the strong pressure from society 'to develop a – previously non-existent – welfare state'. The boom, however, was primarily driven by a speculative and construction bubble. The fact that it has burst is now used as an opportunity to implement a conservative neoliberal project. This means privatisation in the health and education system cuts in social services and rights, while conservative-elitist elements are simultaneously strengthened, for example in the educational system. Making families take on the burden of social security and making women 'fill the gaps opened up by the lack of public provision' implies a 'return to the old Mediterranean model'. Also, economically speaking, Banyuls and Recio consider the 'structural reforms' regressive. Instead of promoting scientific and technological progress, instead of being open to production methods which are more productive and cooperative or which remove barriers to social mobility, they are designed to reanimate a production model which is doomed to failure and which is built on low wages and precarious working conditions. It is the very production model which delivered high growth rates in the period of transition to democracy up to the 1990s, after which the country was put under pressure by the eastward enlargement of the EU, and was partly replaced as a driver of growth by the property boom of the 2000s.

Like Spain, Ireland also experienced a property boom financed by private debt, which led the country into crisis. The growth it experienced came about so rapidly that Ireland – traditionally an emigration country – turned into an immigration country, at least temporarily. When the bubble burst, the debt-to-GDP ratio of around 25 per cent on the eve of the crisis escalated to almost 120 per cent five years later. This was mainly the result of an unprecedented state acquisition of the entire debt accumulated by the speculation-driven banking sector. Out of all the countries 'bailed out' with the help of European bailout funds, Ireland's development is highlighted by the EU Commission as an encouraging example. In his analysis, James Wickham, however, points out the contradictions and downsides of this success story. Apart from the banking sector, the most important growth engines are foreign, mainly US, direct investments. Ireland is especially attractive for its low company taxation levels, which big software and web firms find beneficial to their global business activities. In Wickham's opinion, it is bizarre that the full spectrum of political parties has 'made "our" corporate tax rate into a symbol of national independence which must be defended in front of the other EU member states': 'Far from stimulating any rethink of the national development strategy, the crisis has turned the reliance on FDI into a national fetish.'

National egoism has become even more noticeable within the context of the EU crisis, and the Irish growth model represents a typical example of this phenomenon (similarly, the British government strongly defends the City of London against financial transaction taxes and the German government supports the German automotive industry by resisting strict CO_2 directives).

This also demonstrates the size of the obstacles that stand in the way of those well-matched economic and tax policies which are necessary for a functional currency union. It also shows that, in comparison, it is relatively easy for governments to agree on cuts in social services and the deregulation of the labour market as an instrument to increase competitiveness.

Looking at an analysis of those countries which have come through the 2008/2009 crash relatively unscathed, one common characteristic becomes obvious: The governments in question have taken measures that temporarily break with the neoliberal economic paradigm. The welfare state, with its 'automatic stabilisers', has proven to be a last-resort pillar of stability, even though it is an extremely unpopular lifeline in times of crisis.

Various German governmental coalitions have perfected a certain pattern – adopting one policy in their own country and making up a different one for the faithful media and for other countries, in other words, prescribing medication to others without having first tried it themselves. I explore this hidden irony in the chapter on Germany. Deregulation in the German labour market is not the reason why its economy and labour market survived the dramatic slump of 2008 surprisingly well, nor does it explain the country's relatively robust development since the second half of 2009. Rather, this deregulation has accelerated the growth of imbalances within the currency union, thus greatly contributing to the near crash of the euro in 2010 as well as subsequent near misses. In 2008/2009, however, the core elements of the social model in place before Agenda 2010 (a series of reforms involving the German welfare system and labour market between 2003-2005) was adopted were reactivated, particularly the priority of *internal* flexibility which was made possible by a 'social partnership' supported by the unions with their renewed self-confidence. In addition, something happened for which the rest of Europe had waited in vain during the previous years of economic boom – average wages started to increase, not least because trade unions were now receiving more public support for their wage policies. As a result, for the first time in this century, the German economic cycle was stimulated to a greater extent by the single market than by the export surplus (which remained high). In short, the relatively robust development of the German economy and labour markets can be mainly ascribed to the fact that in the last years efforts were undertaken to at least limit the detrimental effects of Agenda 2010 policies on the labour market.

However, the Federal Government and the media are still promoting Agenda 2010 and it is still being met with public approval. This is due to the fact that German industry is exceptionally successful at an international level, especially for its product-based competitiveness. This too has nothing to do with Agenda 2010 policies, which becomes obvious when one looks at Austria and Sweden. Neither of these two countries saw similar deregulations on the labour market, and, what is more, they both are countries where the economic structural base for value creation has proven to be quite robust. The depreciation of the Swedish Krona only marginally affected the country's industrial sector because Swedish industry is internationally competitive 'despite' the country's high social standards.

When analysing countries with strong economies, another similarity becomes obvious: Germany, Sweden, and Austria are at risk of losing their assets, but in different ways. In the case of Germany, underinvesting in social services and public infrastructure, as well as neglecting the education sector to the detriment of professional education, will undermine future economic success.

France currently finds itself in the midst of such a process. In the French case the widespread inability of economic and political elites in Europe to identify the actual strengths and weaknesses of their individual economic and social models, and to concentrate on overcoming these weaknesses as well as developing existing strengths without ideological blinkers, is especially obvious. The controversy surrounding France's (and also Italy's) economic and political course will possibly play a key role in the question of how seriously the 'competitiveness' standards agreed on in Brussels are to be taken. The Hollande administration continues to cling in cowardly fashion to the dogma of reducing labour costs to promote competitiveness, growth, and employment. The widespread disappointment with Hollande's lack of leadership has led to a large number of those voters who demonstrated in 2012 against 'Merkozy' policies turning to the right. Thus, France is becoming a striking example of the core of Chancellor Merkel's dictum that 'there are no alternatives' to current anti-crisis policies; there is indeed a lack of enforceable and politically credible alternatives.

All change in Europe emanates from the nation-state

'Investor and market confidence' are considered the pivotal elements of the continent's economic recovery. If the confidence of the *people* does not automatically follow, there is a simple solution: declare social and economic problems to be national problems.[4]

This is in fact true to a certain extent. However, we are dealing here with social differences *within* the national states and not *between* them. The economic development models of numerous European countries have proven unsustainable, and now they are to be revitalised by increasing social differences and weakening labour market regulations as well as the welfare state. In the meantime, the governments of stronger economies, with whom the weaker economies formed a toxic symbiosis before the crisis, are monitoring other countries' compliance with the rules of the 'austeritarian' regime. However, this regime is increasingly turning into a self-laid trap preventing both the stronger and the weaker economies from overcoming their own problems. Thus, the members of this 'union of competition'[5] become a burden to each other. They are mainly connected by problems and they are united by a common evil nobody wants to deal with, namely growing imbalances which are increasingly hard to shoulder and which present a challenge to government action in all the national states.

Since all member states have fallen into a trap set collectively by their governments (under the guidance of Germany), from which it seems almost impossible to escape due to difficult to revise and legally-binding decrees at the European level, the conviction is beginning to spread among critics that a progressive reform of the EU's legal regime and the currency union is not feasible in the foreseeable future. Thus, defending social achievements mainly established during the second half of the twentieth century at a national level is now, in their opinion, only possible at this level. In Wolfgang Streeck's words, 'constructive opposition is impossible'; 'the opposition's options in their struggle against the "consolidation state" are reduced to trying to throw a spanner in the works of the capitalist "austeritarian" orientation and discourse'.[6] According to Streeck, it is important to use historically grown institutions and the 'remaining elements of democracy in the national states' as 'brakes on the downhill path towards a democracy-free, single-market state'.

In fact, strategies which are limited to the defence of national achievements have been present for quite some time. They predominate in Northern Europe (for obvious reasons), and trade unions in these countries tend to focus heavily on this task, while their interest in European politics appears quite limited. They have in part succeeded. Nevertheless, they are experiencing a steady decline in their influence, and their institutional power resources are being undermined. These are experiences described by Hans-Jürgen Urban, member of the board of IG Metall, the German Industrial Union of Metalworkers, in his contribution to our volume. He comes to the conclusion that those remaining possibilities of influence should not focus on 'preserving status quo structures, but on making one's own contribution to reconstructing the socio-economic model of development'. This is what he calls using the power of the veto 'constructively', which he considers a key goal of a trade union strategy for dealing with the European crisis. Facing this challenge begins with drafting concepts or reform projects aimed at reconfiguring the socio-economic development model in one's *own* country. This is the necessary basis for implementing a Europe-wide reorientation. Yet this reorientation must be based on a 'pro-European criticism'. The widespread uncertainty as to how to master this twofold challenge is what he calls the 'Europe gap' in trade union strategy.

Trade unions are far from being the only, or indeed most active, opposition forces acting as brakes against the deconstruction of national achievements. In the chapters on Greece and Spain, Maria Karamessini, Josep Banyuls and Albert Recio highlight the role of social opposition to the political crisis management of their governments and the EU. In reading about the actions of social networks and analyses of the large-scale protest movements in these countries,[7] one is struck on both the political and human levels by the great courage and fierce resistance they exhibit. However, Banyuls and Recio also point to their failure to counterpose a clearly defined overall alternative to neoliberal shock therapy. There are vital social movements such as the 15-M Movement, and Social Forums in the areas of health and education, as well as anti-eviction movements. Although these movements focus on very important issues, they are still single issues. However, because of the lack of a credible political alternative to neoliberal politics, with its cuts and deregulations of the labour market, these movements are at present the only answer to the crisis, realistically speaking. Neither opposition parties nor the unions are offering any comprehensive strategies for new development paths.

Exceptionally, in the Greek case, Maria Karamessini can truly say that such a political vacuum no longer exists. The strengthened opposition forces are proposing a growth strategy, which aims at improving the budgetary situation by increasing taxed incomes, implementing a radical tax reform, and by using primary surpluses and external financial support to fight poverty and boost public investments. However, she also points out that such alternative approaches can only be put in place if the EU stops implementing its crisis management policies and if national reform programmes are given some room for manoeuvre. Therefore, alternative crisis management approaches can only be negotiated at an EU level.

Italy is a country which is not under the strict supervision of the Troika or the EU Commission and which still has substantial economic potential. Annamaria Simonazzi provides a harsh assessment of Italy which neatly summarises the complex challenge the country is facing: 'One good thing that this crisis might have produced is to convince Italians that the country is at present on a road to ruin and that there is no external (European or German) nor individual (devolution, Lega Nord) salvation. Only once we have done our homework can we seek, and demand, Europe's help.' She concludes: 'Emergency intervention needs to pave the way for long-term construction: a growth strategy that would mean easing up on austerity for Greece and the other weakened countries and enacting stimulus measures in surplus countries, as well as new rules that prevent the formation of the very disequilibria that led to the present predicament.'

Today, such interaction is inevitable. The questioning and eroding of the social achievements of post-war capitalism started long before the introduction of the euro and the single market. Rules and institutions established within this context may have increased this pressure, but they are not to blame for initiating it. Furthermore, we should not forget that since France's first Mitterrand administration at the opening of the 1980s, no efforts have been undertaken at a national level to pave the way for an alternative to neoliberalism in Europe. Thus, following the pessimistic proposal of focusing on 'trying to throw a spanner in the works of the current system' would simply mean exhausting ourselves in an attempt to conserve past achievements. The solution to this dilemma is to take the bull by the horns. In contrast to past decades, the 'productive reconstruction'[8] of European economies is becoming increasingly less viable if applied on an exclusively national level. During the twentieth century it may have sufficed to cite globalisation to explain this challenge (and the aforementioned French attempt, which was terminated soon after its start, well illustrates this challenge). Today, however, we are facing strong mutual cross-border dependence due to accelerated economic integration and consolidated authoritarian control. Those seeking an answer from the left of the political spectrum should be realistic, understanding that in today's Europe, things often come in pairs: *There must be massive pressure at the national level for the implementation of reform projects in order to provoke unavoidable conflicts at the European level so that EU obstacles to the implementation of national reform projects can be overcome.*

One could argue that the European treaties will not permit certain changes, certainly not changes in the relations of political power in the EU. As regards the treaties, this is only partly true. The proposed 'European Recovery Programme',[9] carefully drafted by the Confederation of German Trade Unions, addresses the possibilities of implementing this plan within the framework of existing institutions. The same is true of the 'Programme for Labour', presented by the Italian trade union CGIL,[10] which points to the room for manoeuvre for reforms at a national level in Italy. However, Council decisions on monitoring policies involving national budgets and economies are obviously firmly established and hard to get rid of, and it would be very difficult to implement a Social Charter having the same legal value as fundamental economic freedoms. However, if we want to achieve progressive change, we cannot limit ourselves to thinking about what is possible. Moreover, we need to think about how to generate a political momentum which could make possible things previously thought impossible. This is the only way that institutions can be changed. In short, it is necessary to think less in institutional categories and more in terms of political processes.

Serious advocacy of economic alternatives, even at the level of a single national state, involving the demand at least to loosen one's shackles (which means deviating from the EU Council and Commission's existing decisions and policies), will put the entire political structure of single market and currency union to the test. Depending on the ability of an individual government that breaks ranks to deal with conflicts and join alliances (it could also exploit the principle of unanimity in the European Council), the other governments in Europe would be called on to deal with this provocation. And then, depending on their fear of 'upsetting the markets' and of a possible domino effect within the currency union, they would, to a greater or lesser extent, have to relax or correct their former policies. Progressive movements and trade unions in other countries would also face a new set of circumstances. Up to now, it could have seemed to them that they inhabit two separate worlds. But in a crisis provoked by politics – instead of by 'the markets' – they would be more likely to act in concert. For critical forces, it would be easier to practice *social* solidarity across national borders, instead of *national* solidarity within their own countries, which is what the 'austeritarian' regime induces them to do.

An institutional framework such as the Maastricht treaty, which gives the green light to almost every kind of neoliberal policy but continues to reject or slow down the achievement of common social standards and most measures for mutual support and economic convergence, cannot be reformed without harsh conflicts, crises, and ruptures. The impulses leading to such an inevitably rocky reform process will come from countries in which the population's desire to put an end to the 'austeritarian' regime and bring about a social, economic, and ecological reorientation of their *own* nation has become strong enough that a conflict with Brussels, Berlin, and other centres of power is inevitable. In the end, 'constructive opposition' at the EU level will only be as effective as the 'constructive opposition' for reforms in the individual countries. From today's perspective, it is hard to imagine such an impulse coming from Germany. What is certain, however, is that everything rests on how impulses from other countries are perceived in Germany and how they are perceived by progressive forces within Germany.

translated by Veronika Peterseil

Literature

Benatouil, Maxime and Sigfrido Ramírez Pérez, *From Industrial Policy to a European Productive Reconstruction*, transform! Discussion Paper No. 3 (2014), <http://transform-network.net/publications/publications-2014/news/detail/Publications/-2790eb1878.html>.

Candeias, Mario and Eva Völpel, *Plätze sichern! ReOrganisierung der Linken in der Krise* [Save Your Seats! The Reorganisation of the Left in the Crisis], Hamburg: VSA, 2014.

CGIL, *Il piano del lavoro. Creating Jobs to Give Italy Future and Growth*, 2013. <http://www.cgil.it/Archivio/EVENTI/Conferenza_Programma_2013/CGIL_Plan_for_jobs_2013.pdf>.

DGB, *A Marshall Plan for Europe. Proposal by the DGB for an Economic Stimulus, Investment and Development Programme for Europe*, 2012, <http://www.ictu.ie/download/pdf/a_marshall_plan_for_europe_full_version.pdf>.

Dufresne, Anne and Jean-Marie Pernot (2013), 'Les syndicats européens à l'épreuve de la nouvelle gouvernance économique' [European Trade Unions and the Challenge of new Economic Governance] *Chronique internationale de l'IRES*, no. 143-144.

Lehndorff, Steffen (ed.), *Divisive Integration. The Triumph of Failed Ideas - Revisited. Ten Country Studies*, Brussels: ETUI, 2014 (forthcoming).

Sauer, Thomas, 'Von Chimären und Krokodilen: Der lange Weg vom sozialen Nationalstaat zum europäischen Sozialmodell' [Of Chimeras and Crocodiles: The Long Way from the Social State to the European Social Model), Thomas Sauer and Peter Wahl (eds), *Welche Zukunft hat die EU? Eine Kontroverse* [Where is the EU Heading? A Critical Examination], Hamburg: VSA-Verlag, 2013.

Streeck, Wolfgang, *Gekaufte Zeit. Die vertagte Krise des demokratischen Kapitalismus* [Buying time. The Postponed Crisis of Democratic Capitalism], Berlin: Suhrkamp, 2013.

Troost, Axel and Philipp Hersel, 'Die Euro-Krise als Zäsur: Eine neue Finanz-, Geld-, und Wirtschaftspolitik in Europa'[The Euro Crisis as a Caesura: A New Financial, Monetary and Economic Policy for Europe], *LuXemburg* April 2012,< http://www.zeitschrift-luxemburg.de/?p=2082>.

Notes

1. This article is based on excerpts from the introductory chapter of the forthcoming book *Divisive Integration. The Triumph of Failed Ideas - Revisited. Ten Country Studies*, ETUI, 2014.
2. Anne Dufresne and Jean-Marie Pernot (2013), 'Les syndicats européens à l'épreuve de la nouvelle gouvernance économique' [European Trade Unions and the Challenge of new Economic Governance], *Chronique internationale de l'IRES*, no. 143-144.
3. Other countries analysed include the United Kingdom, France, Sweden, Hungary, and Austria. The country studies are complemented by analyses of EU crisis policies and the reactions of trade unions to the crisis.

4   Thomas Sauer, 'Von Chimären und Krokodilen: Der lange Weg vom sozialen Nationalstaat zum europäischen Sozialmodell', Thomas Sauer and Peter Wahl (eds), *Welche Zukunft hat die EU? Eine Kontroverse* [Where is the EU Heading? A Critical Examination], Hamburg: VSA-Verlag, 2013, p. 124.
5   Axel Troost and Philipp Hersel, 'Die Euro-Krise als Zäsur: Eine neue Finanz-, Geld-, und Wirtschaftspolitik in Europa', *LuXemburg* April 2012.
6   Wolfgang Streeck, *Gekaufte Zeit. Die vertagte Krise des demokratischen Kapitalismus* [Buying time. The Postponed Crisis of Democratic Capitalism], Berlin: Suhrkamp, 2013, pp. 218, 223, 256.
7   Mario Candeias and Eva Völpel, *Plätze sichern! ReOrganisierung der Linken in der Krise*, Hamburg: VSA-Verlag, 2014.
8   Maxime Benatouil and Sigfrido Ramírez Pérez, *From Industrial Policy to a European Productive Reconstruction*, transform! Discussion Paper No. 3 (2014).
9   DGB, *A Marshall Plan for Europe. Proposal by the DGB for an Economic Stimulus, Investment and Development Programme for Europe*, 2012.
10 CGIL, *Il piano del lavoro. Creating Jobs to Give Italy Future and Growth*, 2013.

EUROPE: A LOCK AND A KEY

Patrice Cohen-Séat

The European treaties jointly developed and voted by the right and social democracy have created a twenty-eight-key lock, which requires all keys to be turned simultaneously if any change in the fundamental direction of the Union's policies is to take place. At the very least, since the less powerful states are to some extent obliged to follow the trend, the hard core of the European structure would have to reach an agreement if any change were to occur. In practice, this gives the most important countries a virtual veto. Within the present political balance of power, therefore, changes in the EU's structure can only be made in the direction of still more liberalism. This is a 'pawl effect': Except in the case of a major political crisis (in which, say, a major country takes the path of disobedience or stands in the way of a move), movement is only possible in one direction, never in the other. Even if everything depended solely on France and Germany, it is highly improbable that both countries would simultaneously elect majorities, each of which decided to break with liberalism. This is, characteristically, the situation in France where a socialist majority was elected in 2012 on a platform of 'renegotiating' the European Treaties. However, this appeared to the newly elected MPs so unattainable that they simply gave up the attempt. Hence the sharp acceleration of François Hollande's drop in popularity as soon as it became clear that this had just been a campaign promise and that nothing would really change on this decisive question.

Thus the system is jammed. The degradation in living and working conditions of millions of people impels them to want 'a change'. But the European structure in fact prohibits it. Under these conditions, the debate distortedly pits those who put stress on the impossibility of change within the European framework, and thus propose to exit it, against those who, pointing to the impotence of each individual nation state to influence the course of globalisation, maintain that exiting Europe or the euro would have still more disastrous consequences. Nearly everywhere the great majority of the population is more afraid of the real or imagined consequences of leaving the European Union or the euro. Even in Greece, where the austerity policies have had truly devastating social effects and have massively discredited Pasok, Syriza's leap forward was only possible because its leaders assured people that they intended Greece to remain in the euro area.

From parliamentary democracy to authoritarian euro-liberalism

The member states of the European Union, particularly those in the euro area, have thus insidiously but radically changed the political system. The nineteenth and twentieth centuries saw the progressive development of regimes called 'parliamentary democracies' in Western Europe, then, after the collapse of the 'socialist' countries, throughout Europe. The parliamentary regimes accompanied the development of capitalism and the considerable social progress that this social formation historically enabled. Their institutions were based on two inseparable principles. On the one hand, universal suffrage, which was gradually conceded, granted citizens some real powers. On the other hand, the affirmation of the unalienable and sacred character of private property placed the 'private' power of capital outside the political arena. This rule, which was written into the 1789 Declaration of the Rights of Man and the Citizen and repeated in the preamble to France's 1958 Constitution, thus limits the sovereign power of the people. Even today, French constitutional jurisprudence is the intransigent guarantor of this – for example by protecting the right of shareholders to make strategic decisions in their own interests in the management of firms or by putting forward the idea that a tax rate of 75 per cent would be 'confiscatory' and therefore illegal.

There is, therefore, a double source of legitimate power in parliamentary regimes – through elections, for political power, and through property, for economic power. It is up to the political power to establish the means for exercising the right of property – but without attacking it or its principles. In such a system, the state can act on the macro-economic framework through monetary and fiscal policies, particularly through its budget and through public property. It can set the rules to be applied in the different sectors of productive activity. But it cannot go further and itself decide on the use of capital or the management of a firm. Only the supporters of socialism have opposed to this – including in the ultimate from of an administered economy – a different regime in which the state would have ownership of the means of production and exchange, thus having in its hands the two kinds of power – political and economic. The respective roles of the state and of the market have, over the last two centuries, been at the heart of the political clashes between left and right and, within the left, between the libertarians and the statists.

But these clashes took place within the framework of each nation-state, which thus could, according to specific conditions, arbitrate between the two sources of power. In France, after the war, the programme of the National Council of the Resistance organised a historic compromise between the two forces present. In this way, more or less everywhere in Europe according to the particular history of each country, there developed what in the end was called – and later denigrated as – *welfare state regimes*. This was a balance in which the state had power to intervene strongly in the economy and to organise and preserve some major social gains: public services and companies, labour rights and status, systems of solidarity, social security, etc. What is new in the present form of the EU's structure is that this compromise can no longer be built in a national framework. In the name of 'free and undistorted competition' the European Union is imposing unification based on the reduced ability of states to act, leaving much greater powers to the markets, that is, to private forms of organising society. Symbolically, one of the most sovereign of all functions, that of issuing currencies (for countries in the euro area) has been taken away from the states to become an exclusively European competence and entrusted, moreover, to an 'independent' central bank.

This is indeed a complete change of regime. The equilibrium that had been built up in the so-called parliamentary-democracy systems between the power of citizens and of money has now been smashed. Above all, there is no longer a space in which this equilibrium could be the subject of democratic discussion. On the one hand, the treaties that establish the EU's new order impose upon the national legislatures, and even on the Union's own institutions, rules that greatly favour the markets, for example by drastically limiting the ability of public authorities to intervene in the economic arena. On the other hand, in those areas where political debate might take place at the European level, the institutions favour inter-state processes. This, quite rightly, gives the citizens of each country the feeling that these issues are beyond their control and that they are powerless. This is why the European elections are the ones with the lowest level of participation. In sum, the EU's structure has transferred a decisive part of the powers of the states to a largely bureaucratic machine that does not obey the fundamental rules of democracy. In effect, political authority is reduced to benefit the powers of money, and democracy has taken a giant leap backwards.

The EU imposes on its constituent countries a liberal regime (in the sense that the role of public powers is in retreat while that of capital is increasing), which, as a consequence, is also becoming authoritarian. Indeed, the most important political conflicts can have no democratic outcome. This is clearly shown by the political debate of spring 2013. How to reduce public expenditure or the cost of labour may be discussed in the national context. Thus François Hollande was able to seize the unexpected opportunity of putting in his place the President of the European Commission, who took it on himself to list the reforms to be carried out in France. Nevertheless, these principles (reduction of public expenditure and labour costs) are imposed on all. This is why the policies of the social democratic left so resemble right-wing policies that they confuse people. It is not due to a lack of imagination, as some commentators like to imagine, but to the need to follow the Union's constituent orientations.

Hence social conflict changes its nature. Since political discussion that could give legitimacy to some choices is impossible, they are imposed authoritatively. And thus social conflictuality changes its nature. If there can be no political debate capable of lending legitimacy to these choices, they will be imposed in an authoritarian fashion. It is then no longer on social and political terrain that contestations and frustrations can be expressed. Social militancy declines in parallel with electoral participation. Instead, sub-political forms of challenging the status quo are developing; the riots in French urban peripheries in 2005, like those which occurred in several major cities in England in 2011, are spectacular expressions of this. With political measures excluded, the response is simply one of law and order. We have entered a new type of political regime: authoritarian euro-liberalism.

This change of political regime has gone virtually unnoticed because it has taken place without any spectacular changes in our national institutional systems. Its tool is simply the legal principle whereby standards set by international treaties (in this case the founding acts of the European Union) are superior to national legislation. Everything is called into question without anything apparently having budged in the domestic institutional and juridical order. The introduction of the neoliberal order in the treaties themselves has dried up political discussion by imposing a certain kind of relationship between the state and the market: the new role assigned to the former is to guarantee the primacy of the latter.

This political choice is imposed on both the right and the left, which from this point on necessarily find themselves essentially in agreement. Authoritarian euro-liberalism has indeed killed democracy.

The challenge of building a progressive Europe

Thus, from the very way it was conceived, the construction of the European Union is one of the principal causes of the democratic regression we have been experiencing over the last forty years. But it would be a pure illusion to imagine a return to the status quo ante, that is, to democratic parliamentary regimes in a national framework. The present situation is actually the solution conceived and carried out by the dominant forces to deal with the deep and irreversible transformations in the production system, particularly the digital revolution, which they themselves had to face. The considerable increase in investments needed particularly for research and development, has made a change in the scale of finance and trade indispensable. In the same way that the nation-states had enabled nascent capitalism to break the shackles inherited from the feudal mode of production, so the creation of continental-scale economic zones has been imposed as part of a vaster movement of worldwide integration whose agents (the IMF, WTO, World Bank, etc.) play a crucial role. Setting the goal of fighting this new political regime of authoritarian euro-liberalism cannot, therefore, be conceived as an impossible return to past democratic forms incapable of meeting the challenges of the very new epoch we have entered. The progressive forces must think out a political system capable of responding to the challenge of globalisation and find avenues of struggle capable of overcoming it.

The system established in the framework of financialised capitalism is quite accurately characterised by the term *governance*.

While the concept of democracy features the plurality of choice – reflecting the conflictual confrontation of socially distinct and mutually opposed social interests – the term governance stresses the alleged efficiency of the management of a given economic order, as defined by the European treaties. In the absence of possible alternatives, the main matters under discussion do not touch on political concepts concerning citizens or social forces, but technical options for experts to deliberate on.

As we have seen in Italy, in Greece, and elsewhere, the establishment of governments of 'technicians', often coming from European economic and financial institutions, tends to replace the search for compromise and political balance that allows the formation of majorities. Neoliberalism, that is, the ideology that reflects the needs of financialised and globalised capitalism, has thus found the political regime suited to it, a regime in which the real debates take place outside the democratic sphere, inside the impenetrable institutions according to the dominant forces' internal balance of power. Thus the political cycle opened two centuries ago with the establishment of parliamentary democracies has come to a close.

The world's major economic areas are characterised by different types of institutional upheaval. The United States, China, India, and Russia, in particular, are continent-nations and therefore very integrated economic areas, which face problems distinctly different from Europe's. The European countries, on the other hand, are faced with the necessity of organising institutional integration on the basis of longstanding national traditions. As it is was not possible in our period to accomplish integration through violence, as had formerly occurred elsewhere, the policy has, since the war, been based on 'small steps' and faits accomplis. More recently, this policy has clashed with a growing movement of rejection of the EU's structure, expressed among other ways by the success of the 'no' vote in France and the Netherlands in the 2005 referenda held on adopting the 'Constitutional Treaty'. Under pressure, the principal political forces of the countries concerned were obliged to throw off their mask and disregard popular sovereignty. In France, this has involved a veritable institutional coup d'état, the right (UMP) and the left (PS) having decided to vote together in Parliament to pass a treaty that over 55 per cent of the people had rejected.

Today we can see, with the rise of the extreme right and of 'Euroscepticism', that this institutional violence, coupled with an unprecedented economic and social crisis, is tending to reach its limits and is exposing the EU's architecture to the danger of disintegration or explosion. However, it has resisted this for several reasons.

Firstly, because of a deeply rooted feeling of its necessity, people have committed themselves to the European Union following two world wars and the hope of 'never again'. This motive remains all the stronger as the world seems increasingly dangerous. Secondly, the idea of 'a powerful Europe' is a way for small or medium sized countries to resist in an increasingly fierce economic war.

The main reason, however, is undoubtedly the absence of a political alternative. The relatively recent creation of the Party of the European Left (EL) has not yet produced a European political project able to unify what we call 'radical' left forces. Between the countries of the East and West, or the North and South, the differences in situation and the conflict of interest are important obstacles. While 'Brussels' is a strong identifier of the present European project, there is, so far, no similar identifier of an alternative left project. It is significant that the EL only played a marginal role in the recent European election campaigns, despite the fact that Alexis Tsipras's symbolic candidacy for the presidency of the European Commission gave it, for the first time, some degree of visibility.

Finally, the European institutions themselves are a self-blocking mechanism.

For all the above reasons, a significant change in the orientation of the building of Europe presupposes a new treaty and thus, in theory, a simultaneous agreement between all the countries of the Union. At the very least, political majorities must simultaneously form in the most important countries in order to propose such a transformation – either by re-negotiating the Treaty or by subverting it. This would be, in the present state of affairs, a completely improbable political situation.

Progressive forces are thus confronted with the literally historic challenge of agreeing on a concept for building Europe. The dominant forces have solved their own problem by establishing an authoritarian regime. Since the policies of members are constrained by the treaties ('free and undistorted competition'), the institutions, especially the Commission, the Central Bank, and the Court of Justice, are the policemen of its rigid orientations. Returning to a democratic regime therefore presupposes inventing a new way of articulating the national and European forms within a new kind of construction. By definition, the treaties we need should not contain any predetermined economic or political model and would be exclusively devoted to affirming the principles and essential objectives of European democracy and defining its institutions. Above all, in contrast to the present construction, the convergence should be founded, in the long term, on respect for the full sovereignty and the free choice of the peoples concerned. This implies that the Union should be *of variable geometry*. A member state, in any area where an essential aspect of its social options is at stake, could thus be able to choose freely whether or not to take part in an area of European policy. It could even negotiate its withdrawal in the event of a complete impasse with its partners, were it the will of its democratically consulted citizens.

Towards a progressive majority bloc

Over and above the institutional dimension, the essential issue is a political constellation that could carry this new conception. It is enough to observe the results of the European election to see that, in most major countries, the stagnation of radical left forces is at too low a level to be able significantly to weigh on the course of events.

This weakness brings us to two interconnected phenomena. On the one hand, the popular social strata that have historically made up the left's main social base are afflicted by increasing electoral abstentionism. On the other hand, the better off strata are hanging on, as best they can, to their post-war gains. The fear of being declassed tends to radicalise in a rightward direction a significant number of people, whose social situation is most fragile and who feel threatened by the crisis. At the other extreme, the best off groups aspire to move up and join the upper social strata. Between these two, a large mass of *middle strata* hopes to preserve its position by not taking the risk of shaking up the system, either at the ballot box or in the streets.

The social bloc that, out of fear or self-interest, supports the dominant forces is, nevertheless riddled by contradictions. In Greece, a virtual laboratory situation, this bloc is split in a crisis situation that has struck violently at the popular and middle strata. This led, in the course of a few months, to a mass transfer of the electorate from Pasok to Syriza. It is obviously impossible to foresee what will follow – especially in a country that does not play a central role in the present European structure. However, Syriza's trajectory shows the possible path for forming an antagonistic social bloc once the progressive forces become capable of proposing an overall project suited to the demands and aspirations of a great part of the disadvantaged popular and middle strata. Unemployment, job insecurity, and poverty have for several decades now been the adjustment variables of a capitalist system undergoing profound transformation. This, in practice, means that the most disadvantaged sectors have borne the brunt of the crisis through cuts in social expenditures and the reduction of public services while being stigmatised by campaigns against state 'handouts'. Fighting against this division between the middle and bottom strata and the isolation of the most disadvantaged, upon which the dominant forces have built their power, is an essential condition for a progressive political outcome, that is, for 'exiting the crisis'. It involves reconciling and articulating the fundamental interests of the disadvantaged groups with those of the broadest possible sections of the so-called middle strata.

This goal presupposes a Europe-wide project. Political and social struggles today are stumbling over the divisions that capitalism has organised at this level and at a world scale. The blackmail of the race to the bottom to improve 'competitiveness' is an objective and subjective obstacle to popular mobilisation. The issue of jobs (i.e., the fear of unemployment) has become the major preoccupation of wage earners, eclipsing any other issue. Under such conditions, the only way to overturn the balance of power, which is so tilted today towards the dominant strata, is to mobilise on an international scale – and particularly on the scale of the European Union.

Thus, however we look at the question, the building of the EU appears to be at the same time the lock installed by the dominant strata to establish and perpetuate their dominance and an indispensable key for combating it. After more than forty years of weakness and setbacks, progressive forces must now realise that their political convergence at this level is an absolute priority. In 1848, putting forward the famous slogan 'Proletarians of all countries, unite!', Marx and Engels explained that this unity should be preceded, in each country, by the victory of the proletariat over 'its own' national bourgeoisie. Since then, the question of whether 'socialism' was possible 'in one country' has become one of the major problems of the emancipatory movement. Contemporary realities are, today, providing at least a partial answer: The only way to fight globalised capitalism is to organise class struggle on the same scale. For Europeans, through timeliness and necessity, this involves working for political unification at the continental scale.

This objective is now on the agenda. For a dozen years – roughly since the creation of the Party of the European Left – there has been a change of scale in political work. The European Social Forums, then the Joint Social Conference, the beginnings of the Alter-Summit process, and some positions taken by the European Trade Union Confederation, show that, faced with the social damage done by European policies, new connections for resistance and working out alternatives are being woven inside the Union. Alexis Tsipras' candidacy for European Commission president also shows that there has been a maturation in this direction. In a situation marked by increasing social suffering and a dangerous disintegration of political systems, we need to prefigure a European alternative for developing a constructive social and political dynamism. No one can foresee what the spark will be that sets off a social movement spreading like a forest fire. Will it be a breach opened in one of the countries of the Union by a political victory of the radical left? Or a significant incident that catalyses social anger? The fact remains that the political responsibility of the forces of this 'radical left' will be decisive in encouraging the emergence of a project and thus of hope in Europe. This is also the condition that could prevent such a movement, if it arises, from ending in adventurism. Peoples of Europe, unite!

AN ALTERNATIVE EUROPEAN INDUSTRIAL POLICY?

Gabriel Colletis

The need for an 'industrial renaissance' seems now to be the object of a fairly broad consensus. Although for a long time industry was considered part of an outdated heritage, industrial jobs are now seen as a crucial factor conditioning the number of jobs, skilled and less skilled, in the service sector.

The usefulness and meaning of a European industrial policy

We see such a policy as having two possible general directions. The first would aim *at taking advantage of the potentials and complementarities of national and regional productive structures in Europe, avoiding, in particular, the imbalances connected to terms of trade and the effects of polarisation.*

The second direction of a European industrial policy would consist of *framing it in a way consistent with both a macro-economic policy directed towards support for activity (through investment but not only) and a policy of promoting efforts in education, training, and research.*

Besides the very unequal development of industry in the different European countries, there are also some profound differences in the composition of productive structures. In certain countries or territories industry essentially produces consumer goods ultimately intended for households, whereas other places primarily produce machines for equipping industrial plants. Still other countries produce energy or intermediary goods that are part of the composition of finished products. These differences in composition constitute a potential for complementarity that could serve as an essential base for the gradual establishment of a European productive system and as a general orientation for European industrial policy. This potential of complementarity has, in the past, been used in certain sectors like aeronautics (e.g. Airbus) or space (e.g. Ariane).

However, several obstacles make this perspective hard to translate into practice. The first is that the most powerful European country, Germany, while known for its production in the capital goods industry is just as much a producer of durable consumer goods and end consumer goods aimed at households. Germany's capacity to produce energy as well as the intermediate products its industry needs is also very strong. While other countries often need things produced by Germany, the converse is not true. With a balance of trade surplus in its strong areas (machinery, cars, chemicals, etc.), Germany has managed to reduce its deficits in areas that, historically, are not its strong points (agro-industry, textile, clothing, etc.). The differences in the level of valorisation of different activities and products, reflected by relative prices, is a second obstacle. A specialised machine tool for cutting gears or a top-of-the-line car do not have the same added value as mass-produced clothing or a ton of coal. Thus a country whose productive composition is focused on activities with a high added value at high prices and where demand is inelastic with regard to price would inevitably dominate at the expense of others. It would sell the others expensive products and buy from them products whose low prices show they contain less added value. Encouraging European complementarity of national or regional productive systems that ignores such an imbalance is equivalent to encouraging the complementarity of a powerful man and his vassals.

The third obstacle comes from the powerful momentums that make activities agglomerate in certain areas called 'focus' zones. Such momentums produce areas of inequality whose cumulative character is hard to overcome. While certain regions in Europe pursue and increase their development by maintaining and attracting specific essential resources, that is, capacities, while deepening the mechanisms of collective learning, others are sinking under the weight of the crisis and under-development, driving into exile the younger and best educated generations. This disorganises the networks of social and productive solidarity where they exist.

Among the weak points of European industrial policy identified by the European Commission itself is internal demand which 'remains weak, undermining European companies' home markets and keeping intra-EU trade subdued after the crisis' (European Commission, IP/14/42 22/01/2014 <http://ec.europa.eu/enterprise/initiatives/mission-growth/index_en.htm)>. It is very hard for all European countries to have a positive balance of external trade and export-led growth. Thus, in all European countries domestic demand, in different degrees and in different ways, plays a central role. Industrial policies, whether European or national, cannot be dynamic and proactive if they are conceived in a depressed macro-economic environment. It is thus necessary to connect industrial and macro-economic policies by injecting the means that are required for them. The strong risk today (especially in France) is that a policy of support for big corporations (in lieu of an industrial policy) associated with a recessive macro-economic policy will only accentuate the outward orientation of these companies although this is one of the prime causes of de-industrialisation.

Rather than devoting disproportionate means to big or very big corporate groups, it would be more sensible for European governments to support economic activity by undertaking massive public investment. Promoting a kind of public investment that is not opposed to the growth of workers' income would indeed combine the advantages of short and middle term measures (the support of activity in the sectors concerned) with preparation for the future. Public investment must cover both plant and infrastructure and must also be oriented towards education, training, research, and innovation. There is no doubt that the fortress of productivity, which has so long protected industry and jobs in Europe, can no longer play this role in the face of the emerging countries. Until conditions emerge for harmonious co-development in the world, it is indispensable that European industry become the crucible of another model of development, placing democracy and labour at its centre through training and the recognition of the abilities of all those who work in the service of human needs today. It is both necessary and possible.

The principles of any industrial policy

Seven principles can guide choices that promote industry:

The first principle: viewing industry as a system. The basic unit of any industrial policy is inter-relation, since industry is a system and not the sum of its actors. It is the density of relations between the actors of the 'productive system' that conditions the efficiency of the whole, which is clearly much more than the sum of the individual performances of each.

The second principle: basing the performance of industry on the recognition and strengthening of the skills of its workers. We think that, more than the saving in time or optimisation of the production process, the potential significance of the new technologies of production that have been announced (e.g. 3D printers and robotics) lies in the capacity to work differently rather than faster. The logic of cost reduction should give way to practices that emphasise innovation.

The new notion expressed by the neologism 'cobotic', which invokes a cooperative kind of robotics, focuses on the needs of the user. Cobotics can be understood as robotics that aims at using or having recourse to mechanical systems of substitution developed to work with people, accompanying them and helping them in particular situations and for particular tasks. As was the case during the computerisation of work stations, cobotics will only really be able to fulfil its promise of a different kind of work if a major effort is made to train people. This effort lies at the heart of industrial policies and must be applied to both technical and organisational skills. The mission of robots is not necessarily to replace people; instead it can assist them. 'Big data' will constitute large stores of structured information, but they cannot replace the human mind. Far from denying the role of skill and experience, the new production and management technologies could accentuate it. The individual and collective capacity to carry out complex tasks, to recombine existing know-how in new configurations, constitutes the essence of technology, defined as the whole of the mechanisms and practices available in a given culture.

From now on, the questions of efficiency and of coordination will assume a growing importance, for two reasons. First, because the individual actors decreasingly have at their command the whole range of skills needed to resolve a problem. Second, because the regulatory mechanisms that ensured the relatively stable and predictable working of economic and social systems have been largely dismantled by the increased opening up of these economies through the deregulation that is causing or intensifying the general instability.

The engineering mechanisms and practices available in a culture, which is what essentially constitute technology, can thrive in a democracy. We therefore believe that democracy in civil society as well as within companies is Europe's only comparative advantage and must be preserved and made fruitful rather than be seen as an obstacle to efficiency.

The third principle: giving life to democracy within the enterprise whose institutional existence is recognised as such. The dominant image of a firm is that of an organisation whose sole aim is to make a profit. Everything happens as if those who own the corporation's capital were the only parties present, being able freely to dispose of the firm as if it were a mere liquid asset.

The process of financialisation, which broadly speaking dates from the 1990s, intensifies all these features and their effects. Not only is profit confirmed as the firm's sole purpose but it in turn is oriented to the shareholders' interests as a matter of priority. Profits and dividends are no longer what are left over from the firm's operations but are considered guaranteed preconditions. Since dividends are announced to shareholders in advance, the sharing of profits and of added value are overdetermined. The effect of this is to restrict both the self-financing of investments and the wage level – these are treated as adjustment variables. Wage earners are expected neither to mobilise their skills nor be associated in the designing of strategy – nor be fairly paid.

The extreme pressure exerted on the firm's costs (especially its wage costs) is not aimed at improving the firm's competitiveness but only its profitability – out of which the guaranteed incomes of the shareholders are paid. Investments are now chosen for their ability to reach a standard of profitability set by the financial markets and the holders of capital. This form of capitalism is far worse than a rentier capitalism that is limited to taking advantage of the condition of past accumulation – it destroys what has been accumulated, eating it up or squandering it.

Recognising the firm as a complete institution in itself, not just a mere capital-owning company, giving it its own managing organ, in which the wage earners would be recognised not in relation to their cost savings but their work contribution, is a central issue for democracy, social peace, and economic efficiency. With the help of available new production techniques, only those wage earners recognised for their competence and ability to directly take part in strategic decisions could be involved at this level, considering the immensity of human needs and the need to preserve nature from the great danger it faces.

Recognised as a common good once it pursues objectives that go beyond those of a mere firm, the enterprise emerges from the classical alternative of the private appropriation of profits and the socialisation of costs and losses. Its governance can be broadened to include, beyond its wage earners and capital providers, representatives of the general interest – those of the territories in which it is active – who could be integrated into the firm's management.

The law must establish this new alternative kind of representation, and EU law could make a positive contribution to this, beyond the present provisions for a 'European company'. The social section of this statute already requires that companies put a mechanism in place for the participation of European wage earners. This mechanism can consist of establishing mechanisms for information and the consultation of wage earners and even for their participation in organs of governance. The first is a move in the right direction, but it is insufficient since the fate of major firms, being strongly marked by their financialisation, has already been radically separated from the future of the national, and even European, fabric.

The fourth principle: promoting long term de-financialising strategies (time). De-financialising must answer to the general principle of re-articulating the economic and the social spheres. This is essential to getting out of the crisis and evolving towards a new kind of social organisation. It is a precondition for all financial regulation with any significant operational scope. The present financialisation follows a general principle that opposes the economic and social to one another, making income depend on the 'factors' of mobility.

The most mobile factor, the financial factor, has established its right of remuneration before that of all the others (industrial capital, and both skilled and unskilled labour), thanks to its extreme mobility and its volatility. The remuneration of labour, whether semi-skilled or unskilled, appears as a 'residue'. The social tensions (e.g. the growth of inequality) that arise from the principle connecting speed of mobility to level of remuneration, but also the economic instability associated with this principle, result, in the current situation, in the impossibility of drawing up compromises and creating the institutions required for a new mode of development. Dealing with time, the speed of mobility of the 'factors', is today the indispensable precondition for putting finance back in its place (in the service of economic and social development) and reducing inequalities.

It is a process that will involve stages, both to put a brake on the liquidity of financial capital and to increase the mobility of labour. Challenging the volatility of financial capital – making it concede that it has to invest rather than just bet money on something – means instituting retardants: taxes on financial transactions, differential taxing of profits according to whether they are re-invested or distributed as dividends, the different taxing of short- and long-term capital gains, the proportional granting of voting rights to shares based on how long they have been held, etc. The 'compartementalisation' of financial activities (one example of which is the separation between the activities of merchant banks and deposit banks) reflects the same logic of favouring relative liquidity at the expense of the absolute volatility of financial capital.

All these reforms could be initiated at the national level, but the most coherent relevance of these reforms lies at the European level. This level will only live up to its potential when there is determined political action by the peoples of different European countries.

The perspective of increasing the mobility of labour must, for its part, not be understood in the spatial sense, as it customarily is, but as a matter of making labour more skilled, of making it specific, developing experience and capacities. Mobility is thus that of workers who change their assignments in accordance with the specific tasks or projects to be carried out. Industry can again become a place of stable and well paid work. This stability, far from meaning the carrying out of a job whose content never changes, should become synonymous with a mobility that is guaranteed by the re-deployable character of its capacities.

The fifth principle: promoting the anchoring of activities (space). Beyond the short term or localised projects that could be developed everywhere to reduce the ecological footprint and protect nature, the durable anchoring of activities in territories or regions is an important aspect of industrial renovation. While the choice of localisation is now mainly based on cost comparisons, those based on an offer of the specific advantages of territories are more lasting. Territories that know how to propose the complementary capacities which enterprises need, by identifying them and organising them in networks, will be able to preserve the local anchoring of the companies in question, and much more effectively than by throwing themselves into a general cost competition.

With this perspective we clearly distinguish between localisation and regionalisation. Rather than proposing generic advantages, always liable to be competed with (offers of real estate, infrastructures, various exemptions), the territories would do well to identify and develop the availability of skills corresponding to the needs of the firms that have gone too far in the practice of outsourcing. A firm would have difficulty in finding specific skills in the areas of competence that it has outsourced. Rather than multiplying a variety of subsidies and exemptions to firms taken in isolation or supporting a number of infrastructure projects through Structural Funds, which show little evidence of being economically effective, this new industrial policy would strengthen the inter-relations between firms (by benefiting from the advantages of proximity to anchor their activities) and could then be called a real policy of a productive system, integrating the actors of the world of research and training.

Rather than only seeking to accumulate and concentrate the protagonists in an area regarded as limited by borders, the public protagonists should in the future seek to encourage productive combinations based on confidence, shared outlooks, and potentially complementary skills. The settling of a firm in a region and its participation in the regional dynamics constitute a wager on the future.

The main role that the public protagonists should play is that of examining these developments and anticipating needs in terms of the complementary capacities of firms. This will require a great improvement in the level of coordination between the public protagonists as well as the strengthening of relations of trust between the public and private protagonists.

The sixth principle: producing for other needs while protecting nature. What to produce and for whom? Production for export or production as a synonym for a more sustained growth cannot be sufficient or even satisfying answers. The degrowth thesis has some solid argument to put forward, which condemn the malaise at work but also the harm productivism does to people and nature. At the same time, it does not always clearly distinguish between growth and development. This approach, while it rightly adopts a critical attitude to the damage done by productivism, ignores the immensity of social needs in poor countries as well as, increasingly, in the developed countries (e.g. in education, health, food, housing, and transport). This question, with the rise in inequality everywhere, has become a central issue for millions of people who are no longer able to feed or house themselves adequately. In this context, while 'growth' does not, by itself, resolve any problem, the converse is also true: Without developing productive activities no progress in covering social needs is conceivable. The difference between growth and development lies precisely in the fact that development implies satisfaction of essential needs such as food, housing, clothing, as well as education and health.

Without subscribing to the degrowth thesis, we nevertheless largely agree with those who advocate an 'ecological transition' and transformations in the structure of employment and the organisation of work. We agree with those who think that a reconversion to more labour-intensive forms of activity is both desirable and possible once the emphasis is placed on the quality of the goods and services provided, the recombining instead of the division of tasks, and the re-localisation of economies.

Rather than a 'green growth' implying that new activities and new kinds of work could arise in Europe on a mass scale in activities involving the management of the environment, we think that one should look at development in another way, a kind of development that no longer considers nature as offering resources (water, air, land ...) that can only have value if they are brought on the market. The development of socially useful production that preserves nature sometimes demands higher capital expenditure but especially requires labour, more skilled than those marshalled by a mass production based on increases in productivity. Providing quality goods and services to consumers and doing so without destroying the environment implies a more complex configuration of work based on a variety of objectives going beyond immediate production.

The seventh principle: establishing protective standards of a new model of development. The change of paradigm that we are proposing will need protective measures and norms – protection against finance, but also against the whole range of deregulatory choices that has pitted workers in general competition with one another through offshoring and dumping of all kinds; protection against the choices that make austerity and decline preferable to the development of productive activities, the only effective remedy to unemployment and deficits; and norms for reconciling the economic with the social, developing useful activities that answer to social needs while protecting nature.

The issue of protectionism is extremely important in the perspective of a new development project. If protectionism is needed, it cannot alone replace an overall project. The approach that we are advocating views protectionism as a means of project development whose intention is political. Most partisans of a policy of protectionism opt for an EU-level protectionism. Theoretically, the EU could be an area where protectionism could be made to work, but on three conditions:

The *first condition of an EU-level protectionism* would be that the European project and institutions be oriented towards development of the economies and productive systems of different European countries. The *second condition* would be that the economic and social situation of the European countries should be more or less similar in order to favour the adoption of common measures that do not provoke significant asymmetries between the countries concerned. The *third condition*, finally, would be that the bulk of the balance of trade deficits contracted by the different countries be with other countries outside the EU. Indeed, what would be the use of measures to protect from countries outside the European Union if the deficits were mainly between the countries? Examining the three 'theoretical' conditions leads to seriously questioning the effective possibility, today, of any protectionism on a European scale. For a long time now EU institutions have not sought to strengthen the development of European countries, particularly not that of their industries. The needed reorientation in constructing Europe is opposed in principle to the content of the present trans-Atlantic so-called 'free trade' negotiations, covering both trade in goods and investments (TTIP: Transatlantic Trade, and Investment Partnership) and services (TSA: Trade and Services Agreement). These negotiations are disarming Europe and the European nations, giving multinational firms the exorbitant power to sue countries if they think a change of legislation harms their interests (see, for example, the Investor-State Dispute Settlement) – not before the national courts but before the International Centre for Settlement of Investment Disputes dependent on the Washington-based World Bank.

A second observation is that the economic and social situation of different European countries, far from converging has never stopped diverging – except that they all share the typical features resulting from the crisis of financialised capitalism. How, for example, can we imagine certain European countries supporting protection measures for certain industries when they totally lack these and they import goods at the lowest possible prices from these very industries?

Finally, as to countries whose trade deficits have contracted – with countries outside Europe or with other European countries – the situation varies. In France's case, apart from trade with China, the principal imbalances are with other developed countries, with Germany in particular. The latter, for its part, has a very positive balance of trade (within and outside the euro area).

It thus appears risky to expect from the present European Union any easy implementation of protectionist measures. This confirms that it is necessary to engage in a reorientation of the EU's construction since the European area is, indeed, the one that seems most favourable for protectionist measures. Because of the size of intra-eurozone trade, it would enable the reconciliation of two figures that globalised capitalism tends to pit against each other – the consumer and the wage-earner. Everything happens as if the consumers had no other choice in maintaining their purchasing power (at least in the short and middle term), that is, being able to buy the products they want, but to 'prefer' imported products at the expense of employment in France and in Europe.

The re-articulation of the interests of consumers, more generally the users of goods produced (whether households which consume or entrepreneurs who buy semi-finished products), with the interests of those who conceive and make them is one of the major reasons for protective measures. The nation seems to be the solidest rampart, likely to be opposed to financialised capitalism and a relevant area for the democratic shaping of an industrial strategy. Open but not offered for sale, the national areas must become the place for initiatives of a new educational protectionism.

Nevertheless, protectionism at the European level, despite difficulties in establishing it, seems the only protectionism conceivable, except by challenging the whole process of economic integration undertaken since the signing of the Treaty of Rome (1957). An eventual protectionism within the community area would destroy the current EU immediately. Within the European area a renewed EU is the institution that would give meaning to the necessary protective measures. It is also the one institution able to provide greater coherence to the connection between increased wages, growth of outlets, and increase of production. The EU, due to the size of its intra-zone trade remains the principal outlet for firms producing in Europe. A gradual increase in the purchasing power of European wage earners would thus privilege the European firms, which could strengthen their production in Europe and re-localise production that has been transferred outside Europe because of the pressure up to now exerted on purchasing power.

Finally, the changes that need to be carried out in the perspective of a new model of development should be made in each of the three spaces – local, national, and EU. These three spaces are intermingled, and the new standards will, most often, be drawn up simultaneously at all three levels. By way of illustration, the present and future wages and working conditions of aeronautic workers are, and will increasingly be, set simultaneously in Toulouse, Hamburg, Munich, Paris, Brussels, and Frankfurt.

Conclusion: for a general change of conceptual framework and an alternative industrial policy

To think that it is possible to establish protections without changing paradigm will only result in failure. It is this paradigm shift that we see as central. A new industrial policy and protective measures are a privileged means or vector. The social forces in Europe must actively campaign for a gradual reorientation but one still supported by the political project of European and national institutions.

No system whatever its area (national or European) – and the EU is indeed vast and complex – can be reformed if it is too open (that is, unprotected). A new development project for Europe presupposes protective standards. The object of these standards would be to prevent externally manufactured products from entering the European Union without restriction if they do not respect the values it intends to promote: the values of labour and the skills incorporated in the products, the value of social relations within the firm, the societal value linked to the great principles based on human rights and protection from a variety of dangers (to health, especially), the values of cooperation and mutually advantageous agreements – and finally, the value of nature. All these values are opposed to the bargaining carried out in secret to impose standards on the peoples that lower the level of protection (TTIP, TISA).

The new industrial development project answers a political aim. This aim cannot exist if it is not carried forward by social forces, if it is not thought out and implemented by the people as citizens.

A LEFT PROJECT FOR RESEARCH IN EUROPE: SOME PRINCIPLES AND PROPOSALS[1]

Marc Delepouve

The policies in force in Europe

Research has a strong impact on human society and life. It should therefore be at the heart of democratic debate and decisions. But research policies are embodied in general policies, which today are oriented towards constantly expanded free trade and major corporations with disproportionate powers. One consequence of these general policies is the intensification of economic clashes inside the European Union and between it and other regions and countries of the world. Hence, there is an increasing subordination of human activities to the imperative to strengthen and defend the EU and its members at the economic level. Public research is being called upon, and is increasingly diverted to this goal. A continuum is being consolidated between a large part of fundamental research and applications or innovations involving the market. Thus fundamental research is in part channelled away from its objectives, shutting out aspects and fields of study with the result that issues of society and of human needs are insufficiently or hardly taken into account even when they are glaringly urgent. The massive use of competitive tenders favours, it is true, some scientific cooperation within Europe but also contributes to a general intensification of competition as well as the subordination of research to financial interests. Projects are under pressure from lobbies and are massively aimed at supporting economic competitiveness. The emphasis laid on societal challenges in recent invitations to tender, particularly in the Horizon 2020 programme, only provides a very inadequate attempt to take these challenges into account.

The support for fundamental research through European Research Council (ERC) scholarships, which encourages excellence, in fact promotes an exacerbated competition between researchers.

An ever growing collusion is occurring between political power and corporate power, especially that of the multi-nationals, leading to the latter's domination of politics and society as a whole. As a result, democracy is weakened and bypassed at the EU, national, and local levels. The public research sector has not been spared, and its subordination assumes different aspects depending on the location, but it is articulated around four axes:

- The major firms and/or the political authorities are playing an increasingly important role in decision-making while personnel representatives are excluded or marginalised.
- Funding by project or by invitation to tender is replacing ongoing funding.
- Evaluations or quality assurance approaches are multiplying based on criteria involving subordination to the corporations' innovation goals.
- The growth of precarity for the personnel; a proliferation of bonuses and the erosion of permanent staff status.

The state has always exercised authority over public research, not only because of its military objectives, but because the power exercised today by the major firms and the political forces has taken on an unprecedented form and breadth.

Asymmetries within Europe

The financial crisis and the option for austerity on a European scale have been accompanied by increased asymmetry within the EU and a collapse of the public funding of research in countries like Greece, Spain, and Portugal. Spanish public research institutions lost 42 per cent of their federal funding from 2009 to 2014; ninety per cent of staff retirements has been followed by the abolition of the jobs involved, accentuating the brain drain towards countries less affected by the crisis and austerity. The sectors not oriented towards economic production have been particularly hard hit. In Spain, the Higher Council for Scientific Research (CSIC) decided to break its contract with Valencia University and the Institute of the History of Science and Medicine, resulting in the latter's demise.

In these countries, not even public research focused on innovation for corporations is spared. This is part of the economic re-composition favouring certain countries, particularly Germany. The budget of the German Federal Ministry of Education and Research has increased by over 26 per cent in the period 2011-2013: 'The objective is to pursue the mobilisation of all the actors in German research, public and private, around strategic issues to encourage the improved innovation of products and the maintenance of German competitiveness at a world level.'[2]

The condemnation of this policy by trade unionists and the scientific community

For the World Federation of Scientific Workers (WFSW), 'the whole world faces a twofold challenge: to redefine the relations between human beings and our planet, and relations among human beings'.[3] According to the European Trade Union Committee for Education (ETUCE) 'Problems and emergencies arise at international level, such as the rapid degradation of the environment of humanity or the growing world crisis of hunger. More generally, our societies are facing more and more complex problems. Research and education have a vital contribution, to conceive and implement solutions.'[4]

The ETUCE thus points to the major issue that research represents for humanity and underlines the sharp contradiction between this issue and the policies of the EU and its member states. These policies have become an obstacle to any research:

- to fundamental research whose object is the broadening and deepening of the field of knowledge, the application of whose results, often unforeseen, are just one of the consequences;
- to targeted research, indispensable to provide answers to needs arising from extremely varied areas – from agriculture and industry to democratic life and emancipation – such as less polluting forms of energy, healthcare, and the maintenance of peace;
- to research serving critical and emancipatory thinking and the ability of society to think about itself and future projects and to mobilise and transform itself to find answers to social questions and for human needs, both contemporary and future.

Repercussions on the work of researchers and on research itself

Concretely, public research is increasingly reduced to supplying innovations and services to corporations, which takes the form of:

- pitting the personnel, the teams, laboratories, and institutions in competition against one another for funding, bonuses, etc., thus curbing cooperation upon which research activity greatly depends;
- the loss of freedom and even truth (or indeed the risk of fraud);
- the drying up of whole areas and spheres of research and the decline of truly innovative research;

- focusing on the short term (a few years) instead of on the time needed for research;
- the fragmentation and dispersal of tasks, and even unmethodical duplication, the proliferation of industrial secrets during research work, and sometimes even when exploiting the results;
- a proliferation of patent registrations, which increases the cost of the results and limits their use.

Research personnel are increasingly subject to the dictates of political and economic authority. In an increasing number of cases the meaning of public research and skills has been diluted. Scientific workers are increasingly led to actively subordinate themselves and their research to narrow and restrictive objectives.

Scientific rigour, the search for truth, and the development of knowledge, as well as its usefulness for society, which account for much of the prestige and attractiveness of research, are today under attack. They are being replaced by the rush to be published, by the motivation to find the needed funding by answering invitations to tender, where each researcher or team candidate strives to play his or her cards right at the expense of others, thus adapting themselves to the criteria of the tenders and the evaluation agencies. Finally, many researchers are increasingly disconnected from the goals of their work, victims, in a sense, of the historic phenomena of enclosure and proletarianisation. In the process, their ideology and even their values are altered.

In the context of the neoliberal economic onslaught, knowledge is the object of privatisation, which clashes with the principles of cooperation and the maximum diffusion of knowledge. The present organisation of research into less polluting energy sources, for example, is largely subjected to this orientation, which impedes the cooperative development of this research work and the achievement of its medium and long term objectives, thus braking the transition to renewables and the struggle against climate change.

There is a similar tendency in the area of healthcare. The poorer countries are the first victims. Nevertheless, some emerging countries have at times succeeded in resisting the pressures and legal attacks from multinational firms holding patents, especially for medicines against HIV and AIDS.

Refounding society for human emancipation and the satisfaction of social needs – refounding research

A left policy for research must be based on principles such as gender equality, equality between regions, which is aided by research, and on scientific freedom, diversity, cooperation, and respect for the different time frames proper to particular kinds of research.

Democracy

There is an urgent need to defend and redevelop scientific freedoms and academic democracy. This requires liberating the university around four axes: the location of power, funding, evaluation, and the status of the personnel. However, this – the priorities and the distribution of financial and human means – cannot be the sole basis of decisions concerning research policies. The political choices must be based on the democratic processes of discussion and decision-making. Researchers must be widely involved in these processes, knowledge and scientific theories being the domain of those who develop them.

Discussions and democratic decision-making must also precede the use or non-use of the results of research and determine their development. Researchers and those who work for the corporations must also be involved.

The use of genetically modified plants for direct field research or of nanotechnologies have given rise to whistle blowers and associations, which are trying to compensate (by sometimes questionable means) for the absence of democratic decision-making. In some countries, debates have taken place on these questions. However, far from being democratic, these have been duels between the pro and contra sides in a pseudo-debate aiming at making the populations accept what had been decided elsewhere.

Finally, if research policy ought to be an object of democracy, it must also serve democracy and not be used against it to control the population. From the local to the EU level, theoretical research must assist a new development of democracy, drawing lessons from history and the human and social sciences, and enriching itself with new tools of communication and collaboration.

Autonomy

The current 'autonomy of the universities' is a financial and managerial autonomy in the framework of economic competition. It is actually a form of subordination. Instead of this, the autonomy of the universities and research organisations ought to be part of a broader approach of making societies autonomous, which would be based on democracy and the application of the principle of subsidiarity.

Cooperation

In order to help provide answers to today's and tomorrow's societal issues and human needs a public plan of research based on European and international cooperation must be established. This requires financial and human resources adequate to the emergency and the seriousness of the global crisis. The plan must address the technological advances and the indispensable transformations of the economic and social system. It must also be based on an analysis of processes that weaken and endanger democracy as well as the conceptualisation and dissemination of ways of reconquering democracy.

Diversity

Research requires the observance of methods and rhythms appropriate to its different fields. It is essential to preserve the difference between fundamental research and applied research in terms of their logic, objectives, and means, while preserving and developing the fertile interrelationships that they have built. It is also essential to preserve a diversity of discipline, which does not mean remaining ossified in a status quo, without evolving; rather, it means striving for enrichment. Finally, ideological and methodological plurality must be defended and encouraged. The wealth and the development of knowledge are based on the diversity and cross-fertilisation of disciplines, schools of thought, and approaches.

In terms of diversity, research in the humanities and social sciences require particular attention because of the political issues they involve.

Freedom

The scientific freedom of researchers and research collectives, within the limits of ethical constraints, must be scrupulously protected and restored where it has been weakened or impeded. These freedoms are indispensable to technological innovation, in particular to future innovation, which is often unpredictable. They are indispensable to research's contribution to democratic life and to a better understanding of the problems with which human societies are confronted.

Transparency

Transparency is a precondition of the freedom of researchers and research teams, a condition of democracy and ethical responsibility. It must be applied to the process of defining research policies, to the management of research (funding, recruitment, careers, etc.), to the course of research activity, and to its results and their practical application. The mass surveillance carried out in secret by the NSA and revealed by the whistle-blower Edward Snowden is a reminder of the importance of this principle.

Basing ourselves on the evolution of research and inter-disciplinarity

A left project for research in Europe must break with the present and with the past, while taking account of the evolution of science without sweeping it all away.

Science has evolved by compartmentalising itself. The disciplines that emerged and were separated out in the eighteenth and nineteenth centuries have continued to subdivide themselves due to the accumulation of knowledge and the dominance of the analytical outlook. In the majority of disciplines a reductionist attitude favoured analysis and static description. But almost none of the questions raised by an emancipatory approach and by the challenges to which humanity must respond can be addressed within a single branch of science – the example of climate is far from being the only one. They require collaboration between existing disciplines (whose development must be respected and preserved), and a contextualisation that runs contrary to the common practices in most disciplines. They require the taking into account of complexity, and, finally, a completely novel development of action-research and participatory research.

Contextualised research

A consequence of the fragmentation of disciplines and the neoliberal management of research is the very weak perception on the part of most researchers of the influences exerted by context (social, cultural, ethical, and natural environments, sponsors, theoretical presuppositions, etc.) on the choices, objects, methods, and output of research – and, conversely, the multiple influences of research output on society.

The strategies of contextualised research do not determine and study the object of their research by isolating and reducing it as much as possible but by envisaging it, and the methods used, in all the complexity of their contexts.

These are strategies that make explicit the interaction between cognitive and social values, contrary to the current myth of research governed purely by cognitive values. The purpose of these strategies is not to replace reductionist strategies but to complement them. Contextualised strategies often lead scientists, alone or with other social actors, to identify research questions that interact with social issues and to immerse these issues in a multi-disciplinary context that can be more or less broad. Thus they open new horizons, which is satisfying from the researchers' point of view on condition that the scientific criteria of their disciplines are guaranteed. The difficulty, however, is the learning of inter-disciplinarity and the possible need to fully involve actors in the research, who are not trained scientists.

The necessarily plural character of the approaches is in no way a relativist one in which anything goes. All roads do not necessarily lead to Rome, even though many in fact do.[5]

Complexity

Over the last quarter of a century, a certain number of converging but not unified concepts have gradually appeared, which are covered by the term 'complex' (or 'complexity') in several scientific disciplines – at first in the 'exact sciences', then in the humanities and social sciences. The subjects of research are not isolated objects, dissected and reduced to the extreme as in the classical analytical approach, but systems whose evolution is due to interactions between the various components of the system. These interactions are multiple, non-linear (that is, without proportionality or an additive relation between causes and effects), and circular (involving retroactions). This new viewpoint has enabled the discovery of unexpected behaviour in systems, behaviour especially characterised by a sometimes extreme sensitivity to initial conditions, and thus a certain unpredictability, and by the existence of organisational levels whose properties emerge from the constituent parts, thus depending on them without simply amounting to them.

The study of these systems, or of complexity, now often uses mathematical models or computer simulations. It generates a way of thinking that radically breaks with established forms of thought (analytic, simplistic, reductionist, and static) though it encompasses them, and thus it is close to dialectical materialism, from which it could benefit and which it could enrich.

The development of sciences of the complex comes up against many obstacles, particularly at the level of official invitations to tender, which brake it, limiting it to some rare sub-disciplines, or sidestep it by confusing the complex with the complicated. To the extent that complexity corresponds to an approach of studying each object or process in its relation to its environment and as a function of the interactions with this environment, which in turn determines its future, this form of thought, more apt to grasp the world and society in all its complexity, should become the basis of rationality and irrigate all thinking, including political thinking. It is a scientific tool, indispensable to most contextualised approaches – and also to approaches for effective social emancipation.

Other political choices

Unconnected to any objective of practical application, completely free research must again become a priority. To achieve this, we must not only give back control to scientists; a plural policy of free research must also be promoted in a voluntarist manner to encourage even the most minority trends to express themselves and work, to encourage newness (which is very different from neoliberal innovation), and back small emerging teams. This research only can work in the long term; it may (or may not) ultimately lead to technical or civilisational progress.

At the same time, some branches of research must be in sync with society. There is an aspect of research that must be oriented to the economy, a form of research whose objective is to contribute to meeting humanity's major challenges, and one that is oriented to emancipation.

The economic recasting of the EU

The EU must initiate a policy of recasting the economic model (production, exchange, transport, and consumption) that reduces its dependence upon international markets. This requires new agreements on international trade and the interruption of all the current negotiations aimed at intensifying free trade and the power of multinational firms. A major contribution from the world of research is needed. In this way, the EU would reduce the intensity of economic conflict and, correlatively, the pressure of the 'knowledge economy' on public research.

Research will require the establishment of democratic organs involving scientists, representatives of firms (researchers and other workers), and citizen representatives. This mechanism will go hand in hand with the development of economic democracy within companies and of political democracy on the local, national, and European territorial levels. The answers provided for each of these issues could take a variety of forms that would depend in particular on the country.

Action-research

The emancipatory transformation of society and the response to the great societal challenges depend on the development of action-research, necessarily participatory and multi-disciplinary. It will involve conceiving, experimenting, analysing, and supporting actions and approaches to social innovation, changes in individual and collective behaviour, the appropriation of techniques and technologies, and the development of democratic life. Action-research also means theorising such actions and approaches and supporting their appropriation by society while working for social progress and for innovative developments.

Diachrony and participatory research

One of the difficulties of a solid and responsible research policy is combining the different time frames of research and society. Public research institutions often deal with questions that necessitate a long-term approach, while social issues often call for short-term responses. To this extent, one cannot envisage defining a research policy solely in terms of problems advanced by the organs of society – it is essential to take into account the time frames and specific logic of research.

It is vital to find ways of linking and synchronising scientific activity and society. Models like the science shops in Europe and community-based research in the United States are attempts at developing such synchronism. Other models are proliferating and make it possible to take into account diversity, priorities, time frames, and interventions. What is important is to note that the relations between scientific work and society are potentially fertile nexuses for scientific development, in particular participatory research in which people who do not have the status of researchers take part in the development of a research activity or in the definition of its objectives.

Plurality of knowledge, democracy, and expertise

Scientific knowledge is diverse. Moreover, some forms of knowledge – narrative, technical, and traditional as well as many others – that are indispensable for a knowledge of reality are not of a scientific nature. The most complete knowledge is based on the combination of a variety of forms of learning. Finally, especially in complex areas, uncertainty and the unforeseeable are important factors and need to be taken into account.

Today we are seeing the substitution of democratic discussion by reports and debate between experts, most often enclosed in a narrow technical field – dehumanised and erasing all complexity, nearly always imprisoned in the framework of neoliberal capitalist dogmas while making much of their claims to having access to *the truth*. Often these reports suffer from major methodological biases, and even manipulations and deceit. The citizens are nevertheless asked to line up behind their conclusions, even though they generally lack the indispensable keys needed to question their validity. As for forms of knowledge that are not based on technical or scientific expertise but essential to wide knowledge and democratic debate, they are too often not called upon. The heritage of Marxist and anarchist thinkers, and the whole spectrum of radical thought movements, are simply brushed aside.

This narrowing tendency is a tool of the current system of control and domination of people.

The idea of expertise must be explored and rethought. Methodological and ethical rules must be established and observed. Firstly, the formulation of the questions must be the subject of a plural debate involving the different parties concerned. Secondly, the political authorities and the media must not decide the choice of experts on whom they call for advice – or at least not decide it alone. Finally, a plurality of forms of knowledge but also of the rigour and quality of expert reports is indispensable. A major principle of expertise in the service of democracy is pluralism. Pluralism of disciplines first and foremost, since on most societal issues the discussions and democratic decisions cannot be nurtured by a single scientific discipline but rather by the crossing of many of them. Then ideological and methodological pluralism since within any one discipline different schools of thought and a diversity of approaches co-exist. Finally, citizen pluralism since expertise is enriched by questioning, comments, and non-scientific knowledge.

A knowledge commons

Privatisation has extended even to the fundamental sciences. More or less indispensable scientific journals, which have to be paid for by their readers or their authors, have considerably raised their prices over the last decade. On both sides of the Atlantic, however, some universities have launched a counter offensive, calling on their research workers to boycott these journals and publish their works with free public access (a boycott that has a limited effect because of the bibliometric evaluation based on these journals). In another area we observe the phenomenon of free software. These movements should be developed to the point of creating free platforms accessible to the public, archiving the results of research work in all areas and backing this with a free system of validation and recognition by peers. This should be part of a new model of research, science, and technology raised to the level of common goods of humanity, whose access should be a fundamental and universal right. The effectiveness of this right requires the refoundation of scientific culture and a deep transformation of education and information systems.

What is the role of the EU?

The EU's research policy must adhere to the principle of subsidiarity and be chiefly aimed at resolving the major challenges facing humanity and Europe. It must encourage fundamental research, its logic, and its ends, in all member countries. It must ensure the application of some principles and pursue certain objectives: international openness and international cooperation; mobility for researchers, freely decided by them; equality and solidarity between European regions and countries; gender equality; academic freedom; democracy in research and in society; improvement of social and work conditions; healthcare; sustainable development; peace; future-oriented studies and critical social analyses, etc.

The institutions and modalities for implementing EU research policy

Certain major research projects, in particular in the fields of particle physics, energy, and space, require international cooperation. The appropriate dimension for such projects is the EU. We must draw lessons from the major European organisations like the EONR (European Organisation for Nuclear Research), the ESA (European Space Agency), and the ESO (European Southern Observatory). This cooperation has resulted in some first-rate discoveries: Higgs Boson (EONR), the evolution of the universe with the Planck satellite, and the rendezvousing with a comet and reduction of its velocity by the space probe Rosetta (ESA). These successes are due to the fact that these areas have largely been freed from economic competition since their costs and time frames (several decades) are such that they are not subject to the criteria of economic profitability, even though their economic benefits can be major, as in the web developed by the EONR. These European research institutions are, above all, based on democracy and cooperation. They enable exchanges and synergies by taking into account the strengths of each country.

Conclusion

Faced with neoliberal global capitalism, it is imperative to develop research on the foundations and models of society, based on the heritage of radical thinkers, Marxists, anarchists, etc., and on the works of anthropologists and historians, but also on democratic and emancipatory experiments, the renewal and multiplication of which is our hope and aim.

To give back to research its full potential breadth, to put it at the service of human rather than financial profitability, a change of conceptual framework is indispensable – the whole economic and social fabric depends on it. The same goes for the development of countries and human beings. Research workers, despite a policy that tends to demotivate them, are deeply attached to their vocation. It is difficult for them to live with the pressures to which they are subjected, the general competitive pressure, and the brakes on their freedom to do research. They have an important role to play in defining and carrying out a policy for the refoundation of research.

Notes

1   On behalf of the Science, Society and Democracy Working Group of Akademia. This article is the result of reflexions emerging from a European seminar organised by Transform! europe in Madrid on 1 February 2014 and written contributions from Irina Castro, Janine Guespin-Michel, Dominique Crozat, and Annick Jacq.

2. <http://www.science-allemagne.fr/fr/la-recherche-en-allemagne/organisation-de-la-recherche/strategie-high-tech-2020/>.
3. <http://fmts-wfsw.org/wp-content/uploads/2014/03/The_WFSW_Newsletter_no07.pdf>.
4. 'Resolution: Fighting the Crisis an Essential Contribution of Higher Education and Research.' ETUCE conference, 2012. <http://etuce.homestead.com/Statements/2012/Resolution_HER_EN.pdf>.
5. Danièle Bourcier, Philippe Brunet, Marc Delepouve, Janine Guespin-Michel, Annick Jacq, Yves-Claude Lequin, and Chantal Pacteau, *La science pour qui?* [Science for Whom ?], Brignais: Éditions du Croquant, 2013.

THE EUROPEAN UNION AND ITS NEIGHBOURS

Lutz Brangsch

Literally on a daily basis, the nature of the European Union's relations with its neighbours is called into question by the never-ending refugee drama on the EU's southern borders, the wars in Ukraine and the Middle East, and the domestic struggles in Turkey and North Africa.

The EU's self-image and its neighbouring states

Any criticism of the EU's relations with its neighbours is, first and foremost, a criticism of the EU's self-image.

The instruments at the EU's disposal for developing its relations with its neighbours do make it possible, at least to a certain degree, to speak of a uniform approach. Equally, though, the treatment of neighbours is characterised by individual nation-states' activities. The divergent actions of individual member states vis-à-vis individual neighbouring states are in fact a political form of division of labour that allows the EU as a whole to react to developments more flexibly. The EU's 'common voice' towards its neighbours is therefore a strange chorus that leaves ample room for the contradictory interests of individual nations and different factions of capital. Some of the clearest examples include the agreement between Hungary and Russia to ensure a nuclear power–based electricity supply and the exemptions from sanctions against Russia that were granted to French armament exporters and Austrian banks.

EU enlargement as a form of intervention

The criteria and instruments of EU enlargement policies establish an externally directed self-image that partners and future members need to adapt to. At the same time, though, this divides the EU's neighbourhood and excludes Russia from the associated forums of communication and cooperation. In principle this is unproblematic on its own; however, it implies that the policy of enlargement is a policy of competition.

Regarding association (under the European Neighbourhood Policy, or ENP[1]), the criteria for accession are currently phrased as follows:

- Stable institutions guaranteeing democracy, the rule of law, human rights, and respect for and protection of minorities;
- A functioning market economy and the capacity to cope with competition and market forces in the EU;
- The ability to take on and implement effectively the obligations of membership, including adherence to the aims of political, economic, and monetary union.[2]

Conditions for access to EU resources, as reflected in the Copenhagen criteria, show the general direction of relations between the EU and its neighbours quite clearly. Enlargement policies, with their corresponding dimensions of association and accession, are an indirect attempt to intervene at the political and social levels. In the case of Yugoslavia, this combined a set of indirect and direct – i.e., military – instruments. Offers of membership to individual former Yugoslav states were connected to clear demands for political reforms, notwithstanding that the pacification of internal conflicts was to a certain degree also a goal. The demand for changes faced by neighbours who wish to become EU members or partners is in itself a characteristic trait of EU external relations. This is also true for cases of direct intervention such as that in Libya in 2011. In his analysis, Inger Solty identifies three key factors motivating intervention in Libya: the 'free flow of oil', the 'co-opting of the pro-democracy movement', and the 're-legitimisation of imperialist war'.[3]

Yet these policies also constitute a hierarchy of democratic and social standards. Conversely, the different degrees of cooperation also mean that with increasing 'distance' there is a corresponding increase in tolerance of certain states' failure to comply with standards, which is the same as saying that partners at different distances are measured according to different standards.

Conceptually, the neighbourhood (like the rest of the world in general) is seen as:

- a space for the provision of resources (raw materials strategy (COM(2011) 25 final))[4], the migration of the labour force, and the exploitation of low social and environmental standards;
- a buffer zone around EU borders (migration regimes, mainly in North Africa);
- a factor in global competition as a market and production site.[5]

This process is reinforced through the export of consultants and experts, through co-operation in the nurturing of future elites, and through support in the development of state and other institutions.

Likewise, the Europe 2020 strategy[6] explicitly states:

> The Europe 2020 strategy is not only relevant inside the EU; it can also offer considerable potential to candidate countries and our neighbourhood and better help anchor their own reform efforts. Expanding the area where EU rules are applied will create new opportunities for both the EU and its neighbours.[7]

In 2014, the tone is a bit more cautious:

> Globalisation is not just about facilitating trade and exchanges. It is about joining global value chains and delivering products, services and technologies that no individual country would be able to produce on its own. It is also about creating the conditions for a balanced partnership and development across countries, starting with Europe's neighbourhood.[8]

At the global social forum in Tunis, Europe's interest in North Africa was characterised in the following terms:

> The logic behind this is very easy: To be successful in global competition the EU wants to have peaceful neighbours willing to be controlled by the EU; it also wants to avoid 'bad surprises' such as social unrest; it wants to protect the EU from unwanted immigration, but at the same time receive highly qualified labour forces. It wants to reduce carbon emissions but at the same time provide the EU with energy and other necessary resources, while of course importing and enlarging the EU's global influence. The main ways to realise this are: 'security', energy partnerships, infrastructure investments, liberalisation and free-trade 'growth' strategies.[9]

Colonial, neo-colonial and/or imperial traditions all resound here. However, new interests or changes in neighbouring countries make it necessary to revise traditional patterns. The accession of Eastern European states changes the determining factors in the relationships with Belarus, Ukraine, and Russia. The debates surrounding the relationship with Turkey flow into the discussions revolving around the EU's cultural identity; the Arab Spring has made it clear how selectively the EU and its member states have applied the criterion of *community of values*. Attempts to selectively expand the *interior* sphere by signing association agreements with Ukraine, Georgia, and Armenia have created new tensions with Russia along well-worn lines, whilst also posing new challenges for enlargement policy as such as well as 'domestic and social policy'. Within these countries, as in Ukraine and certainly in the Middle East and in North Africa, the social question is posed in myriad new ways. Intensive migratory movements from neighbouring regions create, even within the EU, new challenges for the configuration of the social sphere. In this area too, therefore, changes within the EU coincide with changes in the EU's neighbourhood. The role and nature of families, ageing, healthcare, and provision for children and the elderly are only some of the challenges blatantly omitted from the EU's neighbourhood policy.

The EU's absolute helplessness in addressing the Arab Spring as well as the unresolved and escalating conflicts and wars in the Middle East demonstrate that EU schemes to develop its neighbourhood 'to its own liking' and ultimately without an opportunity for independence are now less feasible to implement than ever. Ukraine's domestic crisis must also be understood against the background that the EU, through NATO, has been attempting this since 1997:

> NATO and Ukraine agreed upon a 'distinctive partnership' in 1997. The NATO-Ukraine commission unifies a broad structure of mechanisms, panels, and programmes for dialogue and practical collaboration to support Ukrainian efforts for reform in particular in sectors such as security and defence policy and contribute to the democratic development of the country. Individual NATO members as well as NATO itself support measures and cooperation projects such as strategic counselling, professional development, and the deployment of trust funds, and they send advisors to NATO's liaison office in Kiev (German government communication).[10]

The justification and configuration of plans for an EU police mission to Ukraine follow a similar pattern, which either ignores Ukraine's deep-seated internal contradictions or implicitly reinterprets these contradictions through social state patterns of conflict resolution (German government communication).[11]

The instability of neighbouring regions cannot be resolved if the living conditions for the broad mass of people do not change. Demands for democratisation are hollow as long as there is no socio-economic basis for democracy. Meanwhile, however, demands for the liberalisation of market access and the privatisation of public services (in places where these are public) thwarts the development of any such basis.

In an analysis of the Libyan war in 2011, Erhard Crome concludes that

> preventing further wars in the Middle East will depend on all players realistically seeing and treating this region not only from the perspective of economic and 'security' interests. The current upheavals in the Middle East are a visible expression of the strategic and historic failure of the West's efforts to permanently control, dominate and exploit this part of the world. In turn, these developments will contribute to further global changes.[12]

Changing neighbours

Notwithstanding internal contradictions, the EU and EU member states have indeed constituted an internal and external sphere in line with the Lisbon strategy. This has not provided the anticipated results, however. First of all, the conflicts already described have escalated and new conflicts have arisen (in Ukraine, Syria). Meanwhile, the neoliberal orientation and financialisation of neighbouring societies, also encouraged by the EU, have ended up polarising and destabilising these regions. Moreover, the EU has built strong ties to Saudi Arabia and other oil-rich and financially strong Arab powers, which destabilise neighbouring regions out of their own interests. As in the EU itself, social upheavals repeat themselves. The distinction is that outside of the EU, more or less openly authoritarian political systems have developed that accord religion (Orthodox Christianity in Russia and Georgia and mainly 'political Islam' in the other regions) an important role (Alikberov and Seifert 2014).

Alnasseri describes the issues of the 2011 crisis in North Africa in the following terms:

> To understand the current situation, we must understand the conditions necessary for state power: neoliberal restructuring, the restructuring of social classes, changes to the governing state party, the imperialist embeddedness of the state, brutal disorganisation, and changes to the balance of power within the state apparatus. All of these developments created new contradictions, clashes of interests, and conflicts, which finally erupted due to both increased resistance and regional shifts (including the geostrategic weakness of the US and its allies in the region, economic crisis, political blunders of state parties, and the alienation of parts of the ruling classes and state players).[13]

In the EU's neighbourhood, the balance of power is shifting. Turkey is becoming an ever more influential and confident economic power. Countries such as Russia, Belarus, Ukraine, Iran, and Turkey[14] have developed different variants of capitalism that compete with the EU's social model of capitalism, which was previously predominant. Israel, too, is increasingly capable of asserting its independence vis-à-vis its neighbour the EU (as well as the US). Far from being modifications of West European or North American capitalism, these new variants already have a history of their own. Attempts by international organisations such as the WTO to incorporate them into, and domesticate them under, the 'old' capitalist model are only succeeding to a limited degree. Property relations, social classes, and class interrelationships have developed here on a different basis, which is nonetheless symbiotically tied into the neoliberal model of society. One particularly characteristic trait is the weak position of wage earners. In that sense, Russia and Turkey do not represent past forms of capitalism but rather possible future models.[15] At the same time, this is also provoking new alternative models, such as the democracy and statehood concepts that have developed out of the Kurdish struggle and which are currently being experimented with in Rojava (Syrian Kurdistan).

In Russia, political decision-making processes mainly take place 'in the shadows', and the 'underground economy' comprises around forty per cent of the total economic output.[16] Thus this EU neighbour's actions are governed by a different logic and dynamic and driven by different interests than those that hold sway in the 'old' EU states, whose political systems are based on their welfare state compromise. Accordingly, Russia assesses the EU according to its own logic and classification scheme, not by fitting it into a paradigm established by the EU. Moreover, through its ever closer cooperation with China, Russia, as a BRICS member, is putting increasing pressure on the global power structure dominated by the EU and the US. The EU and US sanctions against Russia are accelerating this process and pulling other states into the new constellation, as highlighted by the violation of sanctions against Russia by a number of Latin American countries.

The EU is changing and being changed by its neighbourhood

In fact, the differences emphasised by official propaganda are compensated by similarities and by the convergence of a set of contradictions to which diverse political forces must adapt. The similarities between people's living conditions and between the social movements is becoming more evident, as are those between the strategies of those in power to resolve conflicts.

The privatisation of the public sphere, the poor working conditions within cooperative chains and value-added chains, the destruction of nature through large-scale projects, and the growing tendencies towards precariousness and poverty are all unifying elements that are beginning to find expression in new forms of protest and organisation. Without being considered global by themselves or others, they are, nonetheless, global from the outset.

In terms of those in power, one salient feature is the increase in the strength of fascist and right-wing populist forces simultaneously with authoritarian forms of conflict resolution. This is true at the levels of the individual state, the EU, and the EU neighbourhood. An extreme example from Germany is the blatant tolerance of fascist tendencies in society by the police and the intelligence community, as became apparent during the court case against the National Socialist Underground right-wing terrorist group (*Nationalsozialistischer Untergrund*, or NSU). At the same time, protests against right-wing extremism are frequently criminalised.

Regarding the role of far-right parties, an analysis of European Parliament elections concludes:

> The social question is linked to national and even nationalist goals, i.e., social policy must be secured nationally, both against the EU Europeans and against asylum-seekers and immigrants from elsewhere. What is at issue is no longer the character of socially, culturally, and pluralistically open societies within the EU and definitely not outside of it. With the linking of social and national issues in such a way as to target not only the nation-state dimension, but also the immigrants, asylum seekers, and refugees within countries, a new revival of value conservatism is arising.[17]

The sometimes violent social debate on the role of religious and ethnic plurality as well as tolerance and its limits (the debates on the hijab, circumcision, and ritual slaughter among others), as well as the radicalisation of the political in religion (political Islam and Christian fundamentalism) are also a result of the neoliberal restructuring of societies both internally and externally as promoted or compelled by the EU. The consequences of these simultaneous processes are widely underestimated. With regard to Ukraine, the combination of nationalism, xenophobia, and social conflicts has been described as a fundamental problem for the prospects of Ukrainian society.[18] An analysis of the social conflicts, though, provides an interesting insight. Whereas the protests against social deficits are organised mainly 'by grassroots movements', nationalist movements are often driven by parties and other established forces. As Anastasiya Ryabchuck writes:

Despite the interest of the media and political parties in highlighting the political and ideological protests in the country, the biggest protests in the last three years were concerned with socio-economic issues: mass protests to oppose changes in the tax code that would have hit small entrepreneurs hard, against changes to the labour code that would have restricted workers' rights, against educational reform that would have encouraged commercialization of higher education, against a cut in subsidies to Chornobyl liquidators and Afghan war veterans – to name some of the biggest protests at a nationwide level. At city level, protests against privatisation of public space (in particular – illegal construction projects in backyards and park areas) or over environmental issues (like the mass protests in the most polluted Ukrainian city of Mariupol) are most common. Cases of corruption and violence on behalf of city officials and police also lead to significant grievances, as in the small city of Vradiyivka, where angry citizens attacked a police station after a rape of a 29-year old woman by three men, two of whom were policemen.[19]

The way the conflict in Ukraine is interpreted, as one fundamentally between Ukraine and Russia, which is the typical reading in the West, is in itself a contributing factor of the current situation. The attitude that a social conflict may never under any circumstances be legitimately carried out in a militant fashion has become the basic perspective of all EU initiatives, an attitude that has fed the looming globalisation of the conflict. At least in this respect, the governments of the EU, Ukraine, and ultimately Russia all agree. The violent reactions to the protests against the Troika's policies and other anti-social measures during the crisis within the EU point in the same direction. Furthermore, these protests reveal that new resistance practices that have developed in the movements and upheavals in EU neighbour states (the Arab Spring) have found echoes in the EU. This questioning of state power is underpinned by a questioning of changed economic power relations as a consequence of globalisation and corresponding social upheavals.

This tendency is most markedly visible in the EU's immigration and refugee policies,[20] which starkly contradict its principles as a 'community of values' and serve as a focal point for all other contradictions. By construing the threat as an ideological one, an internal state of emergency is declared that masks the true problems in society.[21] Frontex, police cooperation, and the restructuring of the military, the partial privatisation of what used to be military or police functions, and privatisations in the field of counter-intelligence and protection of data privacy are all directly or indirectly ideologically motivated and determined by changes in the EU's neighbourhood. Neoliberal globalisation thus inevitably combines with a new nationalist tendency and the rise of nationalistic and right-wing populist political movements and parties, which in turn reproduces instabilities in neighbouring countries, creating the basis for new repressive instruments. At the same time, the democratic rights that are protected within the EU continue to offer relatively favourable conditions for the organisation and self-organisation of emancipatory movements. Still, this is the same democracy that restricts opportunities for immigrants and represses corresponding emancipatory movements in the EU's neighbourhood. This is the catch-22 situation into which the left is constantly thrust and from which it must seek to break free.

Challenges for the left

The developments described can be broken down into the following fissures that are changing the EU both from within and without:

- There is a new *state of competition* in which confident and economically relevant powers are arising in our neighbourhood. Unlike before, these powers are now gaining leeway by building alliances with one another and/or by aligning themselves with powers like China. They build on the blatant powerlessness of subaltern movements (wage earners and farmers), which in turn leads to the development of new variants of capitalism.
- There is a general tendency towards *ideological and cultural upheavals* marked by the growing power of right-wing populism, fascism, and religious fundamentalism. States and society are demonstrating a growing propensity for violence and repression. As in the case of the American war on terror, this has internal repercussions, leading to a new security paradigm and a tendency to accept openly repressive or even military means as politically legitimate.
- A further generally visible tendency is the *globalisation of the social question* and of social upheavals. Social concerns increasingly meet with authoritarian responses, as evidenced by social reforms in several EU member states (which are – based on neighbourhood policy principles – subsequently 'recommended' to neighbouring countries) and Troika or IMF policies (as imposed most recently upon Ukraine). The welfare state compromise appears to be centred on the middle class. This leads central social questions to be either omitted or treated merely as questions of charity. Immigrants in particular, both within and outside the EU, are

excluded from this compromise. Yet migration and escape from conflict have become essential components of today's social questions.
- The relationship between the EU and its neighbours is characterised by changes in the concepts of *statehood* and *democracy* both within the EU and in EU neighbour states. This affects the development of EU statehood, processes of state building (in the Ukraine and other USSR successor states including Russia as well as Kurdistan) along with the restructuring of states (Syria, Iraq, and Turkey), and secessionist movements in Western Europe (the Crimea question). The privatisation of the public sphere, including parts of the government's administration and security services, changes the fields and forms of social struggles as well as the relationships between states. This is an ongoing process that seeks to redefine democracy to exclude participation and incorporation.

Confronted by all these tendencies, the left must still decide where to place its focus. The analysis shows that the evolution of relations between the EU and its neighbours is intimately tied to the EU's internal balance of power. At the same time, this development is a tool allowing it to cement this balance of power, that is, primarily the social balance of power, not the balance of power between member states. The EU's propagandistic combination of economic interests, its aspirations to become a joint political superpower, and its sense of shared moral values, which are all fundamental elements of neighbourhood policy, make it difficult to develop alternatives. The left will be unable to act, whether at the national level or as a global movement, unless it bursts the current logic.

The problem lies in the makeup of the left and its relation to the EU's self-image.

First, the left must overcome the polarising view that regards neighbouring countries' social movements through the prism of governments, a view the left shares to some extent. The left must also break the vicious cycle of engaging in domestic repression (for example against refugees), giving preferential treatment to repressive neighbouring regimes (to ward off refugees and secure economic interests), and expanding the EU's machinery of violence as legitimated by the aforementioned policies.

The crisis in Ukraine serves as evidence that large parts of the left spectrum are still (or once again) caught up in concepts of the nation–state and raison d'état and/or remain preoccupied by the narratives of the 1980s. Commitments made to 'Ukraine' or 'Russia' serve stereotypes that do not stand up to an analysis of the true interests of all sides. This includes a critical review of one's own democratic system. Democracy needs to be clearly understood, without illusions, as a relation, as a balance of power, and as a prerequisite to political action. As such, we must defend democracy and harness it but also criticise its shortcomings. In particular with regard to neighbouring states, we should not hesitate to reiterate that democracy is not a gift that can be granted once. Rather, democracy constitutes an ongoing struggle, in particular against the demands of the new financial oligarchy and in the face of the changes to statehood within the entire region as analysed here.[22]

Second, solidarity between movements in the EU and neighbouring countries needs to be re-created or built anew based on the commonality of problems. Solidarity is currently delegated to party apparatuses. There are hardly any contacts between the members of left-wing parties within the EU and its neighbourhood, posing a significant barrier to joint and individual change. Organisations on the left need to offer opportunities to experience solidarity.

Third, a clear line needs to be drawn and joint action taken in response to all populist, far-right, and neofascist currents. Increasingly, it is nationalist tendencies and not the left that are defining the political framework behind social protests. Emancipatory hopes are pressed into a reactionary framework. Yet belittlement and attempts to confront right-wing populism with some sort of left-wing populism only play into the hands of the far-right.

This is closely tied to a *fourth* challenge, namely to jointly develop an alternative immigration and refugee policy. Papastergiou and Takou outline a possible left-wing immigration policy from a Greek point of view in the following terms: 'Words that play a key role in the preparation of a different strategy for the issue of migration are: legalization, registration, fair examination process of asylum applications, integration, citizenship, international cooperation.'[23]

Fifth, the EU's foreign relations need to be pacified. Violence has not been treated as the means of last resort in the relations with neighbouring states. In fact, when it comes to immigration policy in particular, violence and force against refugees are precisely the response that the EU demands from its neighbours. Tolerance of violence in neighbouring regions, insofar as it serves the EU's interest, breeds new violence. This is clearly demonstrated in particular by the wars in the Middle East, where the constructed constraints allegedly require arms exports and the deployment of military personnel. The same is true for the acceptance of war and the rhetoric of war in Ukraine. This cycle must be broken.

Sixth, a conversation needs to be initiated in society concerning our way of life, the importance of the 'national question', how to deal with tendencies towards religiously motivated political action, and in general there needs to be a debate on moral values.

As a seventh and final point, we need to consider the best venue in which such strategic axes could be coordinated. In principle this should be the Party of the European Left (EL). If the EL is to have a political function, then it will have to ask itself how to organise international solidarity. The interdependence between the EU's self-image and its relations with neighbouring regions, only briefly outlined here, requires a unified position and coordinated action on the part of EL member parties. A national vantage point is not sufficient to develop strategy and communication with the movements in neighbouring regions. In sum, the EU neighbourhood policy aggregates fundamental global conflicts as well as conflicts that exist within the EU. This demands a new level of global action.

Literature

Alikberov, Alikber and Arne C. Seifert, *Religion und Transformation in Zentralasien und Südkaukasus*, Rosa-Luxemburg-Stiftung, *Papers*. Berlin: Rosa-Luxemburg-Stiftung, 2014.

Alnasseri, Sabah, 'Revolutionäre ernten die Früchte selten: Der 17. Bouazizi 2010.' *PROKLA* 41,2 (2011).

Atanasov, Vitaly, 'Three Sources of Ukraine's "Freedom" - Nationalism, Xenophobia and the "Social Issue"', *transform! european journal for alternative thinking and political dialogue* 8/2011.

Baier, Walter, 'Right-Wing Populism in Europe', *Transform! european journal for alternative thinking and political dialogue* 9/2011.

Bundesregierung, 'Antwort der Bundesregierung auf die Kleine Anfrage der Abgeordneten Jürgen Trittin, Dr. Tobias Lindner, Agnieszka Brugger, weiterer Abgeordneter und der Fraktion BÜNDNIS 90/DIE GRÜNEN', *Drucksache* 18/2029, Drs. 18/2198, Berlin: Deutscher Bundestag, 2014.

Bundesregierung, 'Antwort der Bundesregierung auf die Kleine Anfrage der Abgeordneten Ulla Jelpke, Sevim Dağdelen, Petra Pau und der Fraktion DIE LINKE', *Drucksache* 18/2110; 'Mögliche Unterstützung der Bundesregierung für die geplante EU-Polizeimission in der Ukraine', *Ibid.* 18/2327, Berlin: Deutscher Bundestag, 2014.

Çakir, Murat, *Neo-osmanische Träume. Über das Werden einer Regionalmacht. Artikelsammlung*. Rosa-Luxemburg-Stiftung, Papers, Berlin: Rosa-Luxemburg-Stiftung, 2011.

Crome, Erhard. 2011. 'Zum Libyen-Krieg des Westens.' *transform. Europäische Zeitschrift für kritisches Denken und politischen Dialog* (8/2011):28-35.

Dell'Aquila, Dario Stefano, 'Immigration Policies in Italy – Rights, Movements and Imprisonment', *transform! european journal for alternative thinking and political dialogue* 6 (10/2012).

European Commission, 'Communication from the Commission. Europe 2020. A strategy for smart, sustainable and inclusive growth', vol. COM (2010) 2020 final.

European Commission, 'Communication from the Commission to the European Parliament, the Council, the European Economic ans Social Commitee and the Commitee of the Regions. Taking stock of the Europe 2020 strategy', In COM(2014) 130 final/2.

Hildebrandt, Cornelia, 'Analysis of the Results of the European Election of 2014', Berlin: IfG Rosa-Luxemburg-Stiftung, 2014.

Hildebrandt, Cornelia and Jochen Weichold, *Europawahl 2014: Wahlprogramme der Parteien im Vergleich*, Rosa-Luxemburg-Stiftung, *Papers*, Berlin: Rosa-Luxemburg-Stiftung, 2014.

Krysmanski, Hans Jürgen, 'Elgersburger Thesen.' Erhard Crome (ed.), *Internationale Politik im 21. Jahrhundert. Konfliktlinien und geostrategische Veränderungen*, Rosa-Luxemburg-Stiftung Manuskripte 80, Berlin: Karl Dietz Verlag, 2008.

Kubiczek, Wolfgang. 2012. 'Ein System kollektiver Sicherheit in Europa?' In *Gemeinsame Europäische Sicherheit. Konzepte für das 21. Jahrhundert*, ed. Erhard Crome and Lutz Kleinwächter, 13-52. Potsdam: WeltTrends.

Papastergiou, Vassilis and Eleni Takou, *Migration in Greece. Eleven Myths and Even More Truths*. Athens/Brussels: Rosa-Luxemburg-Stiftung, 2014.

Rosa-Luxemburg-Stiftung (ed.), *Flucht und Vertreibung im Syrien-Konflikt. Eine Analyse zur Situation von Flüchtlingen in Syrien und im Libanon, Studien*. Berlin: Rosa-Luxemburg-Stiftung, 2014, <http://www.rosalux.de/publication/40677/flucht-und-vertreibung-im-syrien-konflikt.html>.

Ryabchuk, Anastasiya , 'Right Revolution? Hopes and Perils of the Euromaidan Protests in Ukraine', *Journal of Contemporary Central and Eastern Europe* 22,1 (2014), <http://dx.doi.org/10.1080/0965156X.2013.877268>.

Sedmak, Clemens, ed. 2010. *Solidarität. Vom Wert der Gemeinschaft*. Vol. 1. Darmstadt: WBG.

Solov'ev, A.I., 'Publičnye i tenevye instituty rossijskoy modernizacii', A.I. Solov'ev (ed.), *Vlast' i politika: institucional'nye vyzovy XXI. veka. Politićeskaja nauka. Ežegodnik 2012*, Moscow: ROSSPĖN, 2013.

Solty, Ingar, 'Krieg gegen einen Integrationsunwilligen? Die politische Ökonomie des libyschen Bürgerkriegs und der westlichen Intervention im Kontext der Krise des globalen Kapitalismus', *Prokla* 41,2 (2011).

Vergiat, Marie-Christine, 'A Major Challenge for a Different Vision of the European Union. The Left and Immigration', *transform! european journal for alternative thinking and political dialogue* (13, 2013).

Notes

1   <http://eeas.europa.eu/enp/about-us/index_en.htm>.
2   Stated thus on the current EU website: <http://ec.europa.eu/enlargement/policy/conditions-membership/index_en.htm> as an interpretation of the 'Copenhagen criteria' of 1993 (see Presidency Conclusions Copenhagen European Council 21-22 June 1993).

3   Ingar Solty, 'Krieg gegen einen Integrationsunwilligen? Die politische Ökonomie des libyschen Bürgerkriegs und der westlichen Intervention im Kontext der Krise des globalen Kapitalismus', *Prokla* 41,2 (2011), pp. 306ff.
4   <http://www.euractiv.de/sites/default/files/docs/KOM_Raw_materials-commodities_communication_in_EN.pdf>. For the corresponding 'Raw materials dialogues' with EuroMed states, Russia and Greenland, see <http://ec.europa.eu/enterprise/policies/raw-materials/international-aspects/dialogues_en.htm> and also the European Innovation Partnership (EIP) on Raw Materials <https://ec.europa.eu/eip/raw-materials/en>.
5   This is also reflected in parties' national election campaigns. The German conservative party, the CDU, clearly spells out this priority; see Cornelia Hildebrandt and Jochen Weichold *Europawahl 2014: Wahlprogramme der Parteien im Vergleich*, Rosa-Luxemburg-Stiftung, *Papers*, Berlin: Rosa-Luxemburg-Stiftung, 2014, p. 53. However, the programmatic assertion of Die LINKE, in section 3.6 of its European election programme, is also not very clear: 'We reject the EU neighbourhood policy in its current form. A truly European neighbourhood policy should put the struggle against poverty and for well-being for the largest possible part of the population at the top of its agenda,' <http://www.die-linke.de/wahlen/europawahlen-2014/europawahlprogramm/langfassung/>.
6   <http://ec.europa.eu/europe2020/europe-2020-in-a-nutshell/index_en.htm>.
7   European Commission, 'Communication from the Commission. Europe 2020: A strategy for Smart, Sustainable and Inclusive Growth', vol. COM (2010) 2020 final, p. 23.
8   European Commission, 'Communication from the Commission to the European Parliament, the Council, the European Economic and Social Commitee and the Commitee of the Regions: Taking Stock of the Europe 2020 Strategy', In COM(2014) 130 final/2, pp. 9f.
9   <http://wsf.blog.rosalux.de/2013/03/30/watch-dog-zu-eu-nordafrika/>.
10 Bundesregierung, 'Antwort der Bundesregierung auf die Kleine Anfrage der Abgeordneten Jürgen Trittin, Dr. Tobias Lindner, Agnieszka Brugger, weiterer Abgeordneter und der Fraktion BÜNDNIS 90/DIE GRÜNEN', *Drucksache* 18/2029, Vol. Drs. 18/2198, Berlin: Deutscher Bundestag, 2014, p. 5.
11 Bundesregierung, 'Antwort der Bundesregierung auf die Kleine Anfrage der Abgeordneten Ulla Jelpke, Sevim Dağdelen, Petra Pau und der Fraktion DIE LINKE', *Drucksache* 18/2110; 'Mögliche Unterstützung der Bundesregierung für die geplante EU-Polizeimission in der Ukraine', *Drucksache*. 18/2327, Berlin: Deutscher Bundestag, 2014.
12 Erhard Crome, 'Zum Libyen-Krieg des Westens', *transform. Europäische Zeitschrift für kritisches Denken und politischen Dialog*, 8/2011, p. 34.
13 Sabah Alnasseri, 'Revolutionäre ernten die Früchte selten: Der 17. Bouazizi 2010, *PROKLA* 41,2 (2011), p. 276.
14 For Turkey in particular see Murat Çakir, *Neo-osmanische Träume: Über das Werden einer Regionalmacht. Artikelsammlung*, Rosa-Luxemburg-Stiftung, Papers, Berlin: Rosa-Luxemburg-Stiftung, 2011, p. 133.

15 This is why the concept of varieties of capitalism only insufficiently captures the problem. See <http://en.wikipedia.org/wiki/Varieties_of_Capitalism>.
16 A. I. Solov'ev, 'Publičnye i tenevye instituty rossijskoy modernizacii.' A. I. Solov'ev (ed.), *Vlast' i politika: institucional'nye vyzovy XXI. veka. Političeskaja nauka. Ežegodnik 2012*, Moscow: ROSSPĖN, 2013, p. 303.
17 Cornelia Hildebrandt, 'Analysis of the Results of the European Election of 2014', Berlin: IfG Rosa-Luxemburg-Stiftung, 2014. See also Baier, 'Right-Wing Populism in Europe'.
18 Vitaly Atanasov, 'Three Sources of Ukraine's "Freedom" - Nationalism, Xenophobia and the "Social Issue"', *transform! european journal for alternative thinking and political dialogue* 8/2011.
19 Anastasiya Ryabchuk, 'Right Revolution? Hopes and Perils of the Euromaidan Protests in Ukraine', *Journal of Contemporary Central and Eastern Europe* 22,1 (2014), p. 130.
20 Marie-Christine Vergiat, 'A Major Challenge for a Different Vision of the European Union: The Left and Immigration', *transform! european journal for alternative thinking and political dialogue* 13, 2013.
21 Dario Stefano dell'Aquila, 'Immigration Policies in Italy – Rights, Movements and Imprisonment', *transform! european journal for alternative thinking and political dialogue* 6 10/2012.
22 'What "democracy" (strongly associated with "the West" at least since perestroika, and probably all throughout the Cold War) means is simply a better life. "Democracy" and "Europe" form part of a utopian project that guides the hopes and aspirations of ordinary citizens even in routine daily actions, when they are purchasing a "Euro-product", hoping it will be of superior quality, renovating their flats according to "Euro-standards" or writing a complaint to a local government official accusing him or her of "acting undemocratically". The utopian image of Europe for many is reinforced by the anti-utopian image of Russia looming as a warning of the "worse evil" of authoritarianism' (Ryabchuk, 'Right Revolution?, p. 129).
23 Vassilis Papastergiou and Eleni Takou, *Migration in Greece. Eleven Myths and Even More Truths*. Athens/Brussels: Rosa-Luxemburg-Stiftung, 2014, pp. 51f.

SOME NOTES ON THE SOCIALIST ALTERNATIVE IN POST-YUGOSLAV SPACE

Anej Korsika

What if nobody attacks you?

Stane Dolanc (1925-1999) was one of the most important Slovenian politicians in former Yugoslavia and among a few of the close trusted friends of President Josip Broz Tito. During his political career he held various high posts and argued for a strong, authoritarian rule of the League of Communists[1] of Yugoslavia; he also categorically opposed the nationalist tendencies stemming from various republics. The story goes that during the early 1980s student uprisings in Priština, capital of Kosovo, Dolanc was explaining the situation to representatives of the foreign press. Supposedly he failed to provide any concise political analysis and entangled himself in contradictions. To save his face he changed the subject and began talking about geostrategic issues. Confidently, he asserted, 'If the West should attack us, the Soviet Union will defend us', and if 'the Warsaw Pact attacks us, the West will defend us', insisting that the political stability of the federation was not in question. A German reporter then asked Dolanc, 'But what if nobody attacks you?' This question, which was dodged by Dolanc as self-evidently comical, too quickly proved a sinister prediction of the coming bloody disintegration of Yugoslavia.

'Brotherhood and Unity', the principal motto of the former socialist Yugoslavia, was shattered through wars, genocide, and nationalism, until nothing but nostalgic memories have remained. The trauma of the thorough break-up of Yugoslavia provided for a peculiar state of affairs. A multinational state that shared 45 years of common history and prided itself on the bedrock of its unified uprising against the Nazi occupier suddenly became torn apart by something quite unimaginable, its internal contradictions. It is not our intention, nor is this the time and place, to go into the analysis of the factors in breakup.[2] At this point we can only schematically point out that the breakup process was not a sudden nor a simple affair. It was a long-term process, beginning at least in the 1970s, and it included a complex mixture of foreign factors (the International Monetary Fund and the Non-Aligned Movement) and domestic factors (liberal[3] and nationalist tendencies). All of this must be borne in mind if one is to understand the contemporary heterogeneity of the ex-Yugoslav republics. One could reasonably argue that there is no group of countries that have been so politically and economically tightly knit together but which have then experienced such a dramatic rupture. The common history then does not simplify an understanding of the contemporary situation; it makes it more difficult.

This paper aims at presenting the case of Slovenia, always considered somehow exceptional among the former republics of Yugoslavia. We will present a general political-economic trajectory of its period of transition, its specificities, and ultimately its catching up with the 'textbook case Eastern European transition'. We will then focus on the theoretical and political development of Marxism and socialism, which culminated in the socialist United Left coalition's entrance into the Slovenian National Assembly in 2014. Ultimately, we will try to present the situation in other ex-Yugoslav countries, mainly concerning ourselves with the general state of affairs and a bit more concretely with the progressive theoretical and political forces at work in these countries.

Slovenia: Running the gauntlet of liberalism, conservativism, and social democracy

Ever since the disintegration of Yugoslavia, which was complete by 2004, Liberal Democracy of Slovenia (LDS) was the absolute hegemon of Slovenian politics. Thanks to the good level of organisation of the working class and the powerful trade unions, the Slovenian transition took place much more gradually than in other countries of the former Eastern Bloc or republics of Yugoslavia. Gradual as it was, the Slovenian transition was not without its dark spots (notably, the case of the Erased[4]), which even surpassed some of the effects of the economic shock doctrine implemented in Eastern Europe. Towards the end of 1990s, despite the initial gradualism, an ever more intensified capital concentration began to develop, which was further intensified after the entrance of Slovenia into the European Union in 2004. It was, in fact, the process of entering Euro-Atlantic organisations that was the main political narrative presented by the liberal political bloc, the LDS. Entering these organisations, so the story went, would fulfil the centuries old dream of finally entering the 'European family of nations', as if Slovenia was moving away from the Balkans, especially away from the former Yugoslav capital, Belgrade, and entering the real Europe, by sending its representatives to the new capital, Brussels. As if the Balkans suddenly had a monopoly on all the negative practices, such as corruption, clientelism, negligence, etc. and the EU stood for rationality, the rule of law, accuracy, etc. Indeed, such was the political and popular discourse of the time that one of the most common phrases used to justify anything was 'This is a common European practice'.

Although practically unchallenged in its power for almost twelve years (1992-2004), the liberal bloc had to face its first defeat in 2004, when the conservative bloc under the leadership of the Slovenian Democratic Party (SDS) of Janez Janša, came to power. The defeat of the liberal bloc triggered a dramatic crisis in the ranks of LDS, and the party experienced a gradual process of disintegration, with the continual formation of new parties through which former high representatives tried their luck in future elections. Janez Janša, whose mandate as a prime minister lasted from 2004 to 2008, began his mandate with the proposal to implement a flat tax. After the intense backlash from trade unions, he had to downgrade his ambitions around tax reform and transform the former five tax groups into merely three. A direct consequence of this tax was that the state of Slovenia has diminished its annual tax revenues by some 900 million euros ever since the reform was implemented in 2006. These fiscal shortcomings are now, in times of crisis, dealt with by means of austerity measures and cuts to the public sector, policies that are highly detrimental to people with low incomes and insecure jobs. The wealthy are now able to afford private healthcare, while the mass of the population is 'stuck' with public health services, which are seriously underfinanced and understaffed. In a time of high economic growth (in 2007 the annual GDP growth was a record 7 per cent), the first Janša government carried out a procyclical economic policy. Its results became visible when the Social Democrats (SD) won the elections in 2008 and Borut Pahor became the prime minister. Already in 2008 growth was halved to 3.4 per cent, while in 2009 it collapsed to -7.9 per cent.

The Social Democratic bloc, in comparison with the liberals and conservatives, won its chance to govern in a time when the crisis was already in full swing in Slovenia. Despite fantastic promises, like the ones from the finance minister at the time, Franc Križanič, that the government would double the minimum wage by the end of its mandate (which would mean it would reach around 1,000 euros), nothing of the sort happened. On the contrary, with the proposal for job market reform, similar to the German reform involving 'mini jobs', the government effectively tried to spread the precarious labour regime, endemic to student work, across the whole population. Alongside this reform, it also proposed a pension reform that would raise the pensionable age by another three years. Both proposals were forced to be submitted to a popular referendum, along with two other proposals, one proposing reforms that would limit the extent of illegal work and the other regarding the accessibility of the state archives. All four referendum proposals were rejected by popular vote, the contra vote ranging from 70 to 80 per cent. In 2011 public polls showed that around 84 per cent of the people believed the government was incompetent. In September of 2011 the government fell after a vote of confidence in parliament. Early elections were announced and took place on 13 July 2014. Looking at the last twenty years, what prospects are we currently facing?

How far the mighty have fallen

Let us focus on the last five years in order to best see the exponential growth of the crisis and its human toll. Since 2008 when the state debt was at 22 per cent it has more than tripled and now amounts to more than 71 per cent of GDP. In the same period, the budget deficit has risen from 1.8 per cent to 14.7 per cent. While five years ago the unemployed numbered around 59,000, the figure now is almost twice as high. Politically speaking, the sad state of the Slovenian economy corresponds to the sad state of 'the big three' political blocs we have briefly analysed.

Janez Janša, president of the SDS, the biggest right-wing party, is currently serving a two-year prison sentence. He was charged with partaking in the corruption practices that occurred while he was prime minister when the government approved a substantial order of military vehicles from the Finnish producer Patria. Although he was already in prison when the electoral campaign for early parliamentary elections began, he represented one of the main issues of the campaign. The party built an image of its president as a political prisoner who has already experienced violations of his human rights[5] and is now, once again suffering for the cause of political freedom, etc. His supporters regularly organise protests in front of the Supreme Court in Ljubljana demanding justice for their president. Still the biggest party, numbering more than 30,000 members, it is yet to be seen how long a party can function with its president in prison.

The immense absurdity of the situation is that Janša ran in the parliamentary elections and was voted into parliament. Due to some legal ambiguities concerning the status of an MP in relation to his criminal record, Janša is currently participating in parliamentary sessions while serving his sentence. This bizarre situation is due to the fact that apparently nobody thought of providing specific legislation for such a case. The law is very clear on those

MPs guilty of criminal charges; in this case their mandate is immediately suspended, and they serve out their prison sentence like any other citizen. However, the case of Janša is exceptional because he had already started serving his sentence, then participated in the elections, and was then voted into parliament. Absurd as it is, this now represents one of the main issues both from the perspective of legal experts, who are debating the matter, as well as from the perspective of the media industry, which is intensively reporting on the whole issue. It goes without saying that this negatively effects both the work of parliament and the attitude of the general population towards politics as such. However, the narrative of 'political-prisoner president' did not pay off in the end. In comparison to early elections in 2011, when the party won 26 seats, it has now fallen to 21.

Although the Social Democrats (SD) are currently a member of the ruling coalition, objectively speaking the party is in very bad shape. After a long period of Borut Pahor at its head (he has just been re-elected president of the republic), he was succeeded as party president by Igor Lukšič, a professor of political sciences and a former minister of higher education. His presidency resulted in the party's disastrous results in the European elections. It more than halved its vote in the last European Parliament (EP) elections and lost one MEP. When it became obvious that Lukšič was generating a lot of discontent among the rank and file, he did another manoeuvre and put himself in first place on the party list for the EU elections. This move, however, was unsuccessful, because through their preferential vote, voters have re-elected Tanja Fajon who had already been an MEP in the last legislative period. After this debacle, the party forced Lukšič to resign, and Dejan Židan, two-time minister of agriculture, was named as acting president until the next party congress. Although a more capable politician, this did not help him in the early national elections in July of this year. The party that won the elections in 2008 with 29 MPs, fell to ten MPs in the early elections of 2011 and experienced a further decline in the July 2014 elections, when it was able to elect only six MPs. This is by far the worst result for the party in its more than twenty years of existence.

If the liberal bloc was once unified within the LDS, which governed for twelve years, later, after its electoral defeat, it started to fragment and lost its MPs to other parties (mainly to the SD). Meanwhile, former prominent figures of the so-called 'old LDS' also started establishing new parties; however, none of this offspring, though initially successful, managed to reach the parliamentary threshold. Thus, in 2011 early elections were the first held since 1992, when the former hegemon LDS also failed to enter parliament; the same occurred in this year's parliamentary elections, and it seems safe to say that all thing considered LDS will not experience a comeback. However, the liberal bloc as such recycled itself through 'new' faces and managed to gain substantial power through such manoeuvres. In 2011, the so-called Positive Slovenia, the party of Ljubljana's mayor, Zoran Janković, was established and entered parliament with 28.5 per cent of the votes. Although it was the relative winner, in the end it did not manage to form a government; instead, Janez Janša, was able to form his second government, which lasted for a year (2012-2013). This was a period of intense protest, never before seen on such a scale ever since the workers' strikes at the beginning of the 1990s. In the span of a couple of months from late 2012 to early 2013 there was a series of popular, so-called all-Slovenian upheavals,[6] which protested against both right-wing and left-wing parties. The protestors demanded an end to corruption, more transparent governing, direct democracy, and an end to austerity measures and public cuts. Because of this popular pressure as well as the report of the anti-corruption commission that damaged both the Prime Minister, Janez Janša, as well as the opposition leader, Zoran Janković, the government received a no-confidence vote and fell.

The new government was formed by another prominent member of the former LDS and now a member of Positive Slovenia, Alenka Bratušek, who managed to form a parliamentary majority and lead the government from 2013 to the early elections in July 2014. A new phenomenon appeared in these elections, which can still be perceived as a part of the liberal bloc, the Party of Miro Cerar (SMC). The party achieved a landslide victory and gained a record number of MPs (36), which is more than any party since independence. What is specific to Miro Cerar and his party? Is there something new under the sun? Cerar always presented himself, his policies, and ultimately his party as based on sound ethical principles, objectivity, ideological neutrality, etc. But this is far from the truth. In an article he published last year, 'Why Capitalism?',[7] Cerar argued, 'Now we are already well aware that we have caused the Slovenian financial, economic, and social crisis mostly by ourselves with our unethical grasping after material goods and superficial splendour of all kinds'. It goes without saying that Cerar's government will continue with the privatisation process, austerity measures, and all other policies dictated by Brussels. At the time he wrote his article, Cerar had managed to form the government, and the Finance Minister had already confirmed that privatisation would have to continue, and that strict fiscal policy and public sector cuts were here to stay and would even be intensified. It is also perhaps noteworthy that Cerar, a law professor, has gathered around him a team that largely comes from academia, the idea being that they are unburdened by any specific ideological predispositions but are qualified by their expertise. Such a technocratic moment is reminiscent of the former Italian government headed by Mario Monti, who presented his policies as self-evident and almost natural.

Here we have to do with a clear example of the belief Karl Marx already criticised in Adam Smith, that is, that capitalist social relations represent the natural order of things. Classical political economy, according to Marx, always perceived older production systems and economic beliefs as historical, that is, as having a beginning and an end. However, in explaining the relations in capitalist society, classical political economy represents and perceives this society as natural, as here to stay. Despite such obstinate and unfounded beliefs, there have been, ever since Marx and Engels, organised anti-capitalist forces, which challenged this artificial 'natural order' of things. In the early elections of 2014 one such force managed to enter the Slovenian parliament. The United left (UL), a socialist coalition, elected six MPs, and for the first time since the disintegration of Yugoslavia an openly declared socialist party entered the Slovenian parliament.

Socialist alternative

UL is a coalition of three parties (Democratic Labour Party, Initiative for Democratic Socialism, Party for the Sustainable Development of Slovenia) as well as a fourth group which includes representatives and organisations of civil society. As such it is a unique political formation, both in the sense of the diversity of its components as well as its political programme – democratic, ecological socialism. The UL was the only participant in the European elections that put forward a rational and critical position on the European Union.[8] It emphasised the disastrous and capital-driven austerity measures that are a direct outcome of Slovenia's membership of the EU. UL argued that the actually existing EU is by its very nature an undemocratic organisation, explicitly established to serve the interests of large European capital and oligarchies. Its historical development confirms this judgement since one can clearly see the trajectory of this political project as one that has over time become ever more calibrated to the interests of capital. With the crisis, these contradictions, which have accumulated during the past decades, have erupted and become very visible. The contradiction between European north and south, between core and periphery is, at the end of the day, the contradiction between capital and labour. This disillusionment with the EU project is now clearly visible in Slovenia: ten years ago 90 per cent of people voted in favour of entering the Union, but recent polls show that less than 30 per cent of Slovenians still trust the EU. Being a new and well articulated political force and the sole critic of EU policies, the UL managed to address issues that people have started to feel in their everyday lives and that other parties have ignored.

Despite refusing this type of European integration, the UL never espoused the Eurosceptic position, and it strongly believes that international cooperation and integration is crucial. Instead of advocating the EU, we in the UL argued that we should start building different political foundations, such as would enable us to build a socialist Europe. All this proved to be positive in the early parliamentary elections, which happened less than two months after the European elections. These elections were organisationally, financially, and in all other aspects much more demanding. With very little experience, an extremely short timeline and little to no financial sources, the UL faced a very difficult task. Hundreds of hours of unpaid labour, good organisation, and a consistent and well-communicated programme, gave us the ability to achieve a much greater votes-to-financing ratio than all the other parties. Again, the distinguishing feature was a clear stance against any policies that would benefit capital and further immiserate workers. The UL was the only political group that has categorically opposed privatisation and advocated alternative socialist policies. Instead of further tax cuts for the rich, it proposed higher taxation for capital, a 1:5 ratio between the lowest and the highest wage, and a complete stop to all privatisation, etc. These were policies that clearly differentiated the UL from other 'leftist' parties, especially the Social Democrats. Putting socialist policies back on the agenda was our explicit goal, since these policies can only be implemented with the broad support of the people. Therefore it is even more encouraging that the young (i.e., people from 18 to 24 years of age) have voted strongly for the UL, providing more than fourteen per cent of all votes the UL received. Although this might seem a modest percentage, one should bear in mind that other parties only got an average of one to 2 per cent of the growth rate and that many of those who voted for the UL had abstained from voting altogether in earlier elections.

The success of the UL has certainly had a very positive effect on the progressive forces in the region. However, one must bear in mind that Southeastern Europe, despite or perhaps exactly because of its common history, is currently an extremely heterogeneous political region. Countries like Hungary and Macedonia in effect already have autocratic governments with obvious elements of fascism, and the situation for progressive socialist forces is perhaps the most difficult there. In Romania and Bulgaria such forces are very limited and marginalised, and further constrained by electoral laws.

Apart from the already mentioned protest movement in Slovenia, massive protests also occurred in other Balkan countries, for example Bulgaria and Bosnia. We can agree that these protests all had a common denominator in, broadly speaking, the increasingly worsening living conditions of working-class people. However, the way in which this dissent was articulated took on very different forms. In Slovenia, one of the main motifs of the protest movement was the fight against corruption. An important qualitative step forward was achieved through understanding the protestors' belief that 'they' (the left-wing and right-wing parties and politicians) are all the same. What we tried to further articulate is: 'yes, they are all the same, they are all willing servants of capital'. In Bosnia, the protests and, later, the plenums, were perhaps the most important achievement of civil society since the disintegration of Yugoslavia. For the first time in more than twenty years people started to talk about class instead of ethnic divisions. In Bulgaria, the protest movement was largely characterised by a mistaken belief that the EU can bring about the desired changes. Without going into too much detail or making claims as to how representative the Slovenian protests actually were, it is clear that socialist forces have an enormous ideological task ahead of them.

Currently, ex-Yugoslav countries are perhaps most similar in terms of the level of development of the critique of political economy, i.e., Marxism as a theoretical apparatus. Besides Slovenia, the other strong theoretical centres are especially Croatia and Serbia. Organisations from these three countries have by now experienced a couple of years of intense theoretical cooperation, organising joint conferences, hosting lecturers from the other two countries, etc. This in itself represents a huge and important qualitative leap forward and provides a solid basis for further political work. This being said it should be kept in mind that the social, political and economic situation in each of the former Yugoslav republics is dramatically different. The objective social bases for building a socialist alternative as an organised political force are therefore very diverse. If Slovenia had the best predisposition, countries like Macedonia and Bosnia Herzegovina one extremely difficult places for establishing and strengthening such a political force. The UL provides a positive entity which can encourage and support comrades from other republics. Socialists from these countries now, more than thirty years later, do not face the threat of being attacked by the Warsaw Pact, nor is it imaginable that NATO would have an interest in intervening in these countries, especially since a lot of them are NATO members.

However, it would be wrong to conclude that all is quiet in the Balkans. On the contrary, once again the region is showing itself to be a European periphery, the weakest link in the larger chain of the European Union, and people are now under attack, an attack which comes in the form of austerity measures dictated from Brussels with a local comprador bourgeoisie that willingly collaborates in this economic warfare, that is, class struggle. Once again, the socialists from the region need to concentrate all of their forces on first building strong national political forces and then unifying them into an even stronger regional network, which could and should reach across the borders of former Yugoslavia. This is the only humane and rational perspective for the peoples of the Balkans to effectively challenge, resist, and ultimately completely reject the onslaught of austerity measures and build a socialist alternative.

Literature

Baurmann, Jana Gioa, 'Die Euro-Krise erreicht den Osten', *Die Zeit*, 5 April 2013, <http://www.zeit.de/wirtschaft/2013-04/slowenien-euro-krise#comments>.

Cerar, Miro, ‚Zakaj kapitalizem', *Dnevik*, 17 July 2013, <http://www.dnevnik.si/mnenja/kolumne/zakaj-kapitalizem>.

Gračner, Brigita, Slovenia's 'Zombie Uprising', *Counterfire*, 1 March 2013, <http://www.counterfire.org/index.php/articles/international/16323-slovenias-zombie-uprising>.

Korsika, Anej, 'Impressive performance of the Socialist Forces', transform!, <http://www.transform-network.net/en/focus/the-eu-elections-from-a-left-perspective/news/detail/Programm/slovenia.html>.

Korsika, Anej, 'Slovenia – United in Austerity': <http://www.rosalux.rs/en/artikl.php?id=209>.

Slameršak, Aljoša, 'Slovenia on the Road to Periphery', *The International Marxist Humanist*, 25 June 2013, <http://www.internationalmarxisthumanist.org/articles/slovenia-road-periphery-aljoa-slamerak>.

Notes

1. The Yugoslav Communist Party directly opposed Stalin; as such it was the only one in the history of the Eastern Bloc to successfully challenge the hegemony of the Soviet Union. As a consequence, Yugoslavia was expelled from the Cominform and developed its own path towards socialism. The party changed its name to the League of Communists and developed and pursued the politics of socialist self-management.
2. Here I can only recommend a lecture by Branko Bembič, member of the Institute for Labour Studies and the Initiative for Democratic Socialism, who developed an important basis for such a theoretical approach. One of his most recent lectures *The Shifting Balances of Class Forces in Slovenia*, is also highly informative on this issue. The lecture is available at <https://www.youtube.com/watch?v=3UCx4sfVKQU≥ (accessed 18 September 2014).
3. The liberal trends within Yugoslav communism: Stane Kavcic (a Slovene liberal known for the so-called 'highway affair'), the Croatian MASPOK (Maspok is an acronym for 'masovni pokret' or 'mass movement' – otherwise known as

the 'Croatian Spring' of 1971), or Marko Nikezic in Serbia (a leading figure in the liberal wing of the Serbian League of Communists and purged from the organisation in 1972). These movements opened up fundamental questions, which were suppressed by the League of Communists at the time, but are even more suppressed in public discourse today.

4   'The erasure from the register of permanent residents implemented by the administrative bodies of the Republic of Slovenia was an arbitrary act that did not have any basis in the law, as was established by the Constitutional Court. The erasure mainly (but not exclusively) affected people born in other republics of the former Yugoslavia who had Yugoslav citizenship and also citizenship of another republic of the former Yugoslavia, but lived in the former Socialist Republic of Slovenia where they had permanent addresses.' For more information on some 18,000 'erased' see <http://www.mirovni-institut.si/izbrisani/en/> (accessed 18 September 2014).

5   Janez Janša, once an ardent member of the League of Communists of Yugoslavia, so much so that some have called him 'The Red Khmer' because of his uncompromising orthodox stance, already served a prison sentence at the end of 1980s. At the time he became an outspoken critic of the system, a civil rights campaigner, a dissident, so to say. His imprisonment had a very mobilising effect for civil society as such and a Commision for the Human Rights of Janez Janša was established; it encompassed a wide variety of civil society organisations, movements and individuals, from church to LGBT activists, from ultra-leftist Marxists to nationalist writers and poets. It goes without saying that Janša later changed his tune and became ever more conservative and right-wing, he himself becoming a violator of human rights (e.g. in the case of the Slovenian Erased). When his party members now try to portray the situation as somehow parallel to his imprisonment more than twenty years ago, one can only say: first as tragedy, then as farce.

6   Members of the Initiative for Democratic Socialism as well as foreign reporters have written numerous articles about the protest movement as well as the Initiative, these are just a few:
Aljoša Slameršak, 'Slovenia on the Road to Periphery', <http://www.internationalmarxisthumanist.org/articles/slovenia-road-periphery-aljoa-slamerak>; Brigita Gračner, Slovenia's 'Zombie Uprising': <http://www.counterfire.org/index.php/articles/international/16323-slovenias-zombie-uprising>; Anej Korsika, 'Slovenia – United in Austerity', <http://www.rosalux.rs/en/artikl.php?id=209>; 'No easy way out for Slovenia', *Deutsche Welle*, <http://www.dw.de/no-easy-way-out-for-slovenia/a-16805351>; 'Die Euro-Krise erreicht den Osten', *Die Zeit* <http://www.zeit.de/wirtschaft/2013-04/slowenien-euro-krise#comments>; 'Kuda ide Slovenija', Aljazeera, <http://balkans.aljazeera.net/video/kontekst-kuda-ide-slovenija> (all accessed 18 September 2014).

7   The article is available (in Slovene) at <http://www.dnevnik.si/mnenja/kolumne/zakaj-kapitalizem> (accessed 18 September 2014).

8   For a more detailed analysis of the 2014 European elections in Slovenia, see 'Impressive performance of the Socialist Forces', available at <http://www.transform-network.net/en/focus/the-eu-elections-from-a-left-perspective/news/detail/Programm/slovenia.html> (accessed 18 September 2014).

EUROPEAN ELECTIONS: A SNAPSHOT OF THE BALANCE OF POWER

THE EUROPEAN ELECTIONS: AN ANALYSIS

Cornelia Hildebrandt

Since the European election of 2014, there has been a split across Europe's political landscape. While in the EU's southern countries – especially in Greece, Spain and Portugal – the growing protest against the predominant line of European policy has been articulated largely in a leftist context, a front of dissatisfaction to the right of the conservatives has been emerging in those core countries of the EU which have been less affected by the crisis. The result is a surprising polarisation of the electoral results between the centre and the peripheries of the EU, between and within the political camps, and, to some extent, within the EU member countries.

The results of the European elections describe a continuing shift to the right, with a new quality: nationalist, right-wing populist parties and parties of the extreme right have attracted more than eleven million voters, especially from the conservative camp, so that the electoral share of parties to the right of the conservatives Europe-wide now stands at 22 per cent. These parties have emerged as the real winners of this election.

The result in coming years will be a modification of the hitherto existing lines of confrontation: no longer will they run only between the political camps, along the classic socio-economic lines of conflict, that is, market radicalism vs. the welfare state, or the socio-cultural lines of conflict, that is, an open, liberal society vs. authoritarian, ethnically based shut-off societies within the EU. Now, the lines will also run perpendicular to these, and at the same time perpendicular to the line between the 'EU-integration camp' and the 'strengthening of national political approaches' camp. Here, we would like to discuss these conflicts, and also the results of the party families which competed in the election, on the basis of the following initial comprehensive theses:

Summarising theses

1. The decisions taken by the European Union, particularly those involving the budgetary policies of EU countries, directly affect the lives of its citizens. The elections for the European Parliament – and particularly the electoral participation rate in those elections – reflect the extent to which the EU enjoys societal legitimacy. From 22 – 25 May 2014, 160 million citizens in the 28 countries of the European Union (approximately 43 per cent of the electorate) went to the polls to elect the members of the European Parliament. The results should cause us to stop and think. On the one hand, it was not possible to mobilise the majority of the citizens for these elections; electoral participation reached a historic low in Slovakia with thirteen per cent, and was below twenty per cent in the Czech Republic. In Croatia and Slovenia, only one voter in four went to the polls. Only in two formerly state-socialist countries did electoral participation exceed 35 per cent; moreover, only 35.6 per cent of British and only 37.3 per cent of Dutch voters went to the polls. The European *demos* (Habermas) is weak. Moreover, the results reflect a shift to the right, with the message that nationalist, right-wing populist parties and parties of the extreme right have gained, and they are the real winners of these elections. As a result, the following lines of confrontation are to be expected in the coming years:

2. The course pursued to date by the ruling elites enjoys no support from a considerable portion of the citizenry; rather, it is increasingly being fundamentally rejected, so that 'business as usual' is becoming more difficult. Superimposed on what hitherto has been intra-national lines of conflict is the conflict between EU integration based on the existing foundations – the Lisbon Treaty and the crisis-policy measures – on the one hand and the reinforcement of national policy approaches to defend existing social standards, on the other. Firstly, the conflict line between market radicalism on the one hand and the welfare state on the other, which, with the implementation of European austerity policies by the EU, is no longer a purely national matter; and, secondly, that between authoritarian/ethnic isolation vs. libertarian opening, which is visibly and dramatically expressed in the controversy over asylum and refugee policies.

3. In the context of these modified conflict situations, new right-wing groupings are forming; in two major EU countries, France and Britain, but also in Denmark, they are in the range of a potential majority. As a result, an intra-elite dispute with broad support in the population based on widespread nationalist and fundamental value-conservative

societal tendencies has emerged. For significant portions of the citizenry, nationalist, right-wing populist parties and the parties of the extreme right have assumed the function of the critics of EU policy.

4. This critique has two dimensions: First, it is directed against the market integration being pushed by the existing major conservative and social democratic parties, and against European institutions. The goal, however, is not so much to remove these institutions as to re-legitimise them in national terms: The social question is linked to national and even nationalist goals, i.e., social policy must be secured nationally, both against the EU Europeans and against asylum-seekers and immigrants from elsewhere. What is at issue is no longer the character of socially, culturally and pluralistically open societies, within the EU and definitely not outside of it. With the linking of social and national issues in such a way as to target not only the nation-state dimension, but equally, too, the immigrants, asylum seekers and refugees within countries, a new revival of value conservatism is arising.

5. Second, this critique formulated by the right wing is raising the issue of real deficits of democracy in both European and national institutions. It involves a declaration of war against their representatives, the national and/or European elites; existing deficient democratic procedures and regulations, including democracy as the fundamental value to be striven for in the shaping of society, are being called into question. In view of these developments, an even more strongly disputed development of the EU, and, as a result, a reconfiguration of the forces of the European and national elites is in the offing.

6. For the first time, European parliamentary elections resulted in the greatest growth for those parties which call for withdrawal from the European Union. Especially the electoral results in France and Great Britain are an expression of political crisis in which, for the first time, the European Constitution is being directly called into question. The cause of these developments include the neoliberal policies pushed through 2005 under the Lisbon Strategy, which have the goal of making the EU the most competitive region in the world, at the cost of undermining its democratic procedures and institutions, and radically dismantling its social standards. For the citizens, the EU is thus no longer palpable as a 'community of democratic values', and its social 'use value' is losing support in the societies of the EU countries.

7. The criticism of the orientation of the EU is also being formulated from the left. The family of left parties were able to score their greatest gains at the European level. The number of their seats rose from 35 to 52.

However, they have so far been able to formulate political projects only in a few countries, such as Greece, Spain or Portugal, where they have been able to articulate and represent such projects from the left in a position also within the range of potential majority. However, if Syriza in Greece, the strongest party to emerge from the European elections, with a result of over 26 per cent, were to be faced with the question of forming a left-wing government determined to oppose the dictates of the Troika, the resulting overlap of national and European crises would lead to a confrontation at the European level with constitutional repercussions.

8. The political elites of the conservative and social democratic parties would confront such pressure with a 'grand coalition' at the European level. In this way, the social democratic parties, which are weaker on a pan-European level – they emerged as the strongest political force in only six EU countries – can be integrated and, in this way, stabilised. This will prove necessary particularly because these elections have revealed political crises in some hitherto presumably stable countries of the EU, which have in some cases so far been concealed. This grand coalition is, however, politically under siege, particularly from the right. The political elites, too, are becoming aware of the fact that simple 'business-as-usual' cannot succeed; for this reason, the coalition is internally differentiated, possibly even split. Two options are currently possible: The first is a reduction of the EU's function to that of the confederation with a common market, a solution currently being put forward by Great Britain and Hungary, which is supported by the parliamentary groups of the moderate political right: the European Conservatives and Reformists (ECR), the Europe of Freedom and Direct Democracy (EFDD), and the members of the European Alliance for Freedom (EAF), which has so far failed to establish itself as a parliamentary group. The second would be an attempt to strengthen the integration of the Europe countries, and 'pay' for this with possible loosening up of the austerity policies, in order to achieve rapid economic and social success.

9. It should be realised that the differences between the party families, particularly the two larger ones, the conservatives and the social democrats, is becoming increasingly blurred. For instance, the Italian PD has long since stopped being a classical social democratic party; nonetheless, at the European political level, it supports the social democratic party group (Group of the Progressive Alliance of Socialists and Democrats – S&D). The French Socialists and the Spanish PSOE, too, have undergone a political change of direction toward the position of their conservative

predecessors in government. Among the conservatives, on the other hand, Hungary's FIDESZ belongs to the EPP group at the European level, although its European policy position is considerably closer to that of the two party groups to the right of the EPP.

10. The European Union is in its deepest crisis ever. This crisis has impact not only on particular countries in the southern part of the EU and the periphery, nor only on smaller countries in general; rather, countries which have hitherto been considered part of the economic and political 'core', the countries that have been the mainstay of the EU economically, are also affected. The crisis of the economic regime has become a crisis of the social and cultural dimensions as well. It is now threatening to develop into a systemic political crisis of the EU. The three hitherto strongest party families in the EU Parliament, the conservatives, the social democrats and the liberals, lost over ten per cent of their strength in this election compared to 2009, when 72.4 per cent of the electorate voted for these groups. The conservatives suffered the greatest losses, the liberals much less.

11. The social democrats were unable to profit from these developments; on the contrary, they have lost the support of major parts of their core voter clientele in those areas where they supported the austerity policies of governments, or continued those of predecessor governments. In the past twenty years, they have not been able to link the social question to economic policy in a positive manner. Instead, they have to a considerable degree helped achieve an EU integration that blocks precisely that linkage. In Spain and France, they suffered heavy losses, and virtually imploded in Greece. In some countries, such as the Netherlands, the Czech Republic, or Finland, their results were on a level with those of middle sized or smaller parties.

12. The crises have been caused by both national and European factors, and the countries of the EU have been affected by them in very different ways. The 2014 electoral campaigns expressed this dual nature of the situation more strongly than has been the case in previous elections. In view of the threatening low voter participation rate, most governing parties depended on electoral strategies that were consciously oriented toward national issues in order to mobilise their core base of support. One reason for this was to cover up the 'business-as-usual' political and economic concepts – or the lack of any concepts at all – applied to solving urgent problems, which has determined their policies at both the European and the national levels. That was true of the majority of social democratic parties, many of which suffered heavy losses, but

it was also true of the left parties in countries that were less strongly affected by the crisis. Die LINKE in Germany, too, primarily presented itself as a national party, even though it is fundamentally in favour of a change in European policy. On the other hand, those parties which made the connection between national and European policies the point of departure for their electoral strategies were successful. For the right-wing populist parties, that meant, for example, protection of the 'national element' both against the institutions of the EU and against the corrupt political class. Nationalistic parties such as the UK Independence Party (UKIP) in Britain and the Danish People's Party positioned themselves successfully along this line of conflict, as did France's Front National (FN). To an extent this is also true of Syriza, which made the betrayal in the social sphere the central issue. A vote for Syriza at the same time appeared to be a contribution to the solution of the Greek crisis, and to a change in European policy.

13. The electoral results of the new right express more than just a critique of the constitution of the European Union; rather, the entire range of political institutions, both national and European, is being called into question. The UKIP, FN and the Danish People's Party, together with other right-wing populist parties, describe themselves as parties outside the political system, the democratic values of which they are increasingly questioning. The view that sees nationalistic and right-wing populist 'flukes' in these European elections, meant to 'send a message' to the respective national governments, distorts the perspective of a change in the basic mood of society which, after these elections, will no longer be able to be democratically 'reined in', as has been the case with national elections in the past. UKIP, for instance, operating in an apparently unchangeable political party system in Great Britain, has been systematically underestimated. In national elections, it first appeared as a relevant force in 2010, winning 13.1 per cent of the vote. At the European level, on the other hand, its rise had already been considerable before that. In 1999, at its first try, it won 16.52 per cent, then increased that to 15.64 per cent in 2004, to 16.51 per cent in 2009 and to 27.5 per cent in 2014. For years, the results of the European elections as indicators of a shifting *Zeitgeist*, and as a seismograph for changing societal moods and even political reorientations, have been underestimated. Now however, the electoral results at the European and national levels have tended to converge (see Thesis 1). The design of the European Union has become a domestic policy issue within countries, so that domestic policy has become direct European policy.

14. The Greens' electoral share, 6.66 per cent, represented a slight drop from the 7.47 per cent they had won in 2009. Although they were the fourth-strongest force in the Parliament between 1999 and 2009, they have now dropped behind the moderate right-wing conservative group, the ECR and behind the left group European United Left/Nordic Green Left (GUE/NGL). Nonetheless, the Greens could point to a firm voter base Europe-wide, although they are currently not in a position to expand upon it. The development of a European Green New Deal got stuck at the conceptual level, and in view of the serious social and economic problems at hand, it proved virtually impossible to present it effectively Europe-wide.
15. For the radical left, these elections are an expression of Europe-wide weakness and at the same time a relative success. The left parliamentary group GUE/NGL obtained 52 seats, compared with 35 in 2009. These gains are primarily due to the results achieved by the left in Greece, Spain and Portugal, and also by Sinn Féin in Ireland. The left was successful where it was authentic and concretely in solidarity with those most acutely affected by the crisis, and where it succeeded in forging broad coalitions in open political alliances. For example, the Spanish Podemos ('we can') list emerged directly from the 'indignant' movement 15-M, which was formed out of the social protest against the austerity policies of the Troika, and was supported by the United Left (IU). Together with the likewise strengthened left in Portugal – the CDU and the Bloco Esquerda together got over 18 per cent – and the Greeks, there is a possibility for a southern European transnational cooperative effort which can now once again since 2008, at least in the EP, count on the support of the Italian left as well. In Italy, the success of the 'Tsipras List' was based on an appeal by intellectuals close to the newspaper *Il Manifesto*, which called for the formation of an electoral list of prominent personalities in support of the candidacy of Greece's Alexis Tsipras as the lead candidate of the entire European left. The new left electoral alliance 'A Different Europe' (*Europa anders*) in Austria won fewer votes than the Eurosceptic EuroStop list; nonetheless, these developments are promising.
16. The EP elections in effect reflected a north-south divide for the left parties. While they were successful in southern countries, which have been particularly affected by the crisis, left parties stagnated in the so-called core countries of the EU such as France, the Netherlands, and Germany. They were especially successful where they were able to forge the broadest possible alliances in which those affected by the structural

change of the modes of production and reproduction could be united with those who have now been additionally affected by the crisis-caused upheavals. The ability to address various sectors of society and to incorporate them into alliances is an essential reason for this success. Evidently, the left in the core countries of the EU has not yet been able to forge alliances of various sectors, including the traditional working class, to the extent that this has been possible in the southern countries most affected by the crisis. For example, in France, workers and the unemployed to a large extent voted for the FN. The left in Germany, the Netherlands, and France stagnated.

17. Moreover, even 25 years after the collapse of state socialism, the radical left has, in most post-socialist countries, not succeeded in establishing relevant left parties. Only in the Czech Republic does the Communist Party of Bohemia and Moravia (KSČM) constitute a relevant political force. The Slovenian United Left electoral alliance, which emerged from the Democratic Labour Party (DSD), Party for Sustainable Development of Slovenia (TRS), and the Initiative for Democratic Socialism (IDS), achieved 5.47 per cent of the vote, not enough for a seat, but entered the national parliament two months later with six per cent.

Point of departure and a look back to 2009-2014

Since the last European elections in 2009, the European Union has changed – as has the political situation in Europe as a whole, certainly since the outbreak of the crisis in Ukraine. The transition period after the end of the Cold War ended with the Russian occupation of Crimea, in violation of international law. That changed the role of the EU, which increasingly sees itself as a global actor in a global contest. Consequently, the very divergent social standards in the countries of the EU are being dismantled in favour of a global orientation towards competition, a policy that is being legitimised as the way out of the crisis of public debt into which the EU was manoeuvred by its political elites in 2008/2009 in order to save the banks. Since then, especially in the southern countries of the EU, this has developed into a social crisis with the danger of political instability and social catastrophe. The privatisation of public utilities and the dismantling of public services has been pushed forward under pressure from the EU-oriented institutions the ECB, the EU Commission, and the IMF, which together constitute the so-called Troika. The result has been a growth of social, political, and economic imbalances within the EU, both within and between the countries and regions, and hence dissatisfaction with the dominant policy of its institutions.

The results have first of all been political crises within the countries of the EU, which were expressed by a series of snap elections: between 2010 and 2012 alone, twelve of the fifteen parliamentary elections – nine of them in eurozone countries – were called early; in addition, there were two changes of government without elections. In all these cases, with the exception of Belgium, the degree of severity of the austerity measures taken to solve the crisis – a crisis of the banks – as well as the manner of their concrete implementation, provided the impetus for these new elections. In the case of Greece, this was accompanied by a polarisation of the electorate; in the case of Italy, it caused yet another restructuring of the party system. Since 2010, a number of new 'anti-parties' have been formed, such as the Palikott Party in Poland, Beppo Grillo's 'Five-Star Movement' in Italy, the Pirates and the AfD in Germany, and the Potami Party in Greece. At the same time, changes of government have not resulted in changes in policy. For this reason, the participation of the social democrats in the governments of sixteen EU countries – up from seven in 2009 – cannot be described as a shift to the left. The mass protests against Conservative President Nicolas Sarkozy are now being turned against his Socialist successor François Hollande who is continuing the same policies. But what did all that mean for the elections to the European Parliament in 2014?

Focus on the radical left party family

A review of the results of elections for the European Parliament from 1979 through 2014 would seem to indicate that not much has changed during that period. The moderate conservatives and the social democrats, the two largest party families in the EP, together won over sixty per cent of the votes in all elections through 2009, when they still scored a combined 61.3 per cent; in 2014 however, their combined share dropped to 54 per cent.

This setback was mirrored by the strengthening of the smaller party families, especially the right-wing conservative, right-wing populist, and extreme right-wing parties and groups in the European Parliament, whose combined share now totals approximately twenty per cent. This figure increases by another three per cent if the seats of those right-wing parties which are still not part of any party group, and of the Hungarian FIDESZ party are added; the latter is in the moderate conservative party group, but is open for cooperation with the extreme right.

The social democratic, Green and left party families together won less than forty per cent (approximately 38 per cent). However, this is only a mathematical quantum; it does not stand for any common project. The radical left is currently the only one of the three party families of the left which was able to increase its number of seats, from 35 to 52, although in percentage terms, it fell short of the 7.5 per cent, achieved in 1999 – its highest result to date. More important is the question as to whether it will be able to transform this arithmetical gain into greater political clout. Finally, the liberals have since 1989 been the third-strongest force in the European Parliament, and were able to hold that position in 2014, in spite of losses of three per cent.

Party groups		Voter share 2004	Voter share 2009	Voter share 2014	Gains/ losses
GUE / NGL	United European Left/ Nordic Green left	5.60	4.76	6.92	2.17
S&D	Progressive Alliance of Socialists and Democrats	27.30	25.00	25.43	0.43
Greens/ EFA	The Greens/ European Free Alliance	5.80	7.47	6.66	-0.82
ALDE	Alliance of Liberals and Democrats for Europe	12.00	11.41	8.92	-2.49
EVP	European People's Party (Christian Democrats)	36.70	36.01	29.43	-6.58
EKR	European Conservatives and Reformists	4.25	7.34	9.32	1.98
EFDD	Europe of Freedom and Direct Democracy (right-wing-populist)	4.35	4.35	6.39	2.04
	Independents	4.00	3.67	6.92	3.26
	Total	100.00	100.00	100.00	

The parties of the radical left have been able to hold on to or even expand their positions, at least in those countries in which they have been relatively strong. In the EP 2014 elections, the GUE/NGL parties were able to achieve good or very good results in eight countries – between approximately ten per cent and almost 27 per cent. Leading the way were the left parties in Greece, with 26.6 per cent, Spain (Pluralist Left and Podemos) with over eighteen per cent, Portugal with over 17 per cent, and Cyprus with over 26 per cent. The left improved its results considerably in Finland, reaching almost ten per cent, and held its ground at a high level in the Czech Republic. Moreover, it was able to make gains in Luxembourg (5.76 per cent), Slovenia (5.47 per cent), Italy (4.03 per cent), and Austria (2.14 per cent).

This confirmed a trend that had already been apparent in national parliamentary elections between 2010 and 2014. Syriza in Greece won 26.9 per cent in the elections of June 2012, while the French left of the Left Front won a respectable 6.91 per cent in parliamentary elections that same year. The Swedish Left Party had scored 5.6 per cent in 2010, thus largely maintaining its position (-0.3 per cent), while in Denmark, the Red Green Alliance (Enhedslisten - EL) was able to increase its vote from the 2.17 per cent it had won in 2007 to 6.68 per cent in the elections of 2011; by contrast, support for the Green-leaning Socialist People's Party (Socialistisk Folkeparti - SF) dropped from 13.4 to 9.2 per cent. Currently, the Social Democratic-SF minority government is being supported by the EL. In Finland, too, the Left Alliance (Vasemmistoliitto - VAS) stabilised itself at 8.1 per cent in 2011 (-0.7 per cent from 2007). Since no change in policy had taken place in Finland, the VAS withdrew from the six party centre-left coalition that had existed since 2011 two months before the election. The Spanish United Left (Izquierda Unida - IU) increased from 3.77 per cent in 2008 to 6.92 per cent in 2011. By contrast, the left in Portugal plunged from 9.81 in 2009 to 5.17 per cent in 2011. In the presidential elections in Cyprus in 2013, the AKEL candidate fell far behind his conservative rival. The Left Party in Luxembourg increased its representation in the Chamber to two seats in the 2013 election.

Political conclusion

The left in Europe will need more than merely symbolic solidarity in its own ranks – and that not only in the event of a leftist takeover of power in Greece. The solidarity will have to be palpable as a European phenomenon, and have practical value for people in Greece and other countries of the EU. If a left Greek government places the question of the constitution of the EU on the agenda, the left will have to put forward concrete paths for a new beginning for the EU, and will have to underpin its demands for social, peaceful, and democratic Europe concretely. It will have to take up the experience of the struggle of the 'indignants' just as much as the experience of work in municipalities, and it will have to interlink the experiences and struggles in political institutions instead of juxtaposing them to one another. The European left has the dual task of defending the institutions of democracy in Europe, and at the same time making a contribution to the economic, social, and ecological reconstitution of the foundations of the EU. This is a strategy of fierce confrontation with the new right, of open conflict with the ruling elites, and of a very open search for allies.

translated by Phil Hill

SOCIAL DEMOCRACY CAUGHT IN THE EUROPEAN TRAP[1]

Fabien Escalona and Mathieu Vieira

Political science literature has extensively described social democracy's 'two metamorphoses'. First there was the establishment of social democratic parties as major government parties in the 'Keynesian State' period and then their 'de-social-democratisation' after the 1970s, while the renovation promoted by Tony Blair and Gerhard Schröder was associated with electoral success at the end of the 1990s. The propulsive power of this new social democratic identity was then rapidly exhausted.

Until the last days before the 2014 European elections, opinion polls carried out in EU member countries allowed the social democrats to hope that they could pass the 200-seat threshold in the 751-seat European Parliament (EP) and make good the setback they had suffered five years earlier. Indeed, in 2009 only a quarter of the MEPs belonged to the EP's S&D group, which was at an historically low level.

We will first show that social democracy managed to stabilise its weight in the EP only while continuing to decline in percentage of votes. This result should be seen in the context of the historic trajectory of a political family of parties that we extensively studied in *The Palgrave Handbook of Social Democracy*.[2] We will next address the present state of this family of parties in the middle of capitalism's structural crisis and the dilemmas it faces in the very peculiar regime of the European Union. The social democrats, because of their own history, have tied themselves up in a bundle of constraints — which are creating their present difficulties. For this reason, they will probably not be of much help in putting an end to the austerity that is devastating the European continent. This will be the last point covered by this article.

The electoral stagnation of the social democrats within the European Parliament

In general, after the recent elections, the European Parliamentary groups have kept the same names, but their internal balances have been markedly altered though not in the direction of greater coherence.

The historic groups that form the 'central bloc' supporting European integration have remained the majority. These are the conservative and Christian democrats of the European People's Party (EPP), the liberals of the Alliance of Liberals and Democrats for Europe (ALDE), and last but not least the social democrats of the Progressive Alliance of Socialists and Democrats (S&D) in the European Parliament.

The EP groups only very approximately correspond with the outlines of the political families that political analysts can identify in Europe on the basis of shared socio-historic origins and ideological characteristics. This weak correspondence expresses the de-structuring of national party systems in Europe, highlighted by the decline of some major parties and the emergence of new contentious forces, which, however, often have difficulty in stabilising themselves. Indeed, the gradual ebbing of government parties is reflected in the contraction of the Parliament's 'central bloc' of Europe-wide parties (PES (Party of European Socialists)-EPP-ALDE) from 72.4 per cent in 2009 to 63.7 per cent in 2014.

In this context, the EPP has remained the largest group, while the social democrats have to be content with second place. The net gain in seats, compared with 2009, is seven – from 184 to 191. Importantly, the group's weight is virtually identical to that of 2009, whereas it had been able to hold a third of the seats at the beginning of the 1990s.

Regarding the heterogeneous character of the S&D group, it is striking that its position is due to the contribution of the Romanian contingent, hardly steeped in social democratic culture, as well as the ten extra seats won by the Italian Democratic Party, a centre-left party whose leader, Matteo Renzi, grew up in the Christian Democratic tradition.

Some gains have certainly also been made by the more 'traditional' organisations of the social democratic family, for example in Germany (which will strengthen its already considerable influence within the group and in the Parliament in general) and in Great Britain (whose Labour MEPs nevertheless refused to support the common candidate Martin Schulz). These gains, however, were counterbalanced by poor scores in other countries.

In the Netherlands, the Labour Party scored less than ten per cent, behind the Radical Left and the social-liberal D66; in Hungary and in the Czech Republic some parties already in difficulty saw their score drop by a third;

in Greece (-28 per cent), in Spain (-15.4 per cent), and in Ireland (-8 per cent) these parties paid a heavy price for their participation in 'austerity' governments. In several countries, regardless of regional zones, the weight of social democracy within the left has been diluted, even in those where it maintained its seats as in Sweden and Austria. Thus social democracy has marked time in the European elections (20.2 per cent on average — a historic low) — which is consistent with the declining electoral trend of this political family in the last few years.[3]

The absence of a real social democratic family at the EU level

The state of affairs that *The Palgrave Handbook of Social Democracy* describes supports Stefan Berger's judgement that contemporary social democracy no longer has 'any model, ideological originality or [...] specific and easily identifiable electorate'.[4] Any convergence there may be within the family is due to a lack, or the 'rubbing out', of specific characteristics, which had marked each of its historic components.

The western and eastern social democrats continue to belong to very different political universes that leave little room for exchanging recipes of good practice and adopting common stands. There are marked differences between these two 'distant cousins' as there also are within the so-called eastern branch.

This is notable in terms of the normal orientations of East European parties. Their programme positions are, indeed, particularly orthodox in economic matters. In the West, the social composition of the social democratic electorates is marked by a tendency to a decline in the relative weight of industrial workers and an increase in the weight of the middle strata with a higher level of education.

In the East, there are fairly different configurations that vary from a plebeian kind of support base, both agrarian and working class (as in Romania) to a materially better off electoral profile with graduates such as could be found in centre-right parties (as in Estonia). The Baltic countries have a weak electoral base (in Latvia social democracy is on the verge of extinction) and have a virtually centrist position in the political spectrum.

On the other hand, those in central Europe (the Czech Republic, Slovakia, and Hungary) regularly get between a fifth and two-fifths of the vote and clearly dominate the left in their national political scene. This is also the case in Bulgaria and Romania, where the latter country's social democratic party's particularly high score can be explained by its alliance with the liberals.

It could be thought that the western party configurations could converge with those of the East.[5] Indeed, the volatility of political leaders and electorate, the poor social and ideological roots of the central eastern political parties, and, more broadly, the difficulty of structuring party political systems in societies during a crisis,[6] could be compared with the different expressions of exhaustion of the representative regimes in the West. The downward tendencies of voter turnouts and weight of major government parties, the uneven paths of 'third' and/or 'protest' parties, and the accelerating decline of electoral stability all tend towards this.[7]

The continued decline of European social democracy

Another observation could be drawn from the overview presented by *The Palgrave Handbook*: the virtually universal process of the weakening of European social democracy. This is shown by several phenomena:

- *The difficulty in renewing the body of activists and forming bonds with a mobilised civil society*

    The social democratic parties are no longer mass parties. They have faced a virtual mass exodus of activists since the beginning of the 2000s. This problem involves their capacity to maintain the number of consistent activists but also the aging of the active members.

    In Austria, party membership dropped by half between 1970 and 2000, while the Swedish SP dropped by a third. In the Netherlands, while PvdA membership reached a historic low point in 2012, the proportion of those over sixty years of age rose from thirty to fifty per cent in the last decade. In Luxembourg, a quarter of the members are over 65 and less than a sixth are under 35; in Germany half of them are over sixty and only six per cent are under thirty. The French Socialist Party (PS), on the other hand can boast of relative youthfulness, but the average age is still high, with 61 per cent of its members over fifty in 2011.

    Where the social democrats have maintained strong links with the trade union movement, as in Austria, this puts them out on a limb with regard to other groups, such as the ecological organisations, which can connect with a younger electorate that is increasing in number. However, in most cases, the organic links with the trade unions have crumbled or been long broken. In these cases, other kinds of social movements have not replaced them.

- *A declining capacity to mobilise large sections of the electorate*

    This trend goes back to the 1970s for some of the biggest parties of the social-democratic family, but it is once again noticeable in the recent period. The Finnish SDP, for example dropped below the twenty per cent level in the 2009 European elections and in the 2011 national parliamentary ones and has dropped to 12.31 per cent in the 2014 European elections. The German SDP lost fifteen per cent between the general elections of 2002 and those of 2009, and the Swedish Social Democrats lost ten per cent over the same period. The most impressive drops were suffered by the southern socialist parties following the sovereign debt crises. In Greece PASOK lost its position as a major alternative party.

Only a few parties escaped this tendency to decline in the last decade: the French speaking Socialist Party in Belgium (but not its Flemish equivalent), the Maltese Labour Party (which got back into office in a virtually perfect two-party system), and the few parties that play a secondary role in their respective party systems (as in Ireland and Cyprus). The French Socialist Party (PS) progressed in opposition, but its electoral base remains modest in relation to the power it now has in the Republic.

The fact remains that, compared with the boom after the Second World War, the social democratic family has lost between fifteen and twenty per cent of its electoral strength. This has affected its ability to govern on its own or to lead coalitions and crucially raises the question of alliances. The Dutch, German, Swedish, and Greek cases can be cited as illustrations. Moreover, the eastern social democrats have not escaped the problem of general electoral decline. Having said this, the changes over the last decade are much more dramatic and rapid there, as in the Polish and Slovak cases, and have included some spectacular rises.

- *Ideological confusion*

The attempts to redefine social democracy in terms of a 'Third Way' have fizzled out. The parties most marked by this have discretely distanced themselves from a legacy that continues to weigh on their fortunes, and they find themselves in a doctrinal vacuum. Points of reference are sometimes sought outside the social democratic tradition in trying to structure a discourse that enhances national cohesion and solidarity, but these attempts are not inter-connected and no motivating proposals have emerged in the 2000s.

Nevertheless, the social democrats continue, with a few exceptions, to dominate the left political space. Most of them, at the risk of diluting their historic identity, have managed to open up to new social strata of the post-Fordist era. This has been reflected in the orientation of their programmes, confirming their commitment to improving the rights of women and sexual minorities and including more pro-ecology positions than in the past. Although many of these issues are occupied by other organisations, sometimes with greater coherence and conviction, the social democrats can claim to have more prospects of getting into office and acting on them.

On the organisational level, many organisations have started to open up and make their machinery more democratic by using similar means: direct election of national and/or local leaders, including sympathising non-members in internal votes. The existence of real primaries remains the privilege of Italy, France, and Greece.

It should also be noted that when some major parties invested their sympathisers with real powers of decision, they escaped – momentarily at any rate – the activist decline that hit their counterparts. These attempts at regeneration 'from below' have been accompanied by an attempt 'from above' to Europeanise the social democratic family.[8]

Compared with other political forces, these attempts have been rather successful. The crisis has created a moment of self-affirmation by the Party of European Socialists (PES) through its representatives in the European Parliament and the European think tank, the Foundation for European Progressive Studies. However, the success of this double strategy remains slight. The democratisation and opening of some parties are, in fact, limited.

Social democracy faced with capitalism's 'great crisis'

The 2008 economic crisis had little impact on the doctrinal character or strategic thinking of some social democrats. Its consequences can be gauged by some negative aspects, like the difficulties it presented for left governments facing stagnation in production, soaring unemployment, and sometimes market speculation on the public debt.

The socialist parties of southern Europe were exemplary victims. The return to office that took place after the defeat in the 2009 European elections should not obscure the continued tendency to decline. This can be measured by looking at the social democratic parties among the original fifteen members of the EU, comparing the six-year periods before and after the crisis; the average drop is five per cent. This does not mean that the decline is only due to the crisis – it largely preceded it – but the crisis definitely did not improve the social democrats' fortunes.

Over five years after the start of the crisis, the activity and thinking of the social democrats has remained confined within the previously established pacts, and no political innovation seems to have emerged. On the contrary, the social democrats persist in emphasising two choices, both of them double-edged: European integration and a competitive knowledge-based economy

The social democrats' 'Faustian bargain' with European integration

The social democrats entered into a 'Faustian bargain' that grew as they supported European integration.[9] It is not that opting for Europe was diabolic in itself; the problem is that in seeking eternal life – that is, the maintenance of its status as the major governmental alternative – social democracy risked losing its soul.

Social democracy's opting for Europe was not so much motivated by a possible renewed taste for internationalism as by its desire, after the crisis of the 1970s, to restore the conditions to which it had owed its post-war success. If Keynesianism had failed inside national borders it was necessary to restore it on a continental scale; if the economic sectors that promised high levels of productivity typical of the Fordist era had run out of steam, new high technology sectors had to be encouraged.

Hence the attraction for the social democrats of the project of European integration and their enthusiasm for knowledge-based economics. In both cases, changes were to enable the launching of a new wave of growth, which in turn was to provide a material basis for a new compromise between capital and labour. In this new context, which was more adapted to the regulation of a 'globalised' capitalism, the single currency was to help put an end to currency speculation, and a knowledge-based economy (promoted by the Lisbon Strategy) was to offer the prospect of growth in contrast to the weary Fordist industries.

These beliefs indicate the invariable ideas behind social democratic thinking – productivism and the rejection of conflict when its cost rises – but are paid for by the reinforcement of the neoliberal form of capitalism. On the one hand, social democracy completed its rallying to the European project at a time when the logic of negative integration – measures to regulate, ensure and make durable the establishment of competitiveness between socio-productive systems – was getting the upper hand over the logic of positive integration – harmonisation to control this competition and the private agents.[10] On the other hand, the social democrats did not seek to explore the non-commodified potentials of the knowledge-based economy but in the name of the latter endorsed a Lisbon Strategy replete with neoliberal recommendations.[11]

Perhaps confident that it was possible to correct the defects once the EU system was built, the social democrats embraced European integration at a time when the turn it took undermined the possibility of achieving their hope. The EU's logic, indeed, is not one based on party conflicts, which the social democrats would have needed to establish their own distinct views and escape the consensus that *by default and by the institutional construction itself* is anti-social democratic.

In fact, the EU is distinguished by the absence of real European parties and by the weakness of the connections between the arena of governing (the decision-making arena) and the parliamentary and electoral arena.[12] Its structure is also marked by the tearing away of whole sections of economic policy from the sovereignty of the states and peoples and by a 'pro-market' orientation imprinted in these policies. This is especially visible in the case of the single currency, which completely fulfils its function of currency stability for the financial community but badly fails in ensuring the social cohesion of the population of the euro area, which is under the control of a central bank enjoying a degree of autonomy unparalleled in the world.

Identity and strategy – the price to pay

However, alongside its historic roots in the working-class movement, another hallmark of social democracy as a family is its leading role in defending the 'primacy of politics' over market forces and private interests. Among the ways of ensuring this primacy, which can assume authoritarian forms, it favoured the democratic way.

Although the history of some of its members may have been stained by the repression of popular movements, this family was one of those most concerned with the civic integration of the masses excluded from the political system. Its present support, even though hesitant, for an EU marked by the 'primacy of competition' and the withdrawal of the decision-making process from 'democratic passions' is very costly on the level of the *identity* of social democracy and also on the *strategic* level, since it makes its alternative proposals to neoliberalism unconvincing.

Even non-revolutionary solutions, like a coherent Keynesian revival and protection of companies from capital markets, require the reversal of the institutional constraints in which social democratic arguments are inaudible or divided. Such contradictions could be read between the lines of the manifesto published by the Party of European Socialists for the European elections. A step back from the one produced in 2009, it only contained generalities and did not even mention the European Central Bank.

Since social democracy has difficulty in providing solutions that tackle the deep roots of the crisis, the social democratic stagnation is not just electoral; it also characterises the strategic and doctrinal thinking of this political family. It must clarify its relations with the institutions and with the principles of popular sovereignty if it hopes to reconnect with wider sections of the electorate and with the partners on the left that it will need in order to return to government in certain countries.

Challenging austerity?

The European Parliament has seen its powers increased throughout its existence, even if it still compares negatively to any national lower house. This has been expressed by some striking votes, like the rejection of the ACTA trade agreement because of the danger it poses to freedom of expression and privacy.

But what of the austerity policies in the EU, described as 'crazy' by the economist Paul Krugman?[13] Do the economic deregulations attacked by radical political forces, both in the creditor and the debtor nations of the euro area, have any chance of being dealt with in a new way?

The right-wing radical or national-sovereignty groups carry too little weight and are too isolated to claim any influence on these issues. Similarly, the solutions put forward during the campaign by the left radical leader Alexis Tsipras will not be considered for a single second by the European elites – or would only be considered in the event of an extreme scenario like the imminent collapse of the banking system.

On the other hand, in a more realistic scenario, some expect a moderation of economic policies in the direction of the centre-left, arguing that the balance of forces has shifted in favour of the social democrats. This diagnosis is based partly on the increase in the number of votes they now have in the European Council (a dozen member states have a government or governing coalition led by the left), partly on the slight increase in left EP groups, and partly on the sharp decline of the EPP, which has strengthened the relative weight of the social democrats in the pro-European central bloc.

Recently, several senior leaders of the PES (notably Matteo Renzi, Sigmar Gabriel, and Martin Schulz) have spoken in favour of a softening of austerity[14] to give priority to growth policies. However, although carrying out their proposals would probably make a momentary difference in terms of the struggle against unemployment, it would only represent a variation of the present constraint-based path.

The balance of power remains unfavourable to the European left. Obliged to compromise, the national executives are still dominated by the right. Moreover, political colour only partly reflects the real divergent interests; the challenge for the euro area is to make different socio-productive models live together under the same currency.

As for the European Parliament, as many observers have already noted, the gradual erosion of the central bloc through the growth of the radical left, on the one side, and the radical or extreme right, on the other, makes an even closer cooperation probable between the PES, the EPP, and the liberals (and Greens) in the European Parliament. Yet it is precisely the consensual character of the European political system that makes invisible the specific contribution of the social democrats who find themselves identified with institutions and economic orientations inconsistent with their 'genetic code'.

The fact that the MEPs opposed to the existing European integration are now more numerous will be a means of blackmailing the social democrats. It will probably be used shamelessly by the 'pro-EU' right through warnings that there must be 'compromise or chaos'. Although the social democrats claim to have insisted on conditioning their support of Juncker as president of the Commission, it is by no means certain that they are in a position to set conditions.

Fritz Scharpf has shown in a fairly convincing manner that whatever the preferences of the actors on the European scene, the present structures of the EU, made concrete through its laws and institutions, are profoundly biased against those capitalist economies that are more socialised and that provide more space for state intervention.[15] Instead, they favour the varieties of capitalism closest to a 'pure liberal model', and the national economies are pressured to move towards this model. Thus the EU has a kind of 'natural inclination', which would require exceptional circumstances to reverse, especially after its extension to the countries of central and eastern Europe. This creates a problem for the left that echoes the 'Faustian bargain' mentioned above.

Even if the left recognises this diagnosis, the framework it has in which to act will not be exhilarating. It can either be trapped in a long and uncertain struggle inside the EU, in which it is a minority, or it can pursue a strategy of disobedience and rejection, which will make it hard to gather consensus and runs the risk of isolating the left or exposing it to the danger of hijacking by nationalism.

Literature

Amable, Bruno, Lilas Demmou, and Ivan Ledezma, 'The Lisbon strategy and structural reforms in Europe' , *Transfer: European Review of Labour and Research* 15,1 (2009).

Baldini, Gianfranco Baldini and Adriano Pappalardo, *Elections, Electoral Systems and Volatile Voters*, Basingstoke and New York, Palgrave Macmillan, 2009.

Bailey, David J., Jean-Michel De Waele, Fabien Escalona and Mathieu Vieira (eds), *European Social Democracy During the Global Economic Crisis. Renovation or Resignation?*, Mancheser : Manchester University Press, 2014.

Berger, Stefan, 'Social Democratic Trajectories in Modern Europe: One or Many Families', Henning Meyer and Jonathan Rutherford (eds), *The Future of European Social Democracy*, Basingstoke and New York: Palgrave Macmillan, 2012.

De Waele, Jean-Michel, Fabien Escalona, and Mathieu Vieira, 'La social-démocratie des années 2000' [Social democracy in the 2000s], Fondation Jean-Jaurès, Observatoire de la vie politique, 22 January 2014, < http://www.jean-jaures.org/Publications/Notes/La-social-democratie-des-annees-2000>.

De Waele, Jean-Michel, Fabien Escalona, and Mathieu Vieira, *The Palgrave Handbook of Social Democracy in the European Union*, Basingstoke and New York: Palgrave Macmillan, 2013.

Hanley, Seán, 'Book Review: Origin, Ideology and Transformation of Political Parties: East-Central and Western Europe Compared', *Party Politics* 18 (2012).

Heurteaux, Jerôme and Frédéric Zalewski, *Introduction à l'Europe postcommuniste*, Brussels: De Boeck, 2012.

Krugman, Paul, 'Europe's Austerity Madness',*New York Times*, 28 September 2012, <http://www.nytimes.com/2012/09/28/opinion/krugman-europes-austerity-madness.html?partner=rss&emc=rss&_r=2&>.

Mair, Peter, 'Ruling the Void? The Hollowing of Western Democracy', *New Left Review* 42 (2006).

Martin, Pierre, 'Le déclin des partis de gouvernement en Europe' [The Decline of Government Parties in Europe], *Commentaire* 2013.

Scharpf, Fritz W., *Gouverner l'Europe*, Paris: Presses de Sciences Po, 2000 ; Paul Magnette, *Le régime politique de l'Union européenne* [The Political Regime of the European Union] Paris: Presses de Sciences Po, 2009.

Scharpf, Fritz W., *The Asymmetry of European Integration or Why the EU Cannot be a 'Social Market Economy'*, Working Paper, KFG, The Transformative Power of Europe, No. 6 (September 2009), Berlin: Freie Universität Berlin, 2009, http://www.polsoz.fu-berlin.de/en/v/transformeurope/publications/working_paper/WP_06_September_Scharpf1.pdf?1367706572.

Sloam, James and Isabelle Hertner, 'The Europeanization of Social Democracy: Politics Without Policy and Policy without Politics', Henning Meyer and Jonathan Rutherford (eds), *The Future of European Social Democracy,* Basingstoke and New York: Palgrave Macmillan, 2012.

'UE: Malgré Berlin, la pression monte pour desserrer le carcan budgetaire', *Le Parisien*, 20 June 2014, <http://www.leparisien.fr/flash-actualite-economie/ue-malgre-berlin-la-pression-monte-pour-desserrer-le-carcan-budgetaire-20-06-2014-3939319.php>.

Vieira, Mathieu, 'Does a European Party System Exist? A Conceptual Framework for Analysis', *Cahiers du CEVIPOL* 2011/1, <http://dev.ulb.ac.be/cevipol/dossiers_fichiers/cahiers-du-cevipol-2011-1.pdf>.

Notes

1. This article is based on a paper 'La social-démocratie des années 2000' [Social democracy in the 2000s] written by the authors with Jean-Michel De Waele for the Jean Jaurès Foundation, as well as various articles published in French by Fabien Escalona on the online periodical slate.fr.
2. Jean-Michel de Waele, Fabien Escalona, and Mathieu Vieira (eds), *The Palgrave Handbook of Social Democracy in the European Union*, Basingstoke and New York: Palgrave Macmillan, 2013.
3. After having advanced until 1994, (27.6 per cent of the seats in 1979, 30 per cent in 1984, 34.7 per cent in 1989, 34.9 per cent in 1994), it has experienced a drop since 1999 (28.8 per cent in 1999, 27.3 per cent in 2004, 25 per cent in 2009, 25.4 per cent in 2014).
4. Stefan Berger, 'Social Democratic Trajectories in Modern Europe: One or Many Families', Henning Meyer and Jonathan Rutherford, *The Future of European Social Democracy*, Basingstoke and New York: Palgrave Macmillan, 2012, pp. 13—26, p. 24.
5. Seán Hanley, 'Book review: Origin, Ideology and Transformation of Political Parties: East-Central and Western Europe Compared', *Party Politics* 18 (2012), pp. 793—795.
6. Jerôme Heurteaux and Frédéric Zalewski, *Introduction à l'Europe postcommuniste*, Brussels: De Boeck, 2012, pp. 136—139.
7. Peter Mair, 'Ruling the Void? The Hollowing of Western Democracy', *New Left Review* 42 (2006), pp. 25—51 ; Gianfranco Baldini and Adriano Pappalardo, *Elections, Electoral Systems and Volatile Voters*, Basingstoke and New York: Palgrave Macmillan, 2009; Pierre Martin, 'Le déclin des partis de gouvernement en Europe' [The Decline of Government Parties in Europe], *Commentaire* 2013, pp. 143, 543—554.
8. James Sloam and Isabelle Hertner, 'The Europeanization of Social Democracy: Politics Without Policy and Policy without Politics', Meyer and Rutherford, *The Future of European Social Democracy*, pp. 27—38.
9. David J. Bailey, Jean-Michel De Waele, Fabien Escalona and Mathieu Vieira (eds), *European Social Democracy During the Global Economic Crisis. Renovation or Resignation?*, Manchester: Manchester University Press, 2014.
10. Fritz W. Scharpf, *Gouverner l'Europe*, Paris: Presses de Sciences Po, 2000 ; Paul Magnette, *Le régime politique de l'Union européenne* [The Political Regime of the European Union] Paris: Presses de Sciences Po, 2009.
11. Bruno Amable, Lilas Demmou, and Ivan Ledezma, 'The Lisbon strategy and structural reforms in Europe', *Transfer: European Review of Labour and Research* 15,1 (2009), pp. 33-52.
12. Mathieu Vieira, 'Does a European Party System Exist? A Conceptual Framework for Analysis', *Cahiers du CEVIPOL* 2011/1, <http://dev.ulb.ac.be/cevipol/dossiers_fichiers/cahiers-du-cevipol-2011-1.pdf>.
13. Paul Krugman, 'Europe's Austerity Madness', *New York Times*, 28 September 2012, <http://www.nytimes.com/2012/09/28/opinion/krugman-europes-austerity-madness.html?partner=rss&emc=rss&_r=2&>.

14 'UE: Malgré Berlin, la pression monte pour desserrer le carcan budgetaire', *Le Parisien*, 20 June 2014, <http://www.leparisien.fr/flash-actualite-economie/ue-malgre-berlin-la-pression-monte-pour-desserrer-le-carcan-budgetaire-20-06-2014-3939319.php>.
15 Fritz W. Scharpf, *The Asymmetry of European Integration or Why the EU Cannot be a 'Social Market Economy'*, Working Paper, KFG, The Transformative Power of Europe, No. 6 (September 2009), Berlin: Freie Universität Berlin, 2009, <http://www.polsoz.fu-berlin.de/en/v/transformeurope/publications/working_paper/WP_06_September_Scharpf1.pdf?1367706572>.

FAR RIGHT PARTIES IN THE EUROPEAN PARLIAMENT[1]

Thilo Janssen

With the Treaty of Lisbon, the financial crisis, austerity, public debt, European top candidates for European Commission President for the first time in European Parliament (EP) elections, all political actors in the European Union (EU), including far right parties, have been confronted with dramatic political change on the European level in the last half decade. According to the Eurobarometer, public trust in European institutions fell from a peak of 57 per cent in spring 2007 to 31 per cent in autumn 2013, while trust in national governments declined from 43 to 23 per cent in the same period. This common feeling of political uncertainty was fertile ground for right-wing ideologies in many EU member states. Hence, scholarly analysts, the media, and the political mainstream all expected the nationalist anti-EU parties to do well in the European elections in May 2014. This article examines the far right party election results and the outcome of the parliamentary group-building processes in the eighth European Parliament. The following two questions will be addressed:

- Organisation: To what extent are far right parties organised in the European Parliament?
- Impact: Is far right party cooperation on the European level politically relevant?

In this article the term *far right* refers to all right-wing parties that *by choosing alliances position themselves* further on the political right than the (mostly) centre-right, conservative, and Christian Democratic European Peoples Party (EPP). However, a consequence of this approach is that EPP member parties like Hungary's FIDESZ, whose leader Victor Orbán recently proclaimed the 'end of liberal democracy'[2] in Hungary, are not included in the analysis.

Organisation: to what extent are far right parties organised in the European Parliament?

In fact, as predicted, the far right did well in the EP elections. In three member states right-wing extremists or populists even turned out to be the strongest parties: the Front National (FN) in France, the United Kingdom Independence Party (UKIP) in Great Britain and the Danish People's Party (Dansk Folkeparti - DF) in Denmark. In the EP there are now 176 out of 751 Members of European Parliament (MEPs) who position themselves further on the political right than the EPP. This amounts to roughly 23 per cent, almost a quarter. Out of these 176 right-wing MEPs, two official parliamentary groups have emerged, the national-conservative Europe of Conservatives and Reformists (ECR), and the right-wing populist Europe of Freedom and Direct Democracy (EFDD). A couple of far right MEPs remain without official group affiliation; such MEPs are called non-attached (NA). Official group status in the EP is reserved for coalitions of at least 25 MEPs from a quarter of the member states (which now means seven out of 28).

The first unexpected development after the elections was the way in which the ECR group was reorganised. A look at the right column of Table 1 shows that only six of the former 2009-2014 ECR members were re-elected to the EP. As a consequence, the hitherto most important ECR parties – the British Conservatives (CP), Poland's Law and Justice (Prawo i Sprawiedliwość - PiS), and the Czech Republic's Civic Democratic Party (Občanská demokratická strana - ODS) – decided to open up the group further to the populist right and invited UKIP's former allies DF and the True Finns (Perussuomalaiset - PS), alongside the newly elected Alternative for Germany (Alternative für Deutschland - AfD) and a couple of other small parties, to join the ECR. In the end, the ECR has become the third largest group in the new EP with 70 MEPs from 17 member states.

Table 1: The ECR group after the European elections 2014

	Member State	Party	Result 2014 %	MEP 2014	Result 2009 %	Group 2009-2014
1	United Kingdom	Conservatives	23.31	20 (-5)	27.00	ECR
2	Poland	PiS	31.78	19 (+4)	27.4	ECR
3	Germany	AfD	7.00	7	---	---

#	Country	Party	%	Seats	% prev	Group
4	Denmark	Dansk Folkeparti	26.60	4 (+2)	14.8	EFD
5	Belgium	N-VA	16.35	4 (+3)	6.13	Greens/EFA
6	Finland	True Finns	12.09	2 (+1)	14.0	EFD
7	Czech Republic	ODS	7.65	2 (-7)	31.45	ECR
8	Netherlands	CU–SGP	7.67	2 (+/-)	6.82	ECR/EFD
9	Bulgaria	BBTS+VMRO-BND	10.66	1	---	---
10	Greece	ANEL	3.47	1	---	---
11	Croatia	HSP dr.Starčević	41.42★	1	---	---
12	Latvia	TB/LNNK + VL	14.25	1 (+/-)	7.45	ECR
13	Lithuania	LLRA (AWPL)	8.05	1 (+/-)	8.42	ECR
14	Germany	Family Party	0.70	1	---	---
15	Slovakia	OL'aNO	7.64	1	---	---
16	Slovakia	NOVA	6.83	1	---	---
17	Ireland	Fianna Fáil	22.30	1 (-2)	24.08	ALDE

★ *Result of a three-party coalition that gained three MEPs: two joined the EPP, one the ECR.*

Another surprise was the re-foundation of UKIP's EFD group, now renamed Europe of Freedom and Direct Democracy (EFDD). The day after the EP elections, Nigel Farage's UKIP lost almost all of its allies from the former EFD. The Italian Northern League (Lega Nord - LN) and the Slovak National Party (Slovenská národná strana - SNS) had defected to Marine Le Pen and Geert Wilders' pan-European party European Alliance for Freedom (EAF) before the elections (the SNS then failed in the Slovak EP election), PS and DF joined the ECR, the Greek Popular Orthodox Rally (Laikós Orthódoxos Synagermós - LA.O.S.) was not re-elected. Nonetheless, UKIP refused to join the EAF after having been approached by Marine Le Pen. Farage explained that anti-Semitism would still be 'deeply embedded' in the FN and that he therefore would not cooperate with the EAF. Then UKIP found a new partner in Beppe Grillo's Italian Five Star Movement (MoVimento Cinque Stelle - M5S). The so-called Grillini held an online referendum in which the party members could decide whether they wanted to join UKIP's group or the ECR. 29,584 M5S members participated and 78.1 per cent voted for partnership with UKIP. Next, the Lithuanian former EFD (and EAF) member Order and Justice (Tvarka ir teisingumas - TT) decided to become part of the emerging group, followed by the newly elected parties Sweden Democrats (Sverigedeomkraterna - SD), the Czech Free Citizens' Party (Strana svobodných občanů - SO), and the Latvian Greens and Farmers (Zaļo un Zemnieku savienība - ZSS), making up six national delegations for the EFDD – a seventh was still needed to constitute a group. At this point, Joëlle Bergeron, a French MEP who was elected to the EP on the FN's list, defected from her party. With Bergeron constituting the seventh national delegation, Farage has secured his leadership of one group of far right populists in the EP – despite the inclusion of populist right-wing parties in the ECR and despite Le Pen and Wilders' declared ambition to lead a broad coalition of nationalists in their common fight against the EU. However, the EFDD's existence is very fragile. In October 2014, the Latvian MEP Iveta Gricule left the group, and the EFDD temporarily lost its group status. A few days later, MEP Robert Iwaskiewicz from Poland's Congress of the New Right (Kongres Nowej Prawicy – KNP) was presented as her successor.

Table 2: The EFDD group after the European elections 2014

	Member state	Party	Result 2014 %	MEPs 2014	Result 2009 %	Group 2009-2014
1	United Kingdom	UKIP	26.77	24 (+11)	16.09	EFD
2	Italy	M 5 Stelle	21.15	17	---	---
3	Lithuania	PTT	14.25	2 (+/-)	12.22	EFD
4	Sweden	SD	9.70	2	---	---
5	Czech Republic	Svobodní	5.24	1	---	---
6	France	Independent (FN)	24.95 (FN)	1	6.3 (FN)	NA (FN)
7	Poland	Independent (KNP)	7.15 (KNP)	1	---	---

NA: Non-attached

Eventually, Marine Le Pen and Geert Wilders' (Party for Freedom (Partij voor de Vrijheid) – PVV, Netherlands) right-wing extremist coalition EAF, initially founded as a European party in 2010 by single MEPs from UKIP, FN, FPÖ, Flemish Interest (Vlaams Belang - VB), TT, and one member of the SD, failed to gather enough partners for official group status in the EP. The remaining five EAF parties are the French FN, the Dutch PVV, Austria's FPÖ, Belgium's VB, and Italy's LN. Slovakia's SNS is no longer represented in the EP, and the former EAF allies SD and TT joined with UKIP and

M5S in the EFDD. Like UKIP, the DF and the M5S had already refused Le Pen's invitation to join the EAF before the elections. The SD left the EAF after a scandal provoked by FPÖ lead candidate Andreas Mölzer who had called the EU a 'conglomerate of niggers' ('Negerkonglomerat') and had said that compared to EU regulations Hitler's Third Reich was 'probably informal and liberal'. The media scandal led to Mölzer's resignation and the withdrawal of the SD from the EAF. The SD apparently feared negative consequences from this partnership for the EP elections and the Swedish national elections in September 2014. Shortly before the deadline to register for group status in the EP (midnight, 23 June) Le Pen approached Janusz Korwin-Mikke's KNP (Poland). However, the partnership was rejected by Wilders, reportedly because of Korwin-Mikke's too openly anti-Semitic, misogynist, and homophobic statements. For the present, Le Pen has had to relinquish her goal of leading a broad radical right-wing group in the EP, but this might not be the end of the story. As history shows, defections from far right parties and groups in the EP are very common and could, during the ongoing legislative term, give Le Pen and Wilders the two missing partners needed to form an official group in the EP.

Table 3: The remaining EAF parties without official group status after the European elections 2014

	Member state	Party	Result 2014 %	MEPs 2014	Group June 2014	Result 2009 %	Group 2009-2014
1	France	Front National	24.95	24 (+21)	NA	6.3	NA
2	Netherlands	PVV	13.32	4 (-1)	NA	16.97	NA
3	Austria	FPÖ	19.72	4 (+2)	NA	12.71	NA
4	Italy	Lega Nord	6.15	4 (-5)	NA	10.2	EFD
5	Belgium	Vlaams Belang	4.14	1 (-1)	NA	9.85	NA

NA: non-attached

Lastly, the neo-Nazis and fascists from the European party Alliance of European Nationalist Movements (AENM) are still far from being able to form an official group in the EP. Bulgaria's Ataka and the British National Party (BNP) have not been re-elected. However, Jobbik and FN's old radical faction around Bruno Gollnisch and Jean-Marie Le Pen will most likely find partners in the radical neo-Nazi parties Golden Dawn (Chrysí Avgí – CA, renamed National Dawn (EA) after being faced with criminal charges in Greece) and the German National Democrats (*Nationaldemokratische Partei Deutschlands* – NPD).

Table 4: Non-attached far right parties after the European elections 2014 (in addition to EAF parties)

	Member State	Party	Result 2014 %	MEPs 2014	Group June 2014	Result 2009 %	Group 2009-2014
1	Poland	KNP	7.15	4	NA	---	---
2	Hungary	Jobbik	14.67	3 (+/-)	NA	14.77	NA
3	Greece	Chrysi Avgi	9.38	3	NA	---	---
4	Germany	NPD	1.00	1	NA	---	---

NA: Non-attached

A number of far right parties were not re-elected to the EP (see Table 5), and, in addition, there are nine EU member states without a far right party of electoral relevance in the 2014 European election. In the so-called Programme Countries, Spain and Portugal, no far right parties benefited from the crisis. Ireland, also a Programme Country, has a left-wing and non-chauvinist nationalist party, Sinn Féin, which is part of the United European Left/Nordic Green Left (GUE/NGL) group in the EP. In Romania and Slovakia the Greater Romania Party (Partidul România Mare - PRM) and the SNS failed in the elections. The other four countries without successful far right parties in the EP elections are Estonia, Luxembourg, Malta, and Cyprus.

Table 5: Far right parties that failed to get an MEP elected in 2014

	Member state	Party	Result 2014 %	Result 2009 %	MEPs 2009	Group 2009-2014
1	Bulgaria	Ataka	2.96	11.96	2	NA
2	Romania	PRM	2.71	8.65	2	NA
3	Greece	LA.O.S.	2.70	7.15	2	EFD
4	United Kingdom	BNP	1.14	6.04	2	NA
5	Slovakia	SNS	3.61	5.56	1	EFD
6	Hungary	MDF	---	5.31	1	ECR
7	Austria	BZÖ	0.47	4.58	1	NA
8	Belgium	LDD	---	4.51	1	ECR

NA: Non-attached

Impact: Is far right party cooperation at the European level politically relevant?

The far right party spectrum, now holding a quarter of the seats in the EP, is politically diverse and currently divided into four factions: the ECR and the EFDD as official groups in the EP, and the European parties EAF and AENM. Given the internal division, it is not yet clear how strong the political impact of the 176 far right MEPs will be.

First of all, despite the strong presence of the FN with 23 MEPs, without official group status Marine Le Pen is largely marginalised in the EP. The EAF clearly has lost the competition for domination in the camp of the far right, at least for now. As a consequence, the impact of its members is not likely to be significant for European politics. The AENM, a project of the old FN radicals Jean-Marie le Pen and Bruno Gollnisch with their partners from Jobbik and BNP might even cease to exist.

Secondly, the EFDD is a project which requires further assessment. It is not yet obvious how M5S and UKIP, the two dominant parties in this group, will fit together in the long run. Qualitatively, the EFDD group does not seem to differ much from its antecedent groups Independents/Democrats (IN/DEM: 2004-2009) and EFD (2009-2014). Thus, it is most likely that EFDD will continue to be not much more than a platform for the particular national political ambitions of each of the party delegations involved, and especially those of UKIP's Nigel Farage who declared that he will seek election to the UK's House of Commons in 2015. Nevertheless, since UKIP's success has already provoked a right-turn in British politics and led British Prime Minister Cameron to announce an in-or-out EU referendum for 2017 (provided he is re-elected), EFDD leader Farage's influence on European politics cannot be denied.

Thirdly, the far right group with the most remarkable story of success and probably the strongest political impact on the EU level is the strengthened ECR, now the third largest group in the EP, with Cameron's CP, Kaczinski's PiS, and their new allies in the German AfD, the Danish DF, and the Finnish PS. What will be decisive for the impact of the ECR is how its members will be able to link politics on the national level to common political initiatives in the EP. That ECR member parties are able to have an impact on European policy could be observed in recent events, such as the reinvention of border controls in Denmark, enforced by the DF while tolerating the centre-right Danish government in 2011, the rejection of the Fiscal Compact by the CP and ODS governments in 2012, and of course David Cameron's announcement of a referendum on the United Kingdom's EU membership.

Furthermore, since nationalist tendencies also exist in the EPP – Orbán's FIDESZ being only the most radical example – far right parties might occasionally succeed in pushing the EPP further towards the right, for example in the attempt to restrain individual civil rights. Shortly before the EP elections such a cultural shift towards right-wing authoritarianism was already apparent when two EP reports on reproductive rights for women were rejected by a coalition of the far right and the EPP. This was a surprise since in preceding votes on similar issues the mainstream of the EPP had regularly voted with the culturally liberal political spectrum.

Apart from the larger scale impact of far right parties on European politics, the very existence of these groups is a political factor in itself. Belonging to an official group in the EP is important for many reasons: Access to financial resources, infrastructure, information, staff, media, and speaking time in the plenary are important factors in the quest for political power. For some parties, the EP is an irreplaceable base for the development of political impact also on the national level. It is no coincidence that the leading personalities of several far right parties, including UKIP (Nigel Farage), the FN (both Le Pens), or the AfD (Bernd Lucke) are elected MEPs. UKIP can serve as an example: The British majority voting system makes it very difficult for emerging parties to enter the House of Commons. Thus, Farage chose the EP as his political base, because the representative voting system in EP elections makes it much easier to gain seats. His now eleventh year of EP group leadership is the backbone of his current political success in the UK.

Literature

European Commission, Standard Eurobarometer 81, Spring 2014.

Thilo Janssen, *Die Europäisierung der Rechten EU-Gegner: Rechte europäische Parteien und rechte Fraktionen im Europäischen Parlament vor den Europawahlen 2014*, Studie im Auftrag der Rosa-Luxemburg-Stiftung, Berlin, 2013.

Notes

1 This is a short edited version of an article to be published by the Rosa Luxemburg Foundation Berlin as part of the documentation for the workshop: On the Situation of the Left in Europe After the EU Elections: New Challenges, 22-23 July 2014, Berlin.
2 Zoltán Simon: *Orban Says He Seeks to End Liberal Democracy in Hungary*. On: www.bloomberg.com, 28 July 2014

THE DANISH PEOPLE'S PARTY: A JOURNEY TO THE CENTRE[1]

Inger V. Johansen

The Danish People's Party (Dansk Folkeparti DF)[2] was the big winner of the European Parliament (EP) elections in Denmark with 26.7 per cent of the votes. This represented a rise in the party's votes of 11.2 per cent compared to the EP elections in 2009. The Danish People's Party was also one of the biggest winners of the EP elections within Europe as a whole.

However, there is a crucial distinction between the DF and most of the other extreme right-wing parties in Europe: In studying the development of the DF one discovers one of the most strategically oriented European extreme right-wing parties, less ideological and more pragmatic than many of the others. Other extreme right-wing European parties are doubtless observing and discussing the DF's strategy and policies. To what extent will its success influence other parties in Europe?

Explaining the Danish People's Party's success

That the DF got a quarter of the votes does not of course mean that the Danish electorate has suddenly become extreme right-wing and xenophobic. It would be more accurate to say that it is the DF – basically a populist, xenophobic, nationalist, and extreme right-wing party – that has moved towards, and tried to compromise with, the positions of the broad working classes, rather than the working classes moving towards it.

In keeping with its aim to become an influential party at the centre of Denmark's political spectrum, the DF has joined the group of European Conservatives and Reformists (ECR) – with the British Conservatives – in the European Parliament, and not the Europe of Freedom and Direct Democracy (EFDD), the more right-wing and EU-sceptical group.

Better results in European than in national elections

The DF has less success at the national level, where its support is now 17.9 per cent (according to a 30 June opinion poll)[3] – around 9 per cent down from the EP election result, but still with a substantial increase of 5.6 per cent since Denmark's last parliamentary elections in 2011.[4] It has 5 per cent less support than the Social Democrats and Venstre, the large liberal party, which both muster around 23 per cent support in this poll. The new voters attracted to the party in the EP elections are mainly former liberal Venstre voters and former Social Democratic voters.[5]

As the DF supports the formation of a right-wing bourgeois government after the next parliamentary elections, due to take place before 15 September 2015,[6] it may very well be able to secure a victory for the right-wing bloc of parties, although the party has also recently announced that in the more distant future it might support the Social Democrats.[7]

The DF does not seem to have attracted any EU-sceptical supporters of the radical left, for example from the Red Green Alliance (RGA), which did not stand in the elections but as in previous EP elections chose to support the People's Movement Against the EU, which won one seat, as in 2009.

The explanations for the most recent success of the DF are many, both on the national and EU levels. The most important is the conscious strategy of the DF to capitalise on popular disaffection with the mainstream political parties because of their support of austerity policies and social cuts and these parties' uncritical position regarding the EU. Second, the DF has very adroitly linked this disaffection to the social dumping, or lowering of wages and benefits, provoked by immigration from Eastern Europe due to the EU's free movement of labour. Thus it has connected itself to the general EU-scepticism among a broad section of the Danish working class and many other voters. Third, the DF had a very charismatic and able top candidate in the EP elections, Morten Messerschmidt, who managed to attract the largest number of personal votes (465,758) in the entire history of Danish EP elections. Lastly, a scandal involving Lars Løkke Rasmussen, the previous Prime Minister and Chairman of Venstre, just before the EP elections,[8] made many voters turn away from Venstre and to the DF.

DF populism and real politics

The DF is verbally a very EU-sceptical party, but in reality less so than the Red Green Alliance, for example. It is not opposed to the EU as an institution and system and is not anti-capitalist; it is in fact in favour of the single market but proposes it be reduced by introducing an opt-out on welfare.[9]

Similarly, although the DF voices strong opposition to social dumping, it does very little in reality to counter it and has, in fact, usually voted against countermeasures.[10] Likewise, despite the party's image as a strong supporter of the weak and elderly, its elected representatives in local councils have made compromises, approving cuts in public welfare.

The DF promotes itself as a centre party but in reality votes like a right-wing one.[11] Nevertheless, this populism and hypocrisy does not seem to affect the broad popular view of the DF. During the years of bourgeois rule from 2001 to 2011, the DF pursued the familiar policies of an extreme right-wing party – as reflected in its restrictive immigration policies. These years were extremely successful for the party in terms of political impact, as the DF (with between 12 and 13.9 per cent in the elections) became the parliamentary majority maker of the bourgeois government and used this position to promote and implement their policies in various deals with the government. This led to a serious deterioration in the political and economic condition of immigrants and refugees in Denmark.

It should incidentally be noted that the Social Democratic-led government, which has been in power since 2011, has done nothing to change these policies, apart from abolishing the so-called 'start-up help' together with other 'poverty' benefits, which meant the removal of the lowest category of social benefits for immigrants.

In sum, the main political achievement of the DF has been to become stronger by attracting the votes of the mainstream parties; at the same time it has also been able to move the mainstream parties to the right – especially with regard to immigration policies.

Moving towards the centre of Danish politics

But the DF has also softened its stance over recent years. There is a focused and determined strategy of seeming to move towards the centre of Danish politics, which the DF has deftly pursued for years.

This strategy builds on a solid analysis and understanding of the broad Danish working-class voters, who are generally not attracted to right-wing extremism. By the same token, neither they nor many of the lower-middle-class voters and pensioners, who were among the first to vote in favour of the DF, are attracted to fascism. Nazi or fascist inclinations always constituted a very small minority culture in Denmark. But many of these working-class and lower-middle-class voters were and are concerned with the issue of 'too many' immigrants and refugees, seemingly threatening their jobs or the welfare state. The DF has sought to exploit this reality. The style of the party has clearly become less overtly racist, although for years it had attacked immigrants and refugees, especially of Muslim background, and underlined the importance of being Danish.

However, since the last elections in 2011 the effort to move to the centre has become even more obvious, especially with a new party chairman since 2012, when Kristian Thulesen Dahl replaced Pia Kjærsgaard. With him the party has acquired a new softer style.

The DF was established in 1995 from a split in the Progress Party,[12] a true right-wing extremist protest party, more extreme than the DF ever was. Those who established the new party were fully aware that in order to gain influence they had to create a party able to appeal to a much larger section of the electorate. The DF was not to be a protest party only. In 1998 the DF scored its first breakthrough when it got 7.4 per cent of the votes in the parliamentary elections. After trimming and centralising, and expelling those who opposed this move, it slowly gained more ground. It does not want to appear to be associated with extreme right-wing parties like the French Front National or UKIP in Britain, (which advocate leaving the EU).

Political developments have favoured the DF. Both its impact during the former bourgeois government and now the popular disenchantment with the centre-left government from 2011 have made it possible to attract many Social Democratic voters.

Party membership now boasts a broad cross-section of the population, including trade union members. Members are no longer publicly timid about their membership.[13] A recent study shows that the DF is now the biggest working-class party in Denmark – bigger than the two big mainstream parties – with 26.7 per cent of working-class voters supporting the party.[14] The perspective of the party is clearly to try to turn its recent wins into a stable electorate.

The challenge for the left

The DF's progress, complemented by the mainstream parties' loss of ground, seems to be part of a larger reorientation in Danish politics. The progress of the Red Green Alliance since 2011 – from May to July 2014 it was at around 10 per cent in the polls[15] – is also part of this trend. Just like the DF, the RGA has attracted a huge number of new voters, disaffected with the Social Democratic-led government's austerity policies and attacks on the welfare state. But this only brought the RGA limited success compared to the DF. Therefore the critical strengthening of the DF is clearly a challenge for the Danish left and the RGA.

For a number of years the RGA tried to demonstrate how the DF's verbal assurances of opposing welfare cuts did not match its practice,[16] but without much impact. Recently, one of the RGA parliamentary candidates interviewed together with a DF member of parliament in a Danish daily[17] voiced the opinion that developing a left-wing populism, parallel to the DF's right-wing version, could perhaps help the radical left. But the RGA as a whole regards populism as more of a tactical than a political answer.

There are now also overtures from the Danish Socialist People's Party (SF) to the DF for closer cooperation - for example on concrete issues such as the government's new job reform.[18] SF is politically close to the Social Democrats[19] and a member of the Green group in the European Parliament.

It is important that some of the concerns of DF's voters be taken seriously by the left, and the RGA is thinking about measures to address this and attract disaffected voters who have gone over to the DF. As regards political responses, the RGA is already very critical of the EU – even more than the DF. Developing more EU criticism as such would seem to be important for radical left parties elsewhere in the EU as one way to deal with the concerns and the EU-scepticism of the broad public, which might see extreme right-wing parties as an alternative.

However, since the RGA chose to support the Danish People's Movement and not run directly in the recent EP elections it did not get a chance to fully campaign on left-wing positions, such as connecting its own opposition to the EU's neoliberal economic policies and austerity directly to the opposition by a broad section of the Danish working classes to aspects of austerity policies. Denmark is not a member of the European Monetary Union; nevertheless Denmark's centre-left government has chosen to comply with EU economic policies and the Fiscal Pact. In this area the RGA certainly has an opportunity to reach more of the working-class voters who are presently attracted to the DF. One of the advantages of the radical left is its ability to link criticism of neoliberal policies to anti-capitalism and to develop credible alternatives to liberal and social democratic policies.

Notes

1   This article is based on a paper presented at the International Workshop of the Rosa Luxemburg Foundation: 'On the situation of the Left in Europe After the EU Elections: New Challenges' (Panel: Why are the right-wing parties successful in Europe?), Berlin, July 2014.
2   See the recently updated article on the politics and history of the Danish People's Party <danskfolkeparti.dk/>, English version, in Wikipedia: <http://en.wikipedia.org/wiki/Danish_Peopleper cent27s_Party>. The article also contains extensive references and sources.
3   Altinget.dk, 30 June 2014, <http://www.altinget.dk>, published from the Danish daily *Jyllandsposten*: 'Måling: Dansk Folkeparti redder blå blok'

[Poll: Danish People's Party saves blue bloc of parties] – a poll conducted by Voxmeter for Ritzau.
4. In fact, the 2011 parliamentary elections were the first in which the DF suffered a slight setback, reaching 12.3 per cent compared to 13.8 per cent in the 2007 elections.
5. Altinget.dk, 26 May 2014.
6. Danish parliamentary elections are called by the government, but according to Danish law no later than four years after the previous elections.
7. See <http://da.wikipedia.org/wiki/Dansk_Folkeparti>.
8. Rasmussen had been buying expensive clothes and going on holidays at his party's expense.
9. Press release, Danish People's Party, 27 December 2013. DR (Danish Radio): 'EU valg' [EP elections], 22 May 2014.
10. *Information*, 11 July 2014, <http://www.information.dk>.
11. *Information*, 21 July 2014, <http://www.information.dk>.
12. See <http://en.wikipedia.org/wiki/Danish_Peopleper cent27s_Party>.
13. *Information*, 5 – 6 July 2014, and 8 July 2014, <http://www.information.dk>.
14. According to a Gallup poll conducted by Altinget.dk, February 2014.
15. *Capitalist*, <http://meningsmalinger.dk>, opinion polls of the government led by Helle Thorning-Schmidt II and supporting parties.
16. See *Information*, 5 – 6 July, 2014: The Red-Green Alliance published reports from 2005 to 2008 on the complicity of the DF in social cuts, which the DF was supporting in two out of five local administrations. See also <http://da.wikipedia.org/wiki/Dansk_Folkeparti>.
17. *Information*, 15 July 2014.
18. *Børsen*, 14 May 2014.
19. Until January 2014, SF was a member of the Social Democratic-led coalition government.

THE LEFT IN THE STORM: THE RADICAL LEFT AND THE ELECTIONS IN SPAIN

Luís Ramiro and Jaime Aja

Six years after the beginning of the 2008 economic crisis, the 2014 European Parliament (EP) elections resulted in enlarged representation for the parties integrated in the group of the United European Left-Nordic Green Left (GUE/NGL). This increase was very significant in a few countries where a considerable growth of radical left parties took place. One of the most important surges occurred in Spain. Izquierda Unida (United Left, IU, the organisation created by the Partido Comunista de España – Communist Party of Spain, PCE – in 1986, and in which the Spanish Communists are still the largest component) and its allies grew from 4.2 per cent of the vote in the 2009 EP elections to 10 per cent five years later.[1] This important upturn in IU's electoral evolution was, however, partially overshadowed by what became the big news of election night – the strong electoral showing of Podemos (We Can), a party only launched in January 2014 and very loosely organised at the time of the May EP elections. Podemos, which despite the vagueness of its ideological self-definition had announced it would support the candidacy of Alexis Tsipras for the presidency of the European Commission and join the GUE/NGL group in the EP, obtained 8 per cent of the vote and five MEPs. Taken together, the support for IU and Podemos was the highest share of votes ever received by the radical left in Spain in any kind of election.

    The electoral growth of these two parties took place in the context of a large change in Spanish public opinion, a very relevant modification of the voters' preferences, and, finally, a significant variation in the party system. Ultimately, the 2014 EP election results were part of a political process set in motion by the economic crisis that began in 2008, the implementation of austerity policies since 2010, and the parties' and voters' reactions to the general social, economic, and political emergency, and the turmoil afflicting Spanish society ever since.

The 2014 EP election results in Spain – beyond 'second order' election dynamics

The 2014 EP election results show many striking features. They contrast with the outcome of the previous national elections (2011), and, more importantly, they also indicate a very relevant change in relation to the previous Spanish experience of EP elections.

In some respects, the 2014 Spanish EP elections still fits the 'second order' model. Electoral turnout was low in relative and Spanish terms (43.8 per cent). Yet, despite the fears of a record low participation due to public dissatisfaction amidst a deep economic crisis, turnout was not exceptionally low (in the 2009 EP elections turnout had been 44.9 per cent).[2] Additionally, as is normal with 'second order elections', the government party saw its support diminished very significantly. However, as Table 1 shows, in more than a mere negative result, the support for the main centre-left and centre-right parties, the social democratic Spanish Socialist Workers' Party (Partido socialista obrero español, PSOE) and the conservative Popular Party (Partido popular, PP), plummeted compared to the previous EP elections. In fact, the sum of the two centre-left and centre-right parties (PSOE and, since 1982, PP) was below 50 per cent of the vote share for the first time since democratic elections began in 1977.

Table 1. **Electoral results, European Parliament elections, 2014**

	2014 EP elections, % votes (seats)	*Change from 2009 EP elections, % votes (seats)*
PP (Popular Party, centre right)	26.1 (16)	-16 (-8)
PSOE (Socialist Party, centre left)	23 (14)	-15.8 (-9)
IU-ICV et al. (United Left-Initiative for Catalonia Greens et al., radical left and left-wing Greens)	10 (6★)	+6.3 (+4)

Podemos (Radical left)	8 (5)	+8 (+5)
UPyD (Union, Progress and Democracy, centre right)	6.5 (4)	+3.7 (+3)
CEU (Coalition for Europe, centre right peripheral –Catalan, Basque and others – nationalist)	5.4 (3)	-0.3 (0)
EPDD (The Left for the Right to Decide, centre left peripheral nationalist)	4 (2)	too different for comparison
C's (Citizens, centre right)	3.2 (2)	+3.2 (+2)
LPD (Peoples Decide, left-wing peripheral nationalist)	2.1 (1)	too different for comparison
Primavera Europea (European Spring, left-wing peripheral nationalist and Greens from *Equo*)	1.9 (1)	too different for comparison

Source: Ministry of the Interior. *The four MEPs who belong to IU and one associated to *Anova-Irmandade Nacionalista* are part of the GUE/NGL group jointly with the five MEPs from *Podemos*. One MEP elected in the IU-ICV coalition is a member of ICV and belongs to the Green group of the EP.

Confirming the 'second order elections' hypotheses, several opposition, smaller, and new parties, and parties and coalitions created a few months in advance for the purpose of running in the EP elections, were relatively successful. The centre-liberal UPyD and C's, the centre-left Catalan nationalist ERC, the coalition (mainly) between the Valencian nationalists (*Compromís*) and the Greens (*Equo*), and the left-wing Basque nationalist *Bildu* were among the parties gaining a significant share of votes. This was also the case with IU and Podemos. The growth of smaller parties and the unprecedented decrease in the vote for larger mainstream centre-left and centre-right parties resulted in a new, more fragmented, party system.

However, although the 2014 EP elections in Spain show many features common to less relevant 'second order' elections, its relevance goes beyond them. EP elections in Spain, in contrast to the 'second order' theory, have in fact been characterised by decreasing gains for smaller parties, and the previous 2004 and 2009 EP elections showed a strongly bipartisan distribution of preferences.[3] However, the 2014 EP elections broke not only with the recent experience regarding EP elections in Spain but also the entire Europe-wide record of EP results. As Graph 1 shows, in the 2014 EP elections Spain's smaller parties reached their highest level of support ever in EP elections. Graph 2 shows the relative vote share of smaller parties and larger parties (including the two larger nationwide parties, PP and PSOE, and the two larger Catalan and Basque nationalist parties, the centre-right PNV and the CiU) in national general elections and EP elections. Both Graph 1 and Graph 2 indicate a previous trend towards the decreasing weight of smaller parties, a small and recent change of this trend in the 2009 EP elections and in the 2011 national general elections (when smaller parties began to improve their results), and a drastic growth for smaller parties in the 2014 EP elections.

Graph 1. **Vote for smaller parties, general and EP elections**

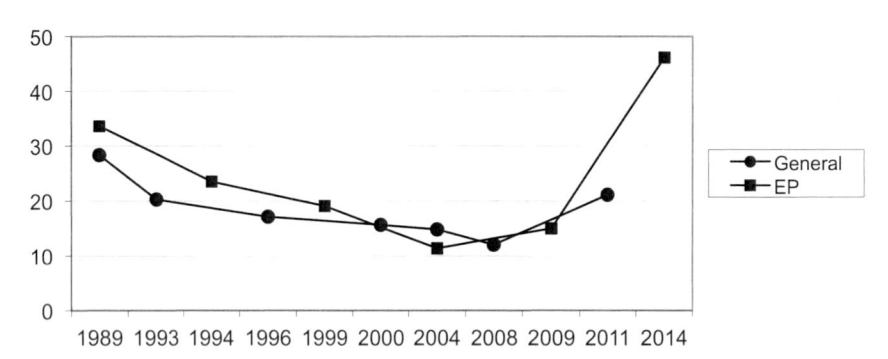

Graph 2. **Vote for smaller and larger parties in general and EP elections compared**

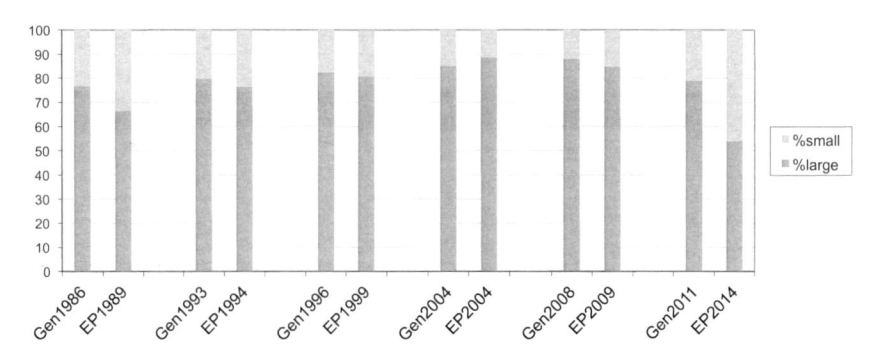

The growth and fragmentation of radical left parties in Spain

The increased fragmentation of the party system after the 2014 EP elections was partly due to the electoral growth of Spain's radical left. However, one of the most striking features of the May 2014 results was that the support for radical left parties in Spain also showed, for the first time since the democratic transition, a considerable internal fragmentation. Two electoral lists that can be classified as radical left gained parliamentary representation and obtained a similar share of the vote: IU grew electorally and Podemos, created five months before the elections, had a spectacular showing.

IU experienced a very relevant vote increase compared to the previous EP 2009 elections (from 3.7 per cent to 10 per cent of the votes), and, leaving aside the different conditions proper to each type of election, its share of votes also grew in relation to the 2011 general elections. From this point of view, IU's results showed an upward trend. Moreover, the support for IU was relatively homogeneous across Spanish regions. Although in some areas IU had a weaker performance, the results in some of the traditionally less 'IU supportive' provinces were relatively high and above the 'usual' figures (with very high numbers, in relative terms, in regions such as the Canary Islands or Cantabria). At the same time, the electoral support for IU in some of its historic strongholds (such as Andalusia and Asturias) was particularly strong. In sum, across regions IU's electoral performance was good, improving its results and lending continuity to a pattern of growth already seen in recent, but different, elections.

However, putting IU's results in the context of its recent electoral trajectory helps nuance the magnitude of its growth. IU grew in the 2014 EP elections from a very low point of departure. Its recent improvement

Graph 3. **Electoral evolution of IU-ICV (PCE-PSUC before 1986), 1977-2014**

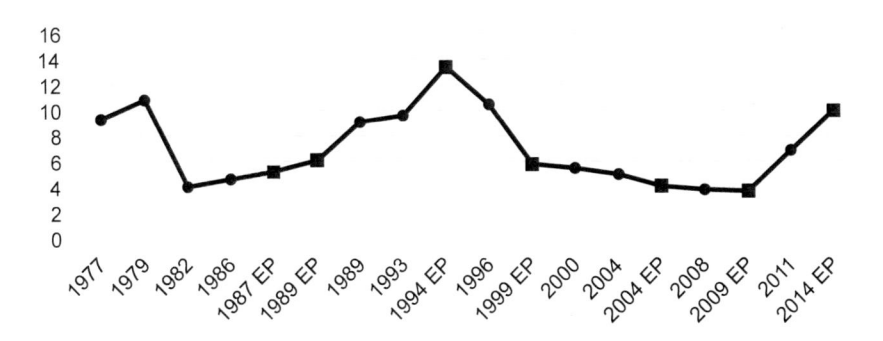

Source: Ministry of Interior

is against the background of its worst ever electoral results achieved in the 2008 (national) and 2009 (EP) elections and a decade-long electoral crisis (1999-2009). As Graph 3 shows, IU grew from an extremely weak starting position, and in its 2014 EP elections results it has not caught up with its highest level of support in the EP elections of 1994.

IU's growth was also lower than forecast by the polls. Leaving aside the very diverse quality of the various polls, and the intrinsic difficulties of predicting election results in an increasingly volatile political environment, IU's results partly occurred against higher expectations. Additionally, the 'intention to vote for IU' indicator produced by one of the most qualified Spanish pollsters, the public institution Centre for Sociological Research (Centro de Investigaciones Sociológicas – CIS), which had showed an uninterrupted growth for IU in the past, ceased to signal this progressing evolution just two months prior to the 2014 May EP elections. To some degree, placed in the context of the evidence provided by previous polls, IU's 2014 EP elections results expressed an arrested growth.

Another important element that contributed to IU's result was that, despite its growth, Podemos was able to gain more votes than IU in several Spanish regions, and in some others it got an almost equal share of votes. That a new party so recently founded and with only a loose organisation on the ground before the May EP elections had been able to electorally overcome IU in some regions was very significant. This was relevant not only because, as Table 2 shows, the number of places in which Podemos overtook IU was relatively high but also because this superior Podemos showing took place in some of the traditional IU strongholds (such as Asturias and Madrid) and in very populated and politically symbolic regions (such as, again, Madrid).

Table 2. **2014 EP elections, IU and Podemos results by region**

	IU, ICV et al.	*Podemos*
Galicia	10.5	8.3
Asturias	12.9	13.6
Cantabria	9	9.2
Basque Country	5.5	6.9
Navarre	9.5	9.3
Aragon	9.4	9.5
Catalonia	10.3	4.6
Balearic Islands	8.9	10.3
Valencian Community	10.6	8.2
Castile-La Mancha	8.7	6.3
Madrid	10.6	11.4

La Rioja	8.1	7.5
Castile- Leon	8.3	8.1
Extremadura	6.3	4.8
Andalusia	11.6	7.1
Murcia	9.7	7.6
Canary Islands	10.5	11
Ceuta	3.4	3.7
Melilla	3.3	2.9

Source: Ministry of Interior. The shaded rows indicate regions where Podemos gained more votes than IU.

Podemos' result was striking for several reasons. With the party founded only five months before the May elections, the results meant they had gained the largest share of votes ever obtained by a new contending party in any EP or general election in Spain. At the time of the EP elections, and despite the frequent and regular presence of its party leader on TV shows during the campaign and even long before the launch of the party, Podemos' ideological self-definition remained vague. Its message made the party resemble radical left populist parties or socialist populist parties, combining classic democratic socialist or radical left positions with an overwhelming emphasis on the confrontation between a corrupted elite (a 'caste') and a morally virtuous common people. Since then, the party has progressed in its political clarification and party building. But a full analysis of its ideology is still pending, leaving aside the accounts by some of the party promoters and founders. One of the most notable recent developments in its clarification of its political and strategic positions is its increasingly open rejection of the left–right division as a determinant of party and political alignments, arguing that this categorisation limits the possibilities of electoral victory for 'anti-regime' parties. This dismissive approach towards the left–right cleavage (which means that the party will not declare itself as left) – aimed at attracting voters ideologically distant from the traditional left electorate – was likely to benefit Podemos' support already by the 2014 EP contest (as we will see later) and is likely to have important implications for the near future.

Although the 2014 EP elections in Spain were not merely the product of the typical 'second order elections' dynamic, they were not a completely extraordinary phenomenon either. The 2014 EP elections could signal a move of Spain's electoral dynamics closer to what is a more general and common pattern in, at least, Western Europe.

In the most recent period many have warned of successive or simultaneous crises: in the capacity of governments to provide welfare to their citizens, the party government model and the diverse party functions, the different pillars of political representation, representative government itself, or even the Western model of democracy and politics.[4] These crises predate the current economic and political crisis of the European Union, have affected every Western European democracy for more than two decades, and have been profusely discussed. They are visible in many symptoms. As to the crises related to parties and electoral politics, these changes, challenges or crises experienced in Western European polities manifest themselves in the form of a significant decline in party membership, electoral turnout, voter loyalty, party identification, party and electoral alignment, and, finally, the weight of larger mainstream parties. At the same time, they are expressed through increases in electoral volatility, 'last-minute' electoral decisions, the appearance of new parties, and, in general, voter dealignment.

Spain exhibited several but not all of these features common to many Western European party systems prior to 2014. Some of them were very strongly visible since the 1980s. Spanish parties have always had particularly weak social links, and there was an important symbiosis between mainstream parties and the state characterised by an overwhelming financial dependence on public subsidies. Episodes of corruption and party patronage were not uncommon before the current explosion of corruption cases, and Spain has been a country with high political disaffection. However, some other features of the democratic crisis were not fully visible or had a minor presence. Above all, the Spanish party system projected strong two-party dominance.

However, the 2008 economic crisis, one of the deepest in Spanish history, triggered a political crisis and a significant change in Spanish public opinion. The public has a negative view of politics, a pessimism and mistrust on a scale never seen before. As the data from CIS surveys show, positive evaluations of the economic and political situations have decreased sharply since the beginning of the economic crisis, and both trends seem to be related.

Graph 4. **Positive evaluations of the economic and political situations**

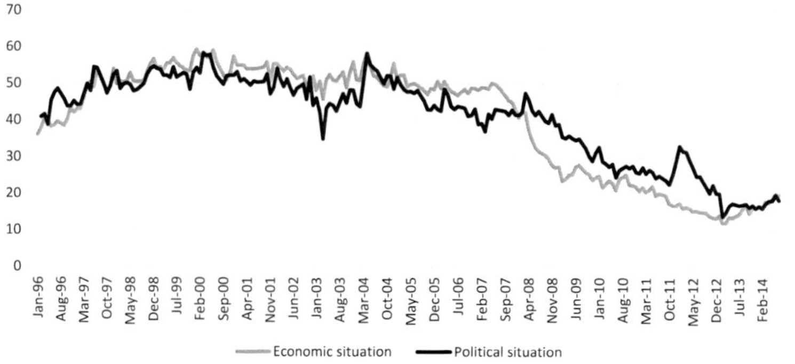

Source: CIS indicators from Barometer surveys

The connection between economic and political crises affected how the performance of government and the main opposition parties is seen. As Graph 5 indicates, positive perceptions of the actions of government and the main opposition party have declined, it mattering little which party is in office (PSOE in 2004-2011, PP since 2011) or in opposition.

Graph 5. **Positive evaluations of government and main opposition party performances**

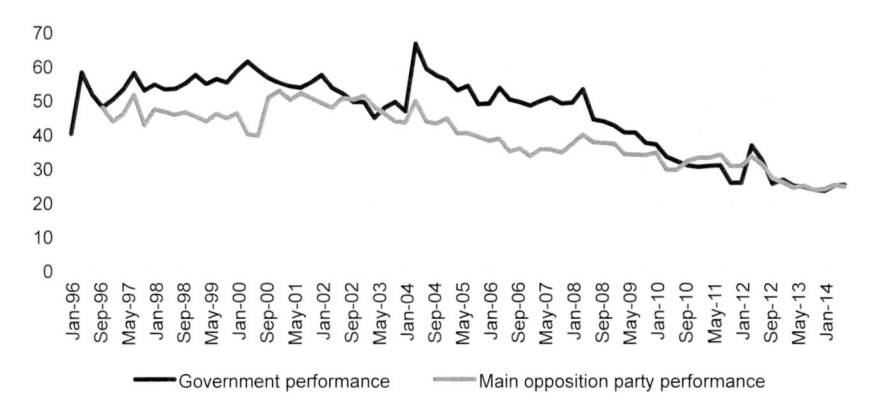

Source: CIS indicators from Barometer surveys

This change in public opinion seems to represent more than mere short-term corrections, with the positive perceptions of the economic and political situations diminishing rapidly since the start of the economic crisis in 2007-2008. Additionally, the change in public opinion entailed a modification in political preferences, already expressed in the 2011 general elections, manifested again in the 2014 EP elections, and, according to public opinion polls, still ongoing. As Graph 6 shows, the support for the two larger mainstream parties has decreased sharply. PSOE's decline began in 2008, before the austerity policies were implemented (in 2010), and it has been unable to recover support despite being in opposition since 2011; in turn, the conservative PP was severely punished by public opinion ever since it came into office that year. While the public lost faith in the capacity of the two larger mainstream parties, the two smaller nationwide parties IU and the centrist UPyD increased their figures in terms of voter intention, transforming the two-party dominance of the Spanish party system. Interestingly enough, the growth of the two smaller parties came to a halt shortly before the 2014 EP elections.

Graph 6. **Voter intention: PSOE, PP, IU, and UPyD**

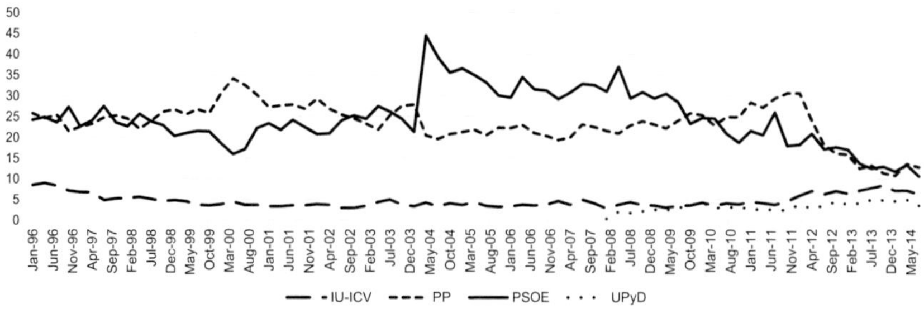

Source: CIS indicators from Barometer surveys.

The left in the storm

New parties, such as Podemos, have successfully taken advantage of the political opportunity structure. Spain has joined the group of Western European countries with more than one radical left party with parliamentary representation (e.g. Greece, Italy, Portugal, France, or Denmark, at different points in time and with obvious differences). Spain also joins the list of party systems where both radical left and green parties are present, with the green party Equo entering the EP. And, finally, Spain also joins the group of countries in which a new and/or populist party gains parliamentary representation – in this case what could be described as a left-wing populist party.

The new political landscape in Spain also points to a new competition within the left in general and, more specifically, within the radical left. The centre-left PSOE, the radical left IU and the newly emerged Podemos – which, even if it does not declare itself to be a left party, can be considered as such – have increased the competition for votes, as well as for activists and other resources, such as media exposure, in the left-to-centre space. The negative change in the voter intention trend for IU at the beginning of 2014 anticipated to a certain degree the limited gains obtained in the 2014 EP elections. At the same time, the strong support garnered by Podemos in the elections signalled the appearance of a new party that appeals to some of IU's voters or potential voters.

In sum, one of the most important outcomes of the 2014 EP elections was the increased competition, volatility, transfer of votes, and fragmentation within the left-to-centre electoral space.

This is clearly illustrated in Graph 7 by the data on the distribution of the left-to-centre party preferred by voters over each position of the ideological scale right after the 2014 EP elections. Voters self-placed in the most left-wing positions (1, 2 and 3) distributed their support among IU, PSOE and Podemos. IU cemented its support with the vote of the more radical left voters (positions 1 and 2) while the PSOE gained the support of the more moderate voters. The PSOE improves and IU worsens their results as we move towards more moderate centre-left positions (3 and 4). As in every western society, the moderate-left (and centrist) voters are more numerous than the radical-left voters, among whom IU was able to win the highest shares in the 2014 EP elections. The strength of Podemos came from its very good performance among radical-left voters while also being able to attract voters from much more centrist and moderate positions, placing the ideological profile of its voters between those of IU and the PSOE.

Graph 7. **Percentage of vote for PSOE, IU, and Podemos in each ideological position, 2014 EP elections (1-10 left-right scale)**

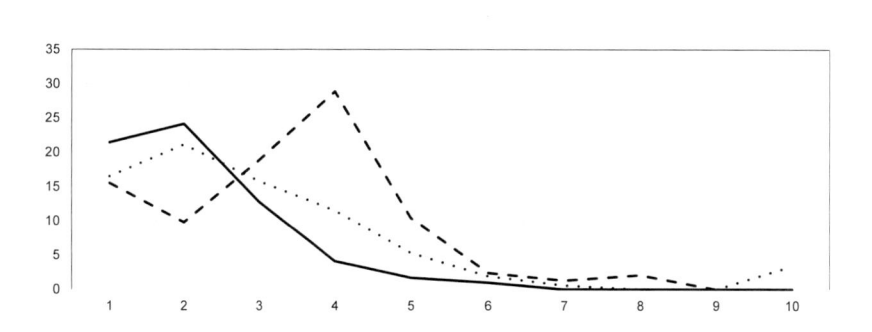

Source: CIS, 2014 EP elections post-electoral survey

This signals the emergence of a complex competitive situation in the near future, in which left-wing parties will be forced to adjust their organisational and political strategies to compete or to cooperate. It is much too soon to analyse the ideology, policies, strategies and electorate of Podemos, as the organisation is still in the process of party building. Nevertheless, despite its vague ideology, or perhaps precisely because of it, it is benefiting from a bandwagon effect with regular improvements of its voter intention numbers in recent polls, which broadens its electorate – and, quite possibly, the heterogeneity of its composition. By contrast, recent polls do not bring such good news for IU, apparently confirming the situation of arrested growth. However, both organisations can anticipate a near future of clarification in terms of strategy decisions. Confronted with their mutual rivalry for votes, IU and Podemos will have to decide whether to collaborate or compete for a partially overlapping electorate in a context marked by a tight electoral calendar; local, regional, and general elections are due in 2015.

Literature

Mair, Peter, *Ruling the Void*, London: Verso, 2013.

March, Luke, *Radical Left Parties in Europe*, Abingdon: Routledge, 2011.

Ramiro, Luís and Joan Font, '¿Una oportunidad para los pequeños? El voto a partidos pequeños en las elecciones al Parlamento Europeo', Mariano Torcal and Joan Font (eds), *Las elecciones europeas de 2009*, Madrid: Centro de Investigaciones Sociológicas, 2012.

Reif, Karlheinz and Hermann Schmitt, 'Nine second-order national elections. A conceptual framework for the analysis of European Election results', *European Journal of Political Research* 8,1, (1980), pp. 3-44.

Notes

1. IU ran within an electoral coalition, Izquierda Plural (Plural Left), with the Catalan Ecosocialist or Left-Green party Iniciativa per Catalunya Verds (Initiative for a Green Catalonia, ICV, which belongs to the European Green Party), the Galician left-wing nationalists of Anova-Irmandade Nacionalista (Anova-Nationalist Brotherhood), several smaller Green parties such as The Greens-Green Option (based in Catalonia) and The Greens Federation, the Galician Espazo Ecosocialista (Ecosocialist Space), the left-wing Basque and Navarrese parties Etzkerreko Ekimena-Etorkizuna Iratzarri and Batzarre (Assembly), the small left-wing party Construyendo la Izquierda-Alternativa Socialista (Building the Left-Socialist Alternative, CLI-AS), and the Catalan branch of IU (Esquerra Unida i Alternativa (United and Alternative Left)).
2. Turnout was 68.9 per cent in the previous national elections of 2011.
3. Luís Ramiro and Joan Font, '¿Una oportunidad para los pequeños?',El voto a partidos pequeños en las elecciones al Parlamento Europeo', Mariano Torcal and Joan Font (eds), *Las elecciones europeas de 2009*, Madrid: Centro de Investigaciones Sociológicas, 2012.
4. See, among many others, Peter Mair, *Ruling the Void*, London: Verso, 2013.

THE ITALIAN VOTE AND THE PROBLEM OF A NEW LEFT POLITICAL ENTITY

Alfonso Gianni

The results of the recent European Parliament elections raise more questions than they answer. Almost all opinion polls and forecasts, even those based on refined socio-political analyses, have shown that people in Italy feel extremely alienated from political reality.

The Italian vote is analogous to that in the rest of Europe, but there are also significant differences: Mainly, fewer people voted in Italy compared to the European average indicating that abstentionism has generally been halted for the first time. If one does not keep the low turnout in mind, one risks overestimating the Democratic Party's (Partito Democratico – PD) approval level: 27,448,000 votes were cast, a total that represents 54.2 per cent of eligible voters, well under the 60.8 per cent of the last European elections in 2009 and the 69.5 per cent of the national elections of just a year ago. For the first time in Italy, in elections of general interest, voter participation has dropped below 60 per cent. Even considering that, exceptionally, the polls were only open for a single day, the drop is still quite significant.

The surprising leap in the PD's percentage – unpredictable and in fact not predicted – is in large part due to this rise in abstention; if absentee voters had not syphoned off votes from other parties, the PD's 2,255,000 votes, though respectable, would not have represented 41 per cent but 31 percent, a full ten points less. The PD did score a success, no doubt, but that success should be evaluated in the context of the impressive loss of votes – around 9,800,000 – suffered by all other parties. If the percentages were to be calculated not based on the actual valid votes cast but on the electorate (that is, those having the right to vote), the context would obviously be very different. Calculated in this way, the PD's votes would be tantamount to 22 per cent of the electors, more than the 18 per cent of its votes in 2013 but *less* than the 25 per cent of 2008.

Ilvo Diamanti, the well-known expert on electoral trends, has concluded that by now abstentionism needs to be understood as a non-voter's vote, that is, as a conscious and willed expression of political opposition without adequate representation. However, the current election results challenge this hypothesis, precisely because the PD ran as the main party in the government. The PD should, therefore, have generated the greatest degree of popular rage or been the principal victim of what has been called anti-politics. Instead, exactly the reverse happened.

The biggest loser in absolute terms, and especially in relation to political expectations, on the eve of the vote was the Five-Star Movement (the movement founded by Beppe Grillo). Contrary to what many of its critics hastened to declare, this defeat is far from signalling the early demise of this movement, as was shown by its next significant victory in a ballot held in one of the cities that symbolises the left: Leghorn. Still, it is clear that the 25 May defeat was a serious one for Grillo. Although sizable portions of Five-Star voters also turned to the PD, they mainly fed abstentionism – as did those lost by the centre-right coalition, the Popolo della Libertà (PdL). No significant voter migration occurred between the PdL and the PD.

And this brings us to the vote for the Tsipras List. It was a success in terms of the reversal of the negative tendencies in the last two national elections, in which the two radical left coalitions – Sinistra Arcobaleno in 2008 and Rivoluzione Civile in 2013 – were defeated. It is rather less of a success if we examine the quantity and quality of the votes in their concrete reality. There were 1,103,203 of them. Taking account, as we inevitably must, of the organised political forces that supported this citizens' list, there were a half million less votes for the radical left coalition than in the national political elections of the preceding year. Many of these votes went to the PD, attracted by the mirage of the 'useful vote'. Others fed abstention. The best results were in the north, with a disturbing loss in the south, in particular in Puglia where the left's votes were halved. The good results were concentrated in cities. Although the urban vote cannot be entirely assimilated to the category of the thinking middle strata (which in any case are in an advanced stage of proletarianisation) and is something more than the typical issues-oriented vote, from the social point of view it does point to an educated electorate. The vote for the Tsipras List also showed a significant component of activist faithfulness, however much this has atrophied due to the poor state of the Partito della Rifondazione Comunista (PRC) and of Sinistra-Ecologia-Libertà (SEL), the former being limited for some time now to the most minimal numbers, the latter in a freefall in the months preceding the vote. However, what is most important is the share of the youth vote. According to IPSOS, 21 per cent of voters for the Tsipras List are less than 24 years old,

39 per cent less than 34, and 8 per cent are secondary school voters. A good investment for the near future, one could justifiably say.

The numbers for the Tsipras List strongly suggest not only that none of the two micro-parties would have passed the electoral threshold alone, but that not even the sum of the two would have resulted in reasonable electoral numbers. This is also confirmed by the regional elections that coincided with the European election in some places. For all of its defects, and they were enormous, the List's underlying project has been successful. Without it the left would have disappeared from the ballots. In sum, without descending into dangerous self-congratulation, the project consisted in the intention to not be oriented to the component parties, basing itself instead on high-profile intellectuals with explicit reference made to Tsipras and the anti-austerity struggle. Its programme was based on a solid critical Europeanism. The campaign – though not without a touch of hauteur – refused to treat the European Parliament election as if it were a national election. The micro-parties were not excluded; their cooperation was accepted, sought, and valued, above all in the first phase of collecting signatures for getting the List on the ballot, which required organisational capacities and traditions that a new list without the parties could not have provided, much less in the short time available.

The construction of this List, as well as the rather less attractive debate that followed around the make-up of the parliamentary delegation, was neither easy nor painless for the organised forces that supported it. Its existence ignited a clarification process within SEL, whose results are still unclear. SEL's second congress, held at the end of January 2014, began very differently from the way it ended. The congress debate profoundly altered the party's initial position, and the majority was won for the Tsipras List, relegating the neutral position between Tsipras and Schulz to the statements of a few leaders.

Even if less evident, a debate has opened up in the PRC, too, which had been incubating for some time, on the fate of the party itself. Because of its decision not to support the List, the Party of Italian Communists (PdCI) has suffered some defections. In addition, explicit declarations of support for the Tsipras List came from parliamentary deputies elected as Five-Star-Movement candidates but who had broken with Grillo. Considering the very narrow margin – a little more than 8,000 votes – with which the List passed the unfair electoral threshold, even small tremors among the potentially left electorate, which on other occasions would be negligible, were decisive for the List's good showing in the end.

This good showing, incontrovertible if the objective results are looked at, makes all the more incomprehensible that sort of longing for dissolution that seems to have taken hold of the List following the more than discussable rethinking Barbara Spinelli did on accepting a possible parliamentary seat. I do not intend to take up the question again here – which I have already publicly called a serious error, not only on the part of Spinelli but also the List's guarantors. I only want to point out that the sense of defeat was and is so deep among the left population – they have to be called this even if their numbers are rather small – that it could not be reversed even by an electoral response that in terms of the timeframe and ways in which it was built is nothing short of miraculous.

Still, what has been said so far is already enough to confirm that a hoped for side effect – which for the future is really the most important thing – of the List's electoral success if not achieved has at least got off to a good start: Right now we are no longer facing the decomposition of the left, even if it is possible to return there, seeing as the 'little family store' mentality – on the part of everyone – has been felt even in the recent electoral campaign and in the succeeding debate. Now we can work concretely to open up a constituent phase for a new political party of the left.

Clearly, every European country needs to construct such a political entity as a point of reference for debate and decision-making in common battles and initiatives to be conducted on a supra-national scale, such as the Party of the European Left can. The reinforcement and renewal of the European Parliament's radical left grouping (GUE-NGL) in terms of politics and ideas, resulting from the protagonist role that Tsipras and Syriza have played, can also help in situations which by comparison are very backward. And among these we have to include Italy, the Mediterranean country in which the left is weakest and must fear for its survival. But only we can carry out the constituent process of constructing a new political party of the left. What is more, it is doubtful that we can look to a model for inspiration. Obviously, I am not speaking of the past but of the present. We often hear people say 'let's create an Italian Syriza', or 'let's do like Podemos'. The sincere spirit of unity that comes through in these statements, the wish to question oneself and start almost as if from the beginning on an exciting new adventure, is clear and very positive. But also too naïve. We have to resign ourselves to the fact that models only become valid *ex post*, never *ex ante*. Certainly, experience resulting from visible errors, above all one's own, could, if there is the intellectual courage to confront them, be useful in avoiding the path just taken from being buried. But not even this is enough to trace a road map. Every route can only be original, thought through, and projected on the basis of the concrete conditions in which one is moving.

In the assembly of the Tsipras List's regional committees held in Rome on 7 June, the expression 'social coalition' kept resonating, often accompanied by 'political coalition'. Explicit reference was made to these concepts both by Marco Revelli and Stefano Rodotà, among others. Both of them, and this is an important point, are motivated to wage counter critique of the insincere and specious criticism made of the Tsipras List, above all by some PD milieus, that it is an operation created by 'big professors'. This conveys the typical contempt for culture on the part of the powerful, or of those who aspire to being such, which has tragic and well-known historical precedents, especially in the extreme-right camp, but not only, since Stalinism, as a system of power, shared this contempt. In reality the drama of the left exploded when it wanted to separate culture from politics, through a twofold and simultaneous operation: make the former sterile and technicise the latter. The aspect of the autonomy of politics which we first have to combat is autonomy from culture, understood as the entirety of diffused knowledge and not as a deposit, access to which is limited to a few chosen illuminati. Perhaps it is enough simply to take up Gramsci's writings. But unfortunately people do so everywhere except in our country, save some laudable exceptions.

We must finally take cognizance of the end of the autonomy of the political, if it ever did exist, and at the same time of the autonomy of the social, since the two levels are interrelated and neither exists in a pure state.

At bottom, it is the end of this separation, which in any case is more conceptual than real, that has determined Podemos' success in Spain and its transformation into a political movement. And it has had a positive influence on the experience of the Tsipras List in Italy – in this case in limited ways and with limited effect due to the pre-existent and persistent history of divisions, often reaching heights beyond the ridiculous, which has studded the experience of Italy's radical left since its inception. To act on a territory like Italy that is neither virgin nor reclaimed is doubtless much more difficult but not impossible.

Paradoxically, we can get a boost from Renzi's scheme of forming a political force that goes well beyond the majoritarian party launched by Walter Veltroni. Renzi's model is that of a catch all party, as many have already observed, a party-government (the updated and modernist version of the party-state in the worst tradition of actually-existing socialism), a party that identifies with and is stimulated by established power, which therefore must preserve itself at all costs. It may do this at times with electoral laws that crush any substance that delegated democracy has (and which makes us yearn for the return of the 'fraud-law' of the 1950s, in which at least a majority bonus was granted to those who had already won it in the field), at times by inserting some redistributive element into the most aggressive neoliberalism in order to garner popular consensus.

To this party of established power we need to oppose a party, in progress, of constituent power working on behalf of society's weakest members. It is a process on the cultural, political, and social level, seamless and without rigid distinctions, not even in the individual biographies of its protagonists, that constructs a new political space, also made up of concrete 'fortresses and earthworks' [of civil society, Eds] (Gramsci). This party must manage to be simultaneously a political coalition and a social coalition, resulting from the convergence and cross-fertilisation of intellectual political experiences and of new movements capable of separating themselves from their own past without recantations, though with substantial rethinking of theory and practice.

It is a difficult course, one that has already led to failure at other times, and is therefore ripe for new disappointments. The electoral affirmation of the Tsipras List and the new size of the European radical left can furnish the anchors and the strength that have up to now been lacking. For this we should not miss the opportunity to expand and provide coalition experiences in the most participatory way possible and starting right now – with great attention paid to horizontal principles of political and human relations, to the need for being rooted socially, at the same time taking great care with the places and moments of the formation of an alternative political-programmatic thinking. And we should pay great attention to that combination of women and men who gave us confidence and have filled us with questions through their vote and their participation in an electoral campaign without any resources other than ideas, passions, and the will to make the left live.

translated by Eric Canepa

EAST OF THE WEST: THE VISEGRAD FOUR

Jiří Málek

The Karlovy Vary Film Festival always presents a series called 'East of the West'. The survey that follows will likewise look at the area east of the West, though in the slightly narrower sense of that part of Central Europe otherwise known as the Visegrad Four – the Czech Republic, Slovakia, Hungary, and Poland (total 106 European Parliament seats – 14.1 per cent).

What happened in this area in the recent elections to the European Parliament (EP)?

Other European countries must certainly have noted the score this area achieved in terms of voter participation in these elections. In the Czech Republic 82 per cent of eligible voters failed to cast a ballot. In this we were overtaken by the state closest to us – Slovakia – which took the prize Europe-wide with 88 per cent non-participation. But the other countries performed similarly: Poland with 77 per cent and Hungary with 71 per cent non-participants. Slovenia and Croatia were also at a similar level. All of the post-communist countries fell below the European average of 43 per cent voter turnout, with only Lithuania slightly above it.

The four states have much in common in their recent history and as a result share very similar social structures. Communist-type parties had governed here; the countries were members of the Comecon and the Warsaw Pact. One could then well expect the political behaviour of their citizens to be similar, and in some ways this is the case – all states that share a communist or, to put it more accurately, socialist past, had below-average voter turnout in the EP elections.

It is interesting though that this voter abstentionism involved all social sectors of the population equally. The proportions between social sectors when turnout is higher in national elections are essentially the same.

216   UNITED EUROPE, DIVIDED EUROPE

Graph 1
Czech Republic: 2009-2014 %

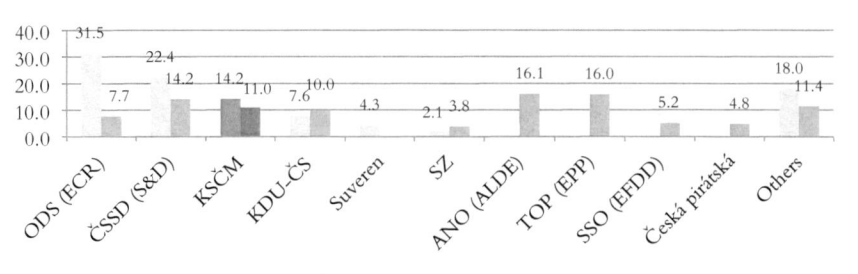

ODS (ECR): 31.5, 7.7
ČSSD (S&D): 22.4, 14.2
KSČM: 14.2, 11.0
KDU-ČS: 7.6, 10.0
Suveren: 4.3
SZ: 2.1, 3.8
ANO (ALDE): 16.1
TOP (EPP): 16.0
SSO (EFDD): 5.2
Česká pirátská: 4.8
Others: 18.0, 11.4

2009 ■ 2014

For an explanation of the EP groups, eg. ECR, S&D, EPP, see the article by Thilo Janssen in this volume.

Graph 2
Slovakia: 2009-2014 %

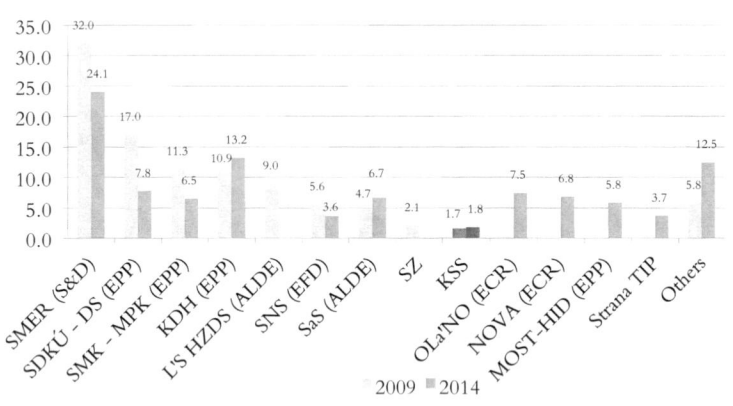

SMER (S&D): 32.0, 24.1
SDKÚ - DS (EPP): 17.0, 7.8
SMK - MPK (EPP): 11.3, 6.5
KDH (EPP): 13.2, 10.9
L'S HZDS (ALDE): 9.0
SNS (EFD): 5.6, 3.6
SaS (ALDE): 4.7, 6.7
SZ: 2.1
KSS: 1.7, 1.8
OĽaNO (ECR): 7.5
NOVA (ECR): 6.8
MOST-HID (EPP): 5.8
Strana TIP: 3.7
Others: 5.8, 12.5

2009 ■ 2014

Graph 3
Hungary: 2009-2014 %

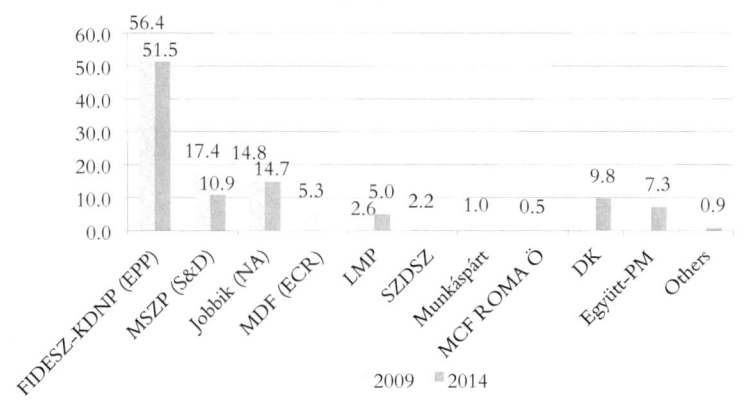

FIDESZ-KDNP (EPP): 56.4, 51.5
MSZP (S&D): 17.4, 10.9
Jobbik (NA): 14.8, 14.7
MDF (ECR): 5.3
LMP: 2.6, 5.0
SZDSZ: 2.2
Munkáspárt: 1.0
MCF ROMA Ö: 0.5
DK: 9.8
Együtt-PM: 7.3
Others: 0.9

2009 ■ 2014

Graph 4

Poland: 2009-2014 %

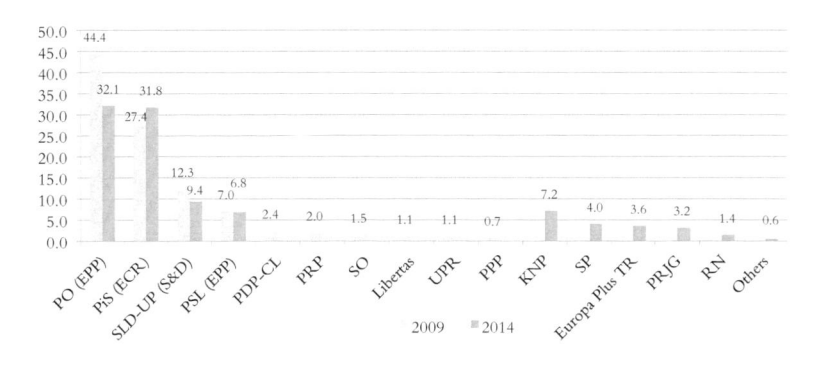

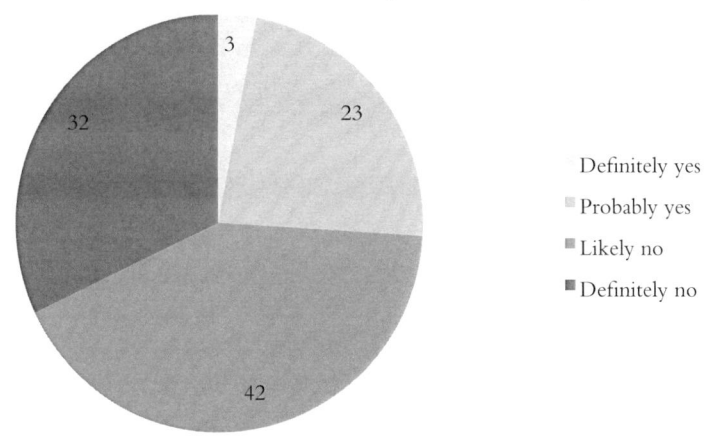

Graph 5

**Democracy in the Czech Republic (2013)
Are you satisfied with the democracy in our country? in %**

Definitely yes
Probably yes
Likely no
Definitely no

There is nothing to support the thesis that non-participation in European elections is equivalent to a condemnation of Europe, an expression of our being closed off within a national, nationalistic context. Citizens distinguish between Europe and its citizens, on the one hand, and the political-economic structures of Europe, on the other. While they identify with the former, many have at least a number of doubts about, or indeed some objection to, the latter. They feel they are Europeans but not content with the contemporary neoliberal European capitalist system, a system that vaunts its democratic character, but skilfully uses every means of manipulating the citizenry to its own advantage in disregard of *demos kratos* (people power). The message sent by non-voters – at least a part of them – can be read that way, too. And why is this more easily perceptible to the east of the West? Perhaps because citizens of the neglected East see certain features more clearly. Just after the fall of communism the slogan 'back to Europe' appeared. These nations went over 'to Europe', but in the meanwhile Europe itself was undergoing a transformation. A large part of the population wanted to be a part of Europe, but did not know what it was they were becoming a part of. And the contradiction between the expectation of brighter tomorrows and the grey reality fed the scepticism and disillusionment of a part of the citizenry. It is important to avoid the easy and erroneous interpretations that are sometimes heard on the left. This is not about a majority becoming disillusioned with capitalism as such but with contemporary neoliberal Central European capitalism.

The actual results of the EP election in central Eastern Europe

While parliamentary elections do enjoy two to three times greater voter turnout in the countries mentioned (CZ 59.5 per cent, SK 59.1 per cent, PL 48.9 per cent, HU 61.7 per cent), none of these countries saw a result in the EP election fundamentally different from their national election results in terms of the political parties' spread. Not even lower voter turnout caused any significant qualitative shift in the distribution of political representation. Representation in EP elections 'copies' the national level in all four countries. No relevant political force either gained or lost ground on account of low voter turnout. It is as if citizens said, 'we won't go to the polls, but we'll maintain the basic proportion'.

It is interesting to compare the situation in the individual Visegrad countries. What differs is how the opinions manifest themselves outwardly, how they are reflected in the political structures resulting from elections.

Let us look at the composition of the legislatures elected in national ballots. It would seem that the four countries could not be more different. In three of them there is no politically relevant entity that could be said to represent the radical left. In two of them (Slovakia and Hungary) there are parties that belong to the Party of the European Left (EL), but these are, with all due respect, marginal parties. In Poland there is not even one party, however small, that is compatible with the EL. And then there is the Communist Party of Bohemia and Moravia (CPBM – KSČM), an EL observer, with its consistent election results of between 11 and 15 per cent. How is it possible? The answer would require a separate analysis, and there is no guarantee that we would reach any shared fundamental conclusions.

We have to go back a quarter of a century. In all of these countries there were communist state parties (with differing appellations). In each country there was massive membership in these parties – the Communist Party of

Czechoslovakia (KSČ) had as a whole 1,700,000 members, with around 1.2 million members on the Czech side and a half million in Slovakia. The political changes in 1989 confronted the communist parties and their members with an existential dilemma. While Poland and Hungary 'set things in motion' in at least the second half of the 1980s, in Czechoslovakia – in the joint state of Czechs and Slovaks – there were no such visible changes. Even Gorbachev's perestroika received a much more ambiguous reception here. On the other hand, the socio-economic situation of Czechoslovakia's citizens was better and more stable than that of Poland and Hungary. In each of these countries the parties and their members sought to set their own course, and in each of them the parties went through a greater or lesser transformation. The transformation consisted of the countries' denying their own governing parties certain monopoly rights, such as a 'leadership role' in society, the absolute dominance of party ideology, or the privileged rights of the cadre. It was also about taking back their own history. In the Czech Republic and Slovakia this also included ways of dealing with people's relationship to the Prague Spring and the half-million KSČ members who had to leave the party in the early days of so-called normalisation. The wave of change and the end of Soviet hegemony at the end of the 1980s had three fundamental consequences for the Central European area: re-orientation to the West, the transformation from a command economy to market capitalism, and the transformation of the system of one-party government to one of free political competition. These constants constituted a basic 'post-communist' political consensus both within the democratic political forces and within the spectrum of public opinion (see Daniel Kunštát, *Za rudou oponou* [Behind the Red Curtain], Institute of Sociology, Academy of Sciences, CR, Prague 2013 – the data presented here rely heavily on this study).

Shared experiences

In Poland and Hungary the post-communist parties accepted the policies of their reform wings. They transformed themselves into 'catch-all parties' closer to the social democratic parties of Western Europe. At the same time, individual bodies of opinion split off. Some of these survive to the present day, but their political impact is quite marginal. Transformed parties came to power in the 1990s as social democratic or socialist parties. Both entered into crises and are now in opposition. It is generally true that the successful transformation of the Czech Communist Party – that is, its cleansing itself of its communist burden, in the understanding of the political mainstream – means its social-democratisation and reformation and the consequent reduction of its membership base.

The process was similar in Slovakia as well. The original Communist party gave rise to the post-communist Party of the Democratic Left (SDL), which shared power in the 1990s. A crisis followed, however, as is typical for the 'reformed' communist parties of the post-Soviet bloc, as did a loss of political positions and voter confidence. Its core moved on to what is now called the Smer-SD ('Direction – Social Democrats') party, which now presents itself as a 'pure' social democratic party. With that, the restructuring of the original Communist Party was complete. In addition to this movement, there were also other post-communist formations, the most distinct of which today appears to be the Communist Party of Slovakia (KSS), which, however, only has about a one per cent electoral following. It is a member party of the EL, although it has lately been almost inactive there. This does not mean, however, that there are no radical left voters in Slovakia; but Smer has absorbed all leftist elements, including those voters. It remains to be seen how long Smer can continue to operate in this way, dependent as it is on its charismatic leader. In the most recent parliamentary elections (2012) Smer received 44.4 per cent of the vote while the KSS won 0.7 per cent. The spring 2014 presidential election, however, saw the Smer chairman and his government defeated; while in the European elections Smer received 24.1 per cent and the KSS 1.5 per cent.

The Czech Communist Party – an exception

The KSČM is a rarity in the Central European area. In none of the other post-communist countries does a communist and little-transformed party play an analogous role in the party system. In none of them does such a party enjoy large and stable voter support. The KSČM never lost the position of a significant and fully relevant political force or the potential that allows it to put pressure on other parliamentary parties.

This 'miracle' has a number of causes. That communists continue to constitute a danger to the state and society, as some pundits from the anti-communist camp maintain, is certainly not true. This line of argument holds that we are seeing a manifestation of 'friends of the old communist systems', who are only interested in regaining their power. A far more accurate view is that in its 25-year development, the KSČM has gone through several phases. In the first period it looked for a new path to the future. There were partial reforms and adaptations to new conditions. The membership base changed too, with part of the original members, including several members of Parliament, leaving and creating new left entities, some members landing in social democratic or even in right-wing organisations. Many of these later vanished, with only the tiny SDS (Party of Democratic Socialism) – an

EL member party – operating in the long term. The Czech communists and their party have been subjected to the pressure of the anti-communist section of Czech society and the new political elites since the early 1990s.

The party's journey started in a ghetto, as it steered an orthodox communist course through a period of stabilisation to the position of sought-after political partner – though it was a party whose partners often had an aversion to it. It was thanks to the fact that its reformation was only partial and to the heavy anti-communist pressure it faced from the outset that it was able to maintain its political position and unity with relative success. The 'centrist' policy that the KSČM leadership has adopted – perhaps more intuitively than deliberately – has proven to be successful in the long term. We must also bear in mind that in the Czech Republic there was no space for a 'new' social democratic party consisting of post-communists (as in Slovakia or Hungary), as the Czech Social Democracy (ČSSD) already existed and had been operating in exile since 1948. At the beginning of the 1990s it returned home where it gradually built up its organisational and core structure until its victory in parliamentary elections (1998). Since the mid-1990s the Czech left has thus hosted a stable structure of moderate and radical leftists represented in practice by ČSSD and KSČM. In Czech society there are of course radical left forces of a non-communist (and sometimes even anti-communist) kind. However, they have never put together a political force of any consequence.

This issue is surrounded by various myths and would-be scholarly opinions rather than relevant facts. Daniel Kunštát's study at the Sociological Institute of the Academy of Sciences presents a relatively detailed analysis of the position of the Communist Party and of its members and voters in contemporary Czech society. Many important, interesting, and, to some, even surprising points emerge from this analysis. Very briefly:

- From the point of view of political science, the Communist Party is understood as an anti-systemic party; even the public sees it as a party that at the very least has reservations about the current system and does not envision merely repairing it. Its policy goal (even in KSČM documents) is modern socialism, albeit very vaguely defined. In terms of policy, the KSČM is seen by the study as a left-wing alternative to Czech Social Democracy. Importantly, it is perceived as such by a large portion of the public, to say nothing of its own voters. The cornerstone of the party's political support are those who were among the defeated in the post-revolution transformation. It is interesting to note that there has yet to be a document compiled by the party that describes a vision for the future – socialism for the twenty-first century. Internal party discussions about such a document are still under way. In any case, the party's supporters neither discuss the concept nor mourn its absence. 'In terms of the political position of voters, the KSČM appears to them to be a collectively organised alternative to the (current) democratic order …' Nevertheless, the KSČM does not endorse anything other than democratic ways and means towards social transformation. The KSČM is not a 'revolutionary' party outside of the democratic framework.

- Anti-communism is gradually becoming stale, and continues to be entrenched only amongst a continuously narrowing group of citizens.
- Communist ideas were never implemented in Czech society as an import from the 'barbarous East', but are a very powerful integral part of our domestic tradition.
- The constituency of communist candidates is neither exclusively nor mostly the 'former communists', as certain commentators are fond of saying. In fact, in 2010 the majority of pre-revolution communists supported political entities other than the KSČM, most of them probably backing the social democrats. The majority of the party's current electorate has nothing to do with the previous Communist Party of Czechoslovakia – the KSČ. The KSČM's constituency is older – 58.6 years on average in 2010 (44.3 is the average for other parties). However, it is civically active – 40 per cent of KSČM voters are involved in various organisations (interest-group, sports, fire brigades, unions, etc.). One third of its electorate are even unwilling to accept the return of 'communism' or any other personal dictatorship. They look favourably on socialism, followed by communism, and least favourably on capitalism and dictatorship. Democracy on this scale is roughly in the middle. At the same time, many of them do not see socialism (communism) and democracy as mutually exclusive systems. They both were received positively.
- The perception of the KSČM by non-KSČM voters is gradually changing. A slight majority of non-communist voters consider the party to be 'totalitarian', but three-fifths of them acknowledge the party has the same rights and obligations as others. There are still two-fifths of non-KSČM voters who think that the party should be outlawed or otherwise restricted in its activities. More than one-third, however, believe that the Communist Party has been transformed into a modern political party, and that it is the only political entity that has not discredited itself. A third of non-KSČM voters also believe that

the party is basically in line with the Czech Republic's foreign policy orientation. Half of them consider the KSČM to represent the poor, and two-fifths believe that 'communists' respect private business.

We are concentrating on the Communist Party because there are not many other left groups worthy of mention. The other radical left forces on the Czech political scene are fragmented and in many ways marginal. They have no significant support even amongst sections of the public that are left-oriented, partly because they do not present themselves adequately and do not offer the citizens a credible vision. On the other hand, there are many left-wing activists doing much praiseworthy and valuable work 'down there' at the municipal level, in non-profit organisations, and as environmentalist or social work activists. Unfortunately, these endeavours have not translated to the higher political levels where they could and should be influencing the processes of decision making.

ELECTIONS IN ESTONIA, LATVIA, LITHUANIA AND POLAND: IN THE SPIRIT OF NEOLIBERAL ECONOMICS AND TRADITION

Krzysztof Pilawski and Holger Politt

Taken together, the three Baltic republics Estonia, Latvia, and Lithuania occupy an area about half the size of Germany. Poland, by contrast, is one of the largest EU member countries.

In other respects too, Poland is very different from the three Baltic states. Unlike Lithuania, Latvia and Estonia, which have to a large degree already experienced the advantages and disadvantages of modern service-oriented societies, Poland still has a mixed economic structure. It has a disproportionately high share of agriculture and a still significant mining sector (particularly hard coal, brown coal, and copper), but also heavy industry and processing industries are particularly important. Poland is now the location for a considerable part of the supply industry for the German economy.

These briefly listed factors generated different effects during the serious crisis years from 2008 to 2010. While Lithuania, Latvia, and Estonia suffered a collapse of their GDPs in a double-digit range, Poland was the only large country in the EU which enjoyed continued economic growth during this period, albeit barely more than one per cent.

The same neoliberal economic spirit dominates in all four countries and the reasons for the important difference referred to here can be attributed to a significant degree to the respective economic structures. Nonetheless, particularly hard coal mining and heavy industry regularly come under serious pressure in Poland; currently, this is particularly true of coal, since production costs cannot stand up to the competition of cheaper imported coal. While Poland is still facing thoroughgoing restructuring processes in some important sectors of the economy and in certain regions, this process has largely been concluded in the three Baltic states. In these countries, there is no industrial work force of any significant size.

All four countries share a common socialist history which lasted from 1945 until 1989, or 1991 in the Baltic states. On the other hand, Poland was not a Republic of the Soviet Union, but rather a People's Republic in its own right. It maintained a significant, if restricted, degree of national sovereignty.

Lithuania, Latvia and Estonia, on the other hand, were Soviet Republics, in which both Russian and the respective national languages were used. In the Baltic Soviet Republics the push by political elites for complete national independence was an important factor in the progressive disintegration of the Soviet Union in 1990 and 1991. Here, important traditions in the history narratives of the countries intersect: the deep systemic transformation after 1989 is seen as an upheaval and a new departure in which the decades of Soviet rule or hegemony could be removed, and the recourse or reconnection to the respective nation-state developments prior to the Second World War became possible once again.

At the European level, it sometimes appears that Poland, Lithuania, Latvia, and Estonia are harmoniously in the same historic-narrative boat. Only a deeper examination will reveal differences which should not be underestimated.

However, that does not change the fact that these four countries generally speak with one voice with regard to issues of the EU's eastern policy, that is, policy towards Belarus, Ukraine, and especially Russia. Among the 28 EU member countries, that fact is hard to overlook. All four of them have long historic experience with direct Russian rule, which lasted between one hundred and two hundred years.

Of course, this somewhat remote past is not the central issue for EU membership, but nonetheless deserves mention here, since it helps explain situations in which these countries frequently adopt common positions not necessarily shared by other member countries. Of course, historical narratives are largely fed within the boundaries of nation-states, but at the EU level, too, attempts are continually being made to obtain grist for one's own mill by citing these contexts.

All four countries border directly on Russia, although in the cases of Lithuania and Poland, this involves only the Kaliningrad Region, a Russian exclave within EU territory. The only other EU country with a direct border with Russia is Finland, which, however, has historic experiences of a specific relationship with Russia based on compromise and good neighbourliness.

Unlike Finland, the former Soviet Republics of Estonia, Latvia and Lithuania are NATO members, as is Poland. All four countries in unison see this membership as an important guarantee of their security and of their national independence. This attitude gained in significance at the time of the European parliamentary elections due to Russian actions in Crimea and other areas of eastern Ukraine.

Even if such fears are certainly also present in Poland, the situation there is still considerably different from that in the Baltic states, where there are significant Russian or Russian-speaking minorities. This is especially the case in Latvia and Estonia, where these groups constitute more than one third of the resident populations. Indeed, these two countries are split societies with respect to many fundamental issues of domestic and foreign policy. This fact is, however, only partially reflected in the landscape of political parties. Recently, moderate forces within the Russian-speaking one third of their populations have in both countries been more successful than radical forces.

Russia's President Vladimir Putin has justified the actions he took in March 2014 in Crimea with the claimed need to protect the Russian population, without even recognising the far-reaching autonomy stipulations that had already existed there. In the capitals of the three Baltic states, this was perceived as a bellwether action. Moscow has long complained about the situation of the Russian-speaking minorities in the Baltic states, often justifiably. The path of gradual acculturation of the minorities to the majority societies, which has been more or less approvingly accepted by the EU, has been only partially successful. One expression of that fact is that in connection with the crisis in the Ukraine, ever more young Russians in the Baltic states have accepted Moscow's offer of Russian citizenship. When Putin thus states that Russia's interests are always affected wherever Russians live, he is referring to Lithuania, Latvia and Estonia.

All these factors were significant for the European parliamentary election in May 2014, even though it was not a polarising plebiscite on any of the currently relevant issues. What was at stake here was the composition of a Parliament for which each country could only elect a certain number of representatives.

The four countries harbour ever fewer illusions about the EU Parliament's possibilities for affecting current EU policy, which is one of the reasons why electoral participation was lower there than in comparable nationwide elections. This is also true elsewhere, however, so it should not give cause for any hasty interpretation that this expresses disillusionment with the EU.

Acceptance figures for EU membership are exceptionally high in Poland, a fact which has not changed, and this is true, too, among ethnic Lithuanians,

Latvians, and Estonians. Surveys of the entire populations of these countries, however, also include the widespread, currently increasingly sceptical views of the Russian minorities.

Estonia

Elections for the European Parliament were dominated by domestic policy issues, and also by the current conflicts in Ukraine and particularly the behaviour of Moscow in that regard. As a result, Estonia's membership in the European Union and NATO received increasing attention. Unlike 2009, there were no major surprises with regard to other domestic policy constellations in the 2014 election. However, electoral participation was only 36.6 per cent (2009: 43.2 per cent) and thus failed to meet expectations.

The six seats elected by Estonians were distributed as follows:

- the liberal Reform Party: 24.3 per cent, two seats, the Alliance of Liberals and Democrats for Europe (ALDE);
- the left-liberal Centre Party: 22.3 per cent, one seat, the Alliance of Liberals and Democrats for Europe (ALDE);
- the conservative Pro Patria and Res Publica Union: 13.9 per cent, one seat, the European People's Party (EPP – Christian Democrats);
- The Social Democrats: 13.6 per cent, one seat, Progressive Alliance of Social Democrats (S&D);
- The independent candidate Indrek Tarand: 13.2 per cent, one seat, joined the Greens/European Free Alliance group (The Greens/EFA).

The Centre Party has traditionally been an important representative of the interests of the Russian minority in Estonia and has a politically moderate, left-liberal orientation with a social democratic accent, so that some observers consider it to be Estonia's real social democratic party. However, in spite of its consistently good election results, it has never been accepted into a governing coalition. In this election too, it took second place, just behind the liberals. The mayor of Tallinn is a Centre Party member.

Indrek Tarand, by profession a TV journalist originally elected to the European Parliament in 2009, once again won his seat, standing on a one-man list. Five years ago, he achieved 25 per cent, which would have been enough to give him two seats in the European Parliament, a fact which was widely viewed as a slap in the face for the other parties. This time, he was able to retain his seat in spite of attracting significantly fewer votes.

Latvia

In Latvia, the continuing conflict in Ukraine, and especially Moscow's behaviour, had a greater effect on the elections than domestic factors. That, too, explains why the governing conservatives were able to win half of the seats allotted to Latvia. A total of five Latvian parties will be represented in the European Parliament. Voter participation, amounting to only 30 per cent, was far below expectations.

Of the eight Latvian seats, the conservative party Unity won four, with 46.2 per cent of the votes. It is a member of the European People's Party group. The other four successful parties, which each won one seat, were: the National Alliance 'All for Latvia!' (14.2 per cent, European Conservatives and Reformists, the right-wing conservatives); the social-democratic party Harmony (13 per cent, Progressive Alliance of Social Democrats group); the Union of Greens and Farmers (8.3 per cent, Europe of Freedom and Direct Democracy group, right-wing populists), and the Latvian Russian Union (6.4 per cent; Greens/Free European Alliance group).

Former Premier Valdis Dombrovskis (2009-2013) will join the Parliament at the head of the conservatives. The country's delegation includes two ethnic Russians, representing the parties Harmony and the Russian Union.

The Socialist Party founded by former MEP Alfred Rubiks failed to win a seat, with considerably less than 5 per cent of the votes. In 2009, Rubiks had been elected to the EP on the Harmony ticket, and had sat with the GUE/NGL group.

Lithuania

Along with domestic issues, the Ukraine crisis was a major issue in Lithuania. Broad sections of the public saw it as a severe burden on bilateral relations with Russia. In addition the relationship with Belarus is relatively close for historical reasons. This is, on the one hand, subject to additional strains due to Russia's action in Ukraine, but, on the other hand, opens up new lines of communication regarding issues vital to both countries.

Voter participation was 47 per cent, higher than in 2009, when only 20.5 per cent of voters went to the polls. One important reason for that was the runoff in the presidential election which was held on the same day.

The eleven Lithuanian seats were distributed as follows:

- The conservative Homeland Union: 17.4 per cent, two seats, EPP;
- the Social Democrats: 17.3 per cent, two seats, S&D;
- the Liberals: 16.5 per cent, two seats, ALDE;

- the nationalistic Order and Justice Party: 14.3 per cent, two seats, Europe of Freedom and Direct Democracy (EFDD);
- the Labour Party: 12.8 per cent, one seat, ALDE;
- the Electoral Action of Poles in Lithuania: 8 per cent, one seat, European Conservatives and Reformists (ECR);
- the Alliance of Peasants and Greens: 6.6 per cent, one seat, The Greens/EFA.

Lithuania's MEPs include one ethnic Russian, Victor Uspaskich, founder of the Labour Party. The party has dropped far behind its former successful results, when it garnered up to 30 per cent of the votes and was the country's strongest party. Valdemar Tomaševski, an ethnic Pole, represents the Polish list.

Overview of the Baltic states

Taken as a whole, the seats of Estonia, Latvia and Lithuania break down as follows between the party groups in the European Parliament: With seven seats, the European People's Party is the strongest group, followed by the Alliance of Liberals and Democrats, with six seats, the Progressive Alliance of Social Democrats with four, the Greens/Free European Alliance and the Europe for Freedom and Direct Democracy group with three each, and finally the European Conservatives and Reformists group with two seats. Only the European People's Party, the Social Democrats and the Greens won seats in all three countries.

The electoral mood emerging from these results is clearly liberal-conservative, while social democratic and green positions are considerably weaker. National conservative and patriotic positions are a factor not to be underestimated in Latvia and Lithuania.

Poland

Since regular parliamentary and presidential elections are scheduled for next year, the elections for the European Parliament was seen by Polish parties as a welcome test of the mood of the country, permitting them to prepare for the upcoming electoral campaigns in a timely manner. However, the electorate did not completely play along, providing a voter participation rate of only 23 per cent, which was surprisingly low.

The current crisis in Ukraine did not affect that, although it has been followed with great interest by the Polish public. However, since all important parties took fairly similar positions here, the hot domestic policy issues were more important in determining the decisions of the voters.

The two major parties, which have been at each other's throats for almost ten years now, crossed the finishing line virtually neck-and-neck. Here, the current crisis in Ukraine may have helped the ruling liberal-conservative Civic Platform (PO). At any rate, the national-conservative Law and Justice Party (PiS) missed its goal of at long last becoming the country's strongest party again. Trailing far behind were the Democratic Left Alliance (SLD), the Polish People's Party (a farmers' party), and the right-wing populist Congress of the New Right (KNP).

Poland's 52 seats were distributed as follows: the liberal conservative PO (EPP) won 32.1 per cent of the votes, with nineteen seats. The national-conservative PiS (ECR) was close behind with 31.8 per cent and also with nineteen seats. The SLD (S&D) won 9.4 per cent, with five seats. The KNP got 9.1 per cent with four seats, and the farmers' party 6.8 per cent with four seats.

Significant was the failure of the left-liberal list Europe Plus, founded by Janusz Palikot and Aleksander Kwaśniewski, which presented itself as an alternative both to the governing PO and to the left-democratic SLD. This is a clear warning to Palikot, whose list will have to fight hard to return to the Polish parliament in 2015.

In the national-conservative spectrum, the unquestioned leadership of the PiS has been reinforced, because other conservative lists failed to meet the 5 per cent threshold, and have since hinted that they plan to approach the PiS with regard to the upcoming elections. A joint national-conservative list would have won no less than 40 per cent of the votes.

One disappointment is the success of the right-wing populist Congress of the New Right, headed by Janusz Korwin-Mikke. This list achieved surprisingly good results, winning four seats in the EP. Korwin-Mikke is a dyed-in-the-wool EU opponent who makes no bones about his rejection of 'European socialism'. On the Ukrainian question, he considers Moscow's actions legitimate, since, for example in Crimea, it was able to implement the right of national self-determination.

translated by Phil Hill

TRANSFORM! EUROPE 2014 AT A GLANCE

Maxime Benatouil

For the last fifteen years, transform! has been working as a horizontal network with alternative thinking and political dialogue at its core. As the political foundation of the Party of the European Left (EL), it has taken an ever more active part in European political debates. 2014 was a year of political challenges marked by the bittersweet lessons of the EU elections. The growth of the left parliamentary group in the European Parliament – the GUE/NGL is now composed of 52 MEPs, instead of 34 in the past legislature – has occurred simultaneously with the reinforced anchorage of the extreme right throughout Europe and with weak voter turnout. Despite the current reassuring narrative of the European Commission and most of the heads of states and governments, the European Union is still in crisis – with very little prospect of recovery ahead. transform! wishes to open up spaces and create dynamics so that a new cultural and political hegemony may emerge. It is in this sense that its two core projects must be understood.

The project 'Strategic Perspectives of the European Left' allows for a transnational space of continuous discussion on the challenges faced by left parties across Europe and the evolution of the political landscape, while the project 'Crisis in Europe – Crisis of Europe. There are Alternatives!' provides social and political actors with thorough analyses of the crisis' multidimensional aspects (political economy, citizens' perceptions, existing alternatives, etc.). In addition, transform! works closely with the Party of the European Left on a regular basis – as is shown by the yearly joint Summer University – but also on occasional common initiatives – such as the European conference on issues of debt. As a progressive network, it also supports the anti-austerity social movements and their attempts to unite at the EU level in a very active fashion. It took part in numerous initiatives launched by key actors of the movements – such as the 'European Days of Action' or the

'Decentralised Day of Action Against Free Trade Agreements' – and plays an important role in the Alter Summit network. Moreover, transform! europe fosters a flexible cooperation framework for European critical researchers organised in different working groups under the name Akademia. Last but not least, transform! issues a monthly newsletter with information on its activities, as well as on those of its members and observer members. The yearbook you are holding in your hands is the first of its kind and replaces the journal that had played a central role in transform! europe's publication strategy for the past seven years.

Strategic perspectives of the EL

2014 has been a particularly rich year with regard to politics. It was marked by the European elections, and their first attempt to lead a transnational electoral campaign with European political parties nominating their top candidates for the European Commission presidency. After his unanimous nomination at the 4th Congress of the Party of the European Left (EL) in Madrid on 13-15 December 2013, the leader of the Greek party Syriza, Alexis Tsipras, gave strong visibility – and voice – to a hitherto little known alternative project for a progressive, social and ecological change of course in the EU. To some extent, this early process of Europeanisation allowed left proposals for another Europe to reach further than the traditional circles of EL parties. The GUE/NGL parliamentary group grew significantly, mostly thanks to its affiliated parties' impressive results in the Southern European countries.

transform! europe deployed its capacity as a European network made up of 27 organisations from 19 countries to cover the European elections in the most thorough way possible, with first assessments accessible as soon as the polling stations closed, video interviews sent by our member organisations, national reports dealing with the new restructuring of political landscapes, etc. A website 'The EU Elections From a Left Perspective' was established in cooperation with Germany's Rosa Luxemburg Foundation (RLS) and the French journal *Regards*.[1]

Next, the RLS and transform! europe held a joint two-day workshop in Berlin on the new challenges ahead for the left after the European elections. With participants from the academy and the world of politics, very important issues were tackled – such as the strength of left parties in comparison with the social democrats and the greens, left responses to the rise of the nationalist and extreme right, but also the geopolitical earthquake in Eastern Europe seen from a left perspective. It was a huge success, and the workshop might become a not-to-be-missed annual event for academics and progressive politicians interested in the challenges for the left in Europe and the evolution of the political landscape in general. At the end of 2014, these themes were echoed by a day of study in Paris that Espaces Marx dedicated to the structural crisis of European social democracy and the challenges for the radical left.

The Nicos Poulantzas Institute gave a new impulse to the project 'Strategic Perspectives of the European Left'. The impressive results of Syriza for both the European and regional elections further anchored its presence on the Greek political landscape, and sharpened the practical questions concerning its potential national victory. It is in this context that the project's thematic focus shifted towards study of the democratisation of the state – more particularly, study of the police in Europe and how the left should address this issue. In the last half of 2014 Giorgos Papanicolaou (Teesside University) and Giorgos Rigakos (Carleton University) presented a Working Paper dealing not only with the varieties of police organisational models, but also with the crucial question of the relations between police and democracy in times of crisis, with possible left responses involving a reorganisation of internal police structures. The paper was presented at a two-day workshop that gathered together criminology professors and other experts from across Europe.

'Crisis in Europe – Crisis of Europe – There are Alternatives!'

The project 'Crisis in Europe – Crisis of Europe' is the second pillar of transform! europe's activities. The crisis that broke out in 2008 has developed into a systemic crisis of capitalism. It has damaged whole swaths of the economic, social, democratic, and environmental fabric of European societies. The severity of the crisis is exemplified by further economic stagnation and the increasingly higher risk of deflation – not to mention the ongoing pressure on welfare systems that goes hand in hand with citizens' alienation from politics. What Europe has been experiencing is not another merely temporary disorder that can be fixed with the recipes applied up to now – reducing the external imbalances, correcting the public deficits, and implementing structural reforms against labour law and social policies. It is a crisis of much greater depth, one that jeopardises the social contracts regulating the capital-labour relation that laid the very foundations of most of the post-Second World War (western) societies, affects their entire political system, and provides fertile ground for the further anchoring of extreme-right political forces. transform! aims to support alternatives, as well as to contribute to their formulation. Alternatives to the neoliberal order exist. They operate at different levels of action – the grassroots level, with the struggle over the commons and social re-appropriation, or the European level, with proposals of recovery plans capable of re-launching the industrial sector throughout the continent while meeting the environmental and social challenges of our times.

In early 2014, the first workshop of a cycle dedicated to perceptions in the crisis was held to deal with questions revolving around the crisis of political consciousness in Europe. Previous research, as well as fruitful discussions between public-opinion specialists and social scientists from Germany, France, and Greece showed that the state of political subjectivities was linked to the intensity of the crisis. The primary goal was to comprehensively study the causes behind both revolt and resignation. It turns out that representations of labour – such as dependence on wage and low-cost employment policies – play a very important role in the mechanisms of resignation. Change will remain out of reach if the relation between the left and labour is not renewed. To more accurately respond to employees' needs and to become emancipatory policies, alternative proposals must take into account their representation in terms of work statutes and production conditions. This research project relies on a combined approach bringing together different social realities and subjectivities related to labour through a dialogue between France and Germany. It is of course open to other countries' perspectives. Beyond national particularities, the idea is to find out whether or not common issues and perspectives can be identified in order to nourish the investigation and formulation of alternatives capable of simultaneously challenging neoliberal hegemony and gaining popular support.

While a deflationary spiral in the euro area threatens its already weak economic health, and that of the global economy as a whole, the European Commission and most of the European Council are sticking to the neoliberal recipes they have been administrating for over six years. transform! is convinced that only a massive European recovery plan will allow us to tackle the crucial economic, social, and environmental challenges ahead. The EU has announced a new policy dealing with European industry, and it is of utmost importance to analyse it properly. The debate on the 'alternatives' (reindustrialisation, industrial rebirth, productive reconstruction, etc.) is gaining weight and relevance within the left, the trade unions, and the academic world. The work undertaken in 2013 within the framework of the Akademia network (for more on this network see below), as well as the availability of new partners, will allow us to push forward our responses for a positive exit from the crisis and to enhance our voice among different European progressive networks: trade unions, economist networks, European parliamentary groups, etc. The new working group on industry's kick-off meeting led to the elaboration of a collective discussion paper providing readers with a thorough analysis of the European industrial landscape and – more importantly – with a set of recommendations for academics, policy-makers, as well as social actors. The paper is to be presented and discussed in a large public conference in 2015.

Initiatives dealing with the commons have emerged throughout Europe – whether involving the implementation of a citizens' management of water services or the collective takeover of a firm in difficulty. It is increasingly seen as a bottom-up practice that challenges the very essence of capitalism. In this, it is not a question merely of 'state-managed common goods'. The 'commons' refer to a set of social relations between individuals jointly exploiting resources in accordance with usage, sharing, and co-production rules. Together with Espaces Marx and the Copernic Foundation, transform! participated in a European seminar held in Paris in on 7 – 9 November 2014 dedicated to successful practices of social appropriation and commons in Europe, as well as to an examination of the self-management of public services. Grassroots activists and academics from across Europe shared their views and experiences on an alternative social model in the making.

In order to contribute to the European debate on the political crisis and the multiple forms it takes, a transform! Discussion Paper on the extreme right was published and is currently being discussed in Europe. The paper provides an analysis of the conditions that paved the way for the further anchoring of the extreme right, as well as considerations on the strategies to be adopted to counter it. The struggle against the rise of the far right is of the utmost importance for transform!, which was one of the main organisers of the Alter Summit Conference in Budapest dedicated to these issues.[2] Also with regard to the multifaceted political crisis, another research angle related to the latest stage of post-war democratic capitalism – formerly based on a compromise between labour's and capital's aspirations – and what could come next will be explored in the course of 2015.

transform! and the Party of the European Left – a fruitful cooperation

As the political foundation of the EL, transform! has a special relationship with the party. The EL-transform! Summer University became an event impossible to miss for those interested in the situation of the left in the European political landscape, as well as in left alternative proposals on a wide range of issues – from the role of Europe in the world to anti-austerity social struggles, and much more. Once a year, at this occasion, representatives from the foundation and the party create the conditions for a dialogue with political and social activists from across Europe. In addition, transform! is present in numerous press festivals affiliated to left parties. These events are unique occasions to relate to grassroots political activists and concerned citizens, and to be informed about our objectives and activities.

In 2014, one of the highlights of this cooperation was the international conference held in Brussels. transform! and the EL brought together economists, civil society activists, and politicians to discuss alternative solutions to the debt crisis. The idea that austerity was not solving the sovereign debt crisis, but rather fuelling it, was the principal motivation for organising this one-day conference. One of the main lessons learned from the rich discussions was that solving the debt problem alone will not be enough to revitalise the economy; it requires developing alternatives involving taxation, the distribution of wealth, and investments in favour of a new model of social and ecological development.[3] transform! and the EL are currently working on a very large initiative entitled 'Forum of Alternatives', which intends to give the floor to actors from the social, cultural, economic, and political arenas willing to contribute to shaping a progressive future of solidarity and social justice. The 'Forum of Alternatives' is to be held in Paris in May 2015.

transform! and the European social movement(s)

The European elections, in a context of deepened recession and global austerity, were seen as an opportunity for the social movements to seize. An opportunity not only to spread the word on the ongoing struggles among European citizens, but also to trans-nationalise local and national initiatives against austeritarian measures and for the establishment of a true democracy – therefore giving hope that a grassroots response promoting a progressive Europe was possible. As the European network for alternative thinking and political dialogue, transform! took part in many joint actions of the social movements that occurred throughout the year 2014.

Indeed, a week before the May 2014 elections, an international week of decentralised action was launched. Under the label 'European Days of Action', a broad alliance of social movements, trade unions, citizen movements, think tanks and progressive political parties decided to take action against austerity programmes and privatisation resulting from the EU's crisis management.[4] The People's Tribunal on EU Economic Governance was one of the numerous events held on this occasion and was jointly organised by transform! europe, Corporate Europe Observatory and the Transnational Institute. It assessed six years of crisis and four years of new EU economic governance measures and Troika policies by giving a voice to 'witnesses' from across Europe and different backgrounds: Greek grassroots activists against the privatisation of the Thessaloniki water company, a Portuguese trade unionist, an Austrian social scientist focusing on the consequences of austerity policies on women, etc. A panel of judges, made up of representatives of the organisations in charge of the event, listened carefully to the testimonies and delivered their judgment on the consequences of the crisis management. They made their verdict very clear: a social regression is occurring in Europe, wrong policies have been implemented, the lack of democratic legitimacy must be confronted, and human rights violations have been witnessed where the strongest austeritarian policies were implemented. To conclude the People's Tribunal, a set of alternative measures to reverse the trend was made public.[5]

Another highlight this year was the European Summer University for Social Movements organised by the network ATTAC Europe. More than 2,000 people from across Europe and beyond attended the event in which transform! participated as one of the co-organisers. Through a major seminar divided into three sessions, transform! europe gave the floor to academics, trade unionists, social movements activists and progressive politicians in order to address some of the most critical issues faced by the European Union: austerity policies and alternatives, European trade unions' response to the crisis, the new political landscape after the EU elections, citizens' perceptions in the crisis, and the electoral turnout, as well as the relations between social movements and new political constructions.[6]

Launched in June 2013, but resulting from many months of arduous work with representatives from European trade unions and social and citizens movements, the Alter Summit network aims at creating a European social and political front for the struggles against austerity and the authoritarian turning point in EU integration. Its ambition was, and remains, to establish a positive force for alternative proposals. transform! has been very actively involved in the Alter Summit process, whose roots can be traced back to the European social movements and, more recently, to the Joint Social Conference. The collective work led to a manifesto,[7] the network's 'common good', gathering together the shared priorities and calling for a 'democratic, social, ecological, and feminist Europe'. As confirmed at its last General Assembly held in September 2014, the Alter Summit has continued to tackle the issues that shake up today's Europe with focuses on alternatives to austerity policies, the struggles against Free Trade Agreements, and the political confrontation with extreme and nationalist right-wing forces.

Akademia Network – an initiative of transform! europe for a network of critical researchers

In the context of a multidimensional crisis of such depth, there is new potential for cooperation between critical researchers and the EL, as well as a strong motivation to build political and intellectual dynamics not only to break with neoliberal logic, but also to contribute to providing alternatives. The struggle for a new cultural hegemony has become crucial in both the intellectual and political arenas. With the launch of the Akademia network, transform! europe is attempting to promote a flexible and fruitful cooperative framework for critical researchers from across Europe towards the achievement of this goal.

The harsh deterioration of the economic and social situation has led to a political crisis of unmatched intensity. Some even refer to a crisis of representative democracy as a whole. Large parts of the European population – especially the most fragile, those who actually most need politics in their daily lives – have stopped thinking that politics can solve their problems or that politicians want to do so. This has produced a very new situation, and it is unlikely that old political recipes will meet the challenges. By bringing together critical academics, social actors, and progressive politicians, the Akademia network seeks to open up new spaces for discussion and will, ultimately, provide responses to the daunting challenges faced by European societies.

At the present time, three working groups tackling issues as diverse as political economy, European history, and science and democracy are active in the Akademia network. A significant number of activities were launched in the previous year, from the organisation of workshops and international conferences to the publication of discussion papers – always with a transnational European dimension. The flexible structure of the network allows for creating new working groups, depending on researchers' needs. In fact, new working groups will be launched in 2015. They will be dedicated to the trade unions and the new challenges posed by the neoliberal restructuring of labour markets, the state of social rights at a time of the normalisation of precariousness, as well as the strength and weaknesses of the European social movement(s) in the making.

Following up the workshop held by the transform! Economist Working Group (TEWG) at the 2013 EAEPE[8] annual conference in Paris on productive reconstruction, a discussion paper[9] was published. The paper aims at putting on the table a single document capable of providing the reader with a synthetic overview of what is at stake in the political and intellectual debates on industrial policy and productive reconstruction, and which studies the position occupied by industrial policies within the European institutional architecture. New issues dealing with concrete aspects of productive reconstructions – such as the role of the third sector (solidarity and collective economy, democratic participation, mutual interests, etc.) and trade-related issues from a left perspective – will be explored in the near future with the cooperation of the Nicos Poulantzas Institute.

The Akademia Working Group on Critical History held its initial meeting in February 2014 in Paris. It gathered a large number of historians from across Europe – from Spain to the Czech Republic, and from Greece to France – as well as the honorary MEP Francis Wurtz (member of the 'House of European History' board) and the MEP Marie-Christine Vergiat (GUE/NGL – Front de Gauche). Given the scope of the EU project, the House of European History, which is aimed at providing a European public history, with all that this means for the left in general, it was only natural that it was at the centre of the discussions. The question of the 'red thread' of European integration was also addressed, namely the contribution of the social movements and the political left in constructing Europe. As decided at the first meeting, a larger conference to take place in the end of 2014 would be the occasion to discuss the dangers of public misuses of European history and to lay the basis for a different narrative, focused on social and progressive struggles, anti-colonialism, and anti-neoliberalism.[10]

As the outcome of a fruitful working process, the Akademia Working Group 'Science, Society, and Democracy' organised a two-day conference in Madrid in early 2014 – together with an important range of partners such as Espaces Marx (France), Europe for Citizens Foundation (FEC, Spain), the Foundation for Marxist Studies (FIM, Spain), the GUE/NGL, the EL, and transform! europe. Entitled 'University, Research, and Science in Europe: Resistance and Alternatives',[11] the conference addressed the disastrous consequences of neoliberal research and university policies – with a focus on the Bologna process and Horizon 2020, the EU Framework Programme for Research and Innovation. Speakers from across Europe and various academic disciplines raised awareness about national resistances and discussed alternative proposals capable of providing Europe with progressive policies. The Working Group is publishing an analysis of an alternative public research policy for Europe – with policy recommendations for the EL – in the current issue of the present yearbook (see the article by Marc Delepouve). In 2015, the Working Group 'Science, Society, and Democracy' will study issues related to alternative energy policies – whose relevance is being confirmed on a daily basis, whether in terms of the upheavals in the geopolitical order or in discussions of how to exit from the European crisis.

Given the increasing significance of the Akademia network, transform! europe will convene an annual Akademia meeting in order to give to the Working Groups' members, and to critical academics willing to come on board, the opportunity to meet, present their work, exchange views, and develop together the frameworks of future joint collaboration within the Akademia network.

Notes

1. <http://transform-network.net/focus/the-eu-elections-from-a-left-perspective.html>.
2. See the Alter Summit theses on the struggle against right-wing extremism in Europe, <www.altersummit.eu/accueil/article/theses-on-the-struggle-against>.
3. See the full conference report, <www.transform-network.net/uploads/tx_news/Benatouil_Report_EL_Transform_DebtConference_01.pdf>.
4. <http://mayofsolidarity.org/>.
5. <http://corporateeurope.org/printpdf/1853>.
6. For the full report see <www.transform-network.net/blog/blog-2014/news/detail/Blog/transform-europe-at-the-attac-summer-university.html>.
7. <http://www.altersummit.eu/manifeste/article/the-manifesto>.
8. The European Association for Evolutionary Political Economy is a major association of heterodox economists working at the EU level, <www.eaepe.org>.
9. <http://transform-network.net/focus/discussion-papers/news/detail/Programm/from-industrial-policy-to-a-european-productive-reconstruction.html>.
10. For more information on the topics and the speakers and a full report, see transform! europe's website, <www.transform-network.org/home.html>.
11. See the short report, <http://transform-network.net/blog/blog-2014/news/detail/Blog/university-science-and-research-european-resistances-and-alternatives.html>.

AUTHORS AND EDITORS

Jaime Aja, University of Córdoba (Spain), works on industrial relations and political behaviour. He is director of Fundación Europa de los Ciudadanos.

Walter Baier, an economist in Vienna, was National Chairman of the Communist Party of Austria (KPÖ) from 1994 to 2006. He was an editor of the Austrian weekly *Volksstimme* and from 2007 has been Coordinator of the transform! europe network and editor of its journal *transform!*. His latest and forthcoming book is *Linker Aufbruch in Europa?* [Left Breakthrough in Europe?] (Edition Steinbauer, Vienna).

Étienne Balibar is a French philosopher and Professor Emeritus at the Université Paris X Nanterre. Currently he is a Distinguished Professor of French, Italian and Comparative Literature at the University of California, Irvine. He is among the leading exponents of French Marxist philosophy and the author of, among many other books, *Spinoza and Politics*, *The Philosophy of Marx* (1985), and co-author of *Race, Nation and Class* (1988).

Maxime Benatouil is a Brussels-based project assistant and junior researcher at transform! europe. He holds an MA in sociology and political science (European Studies) and is working on transform's core project 'Crisis in Europe – Crisis of Europe', as well as for the transform! Akademia Network.

Joachim Bischoff is an economist and co-editor-in-chief of the journal *Sozialismus*, Hamburg. His latest publication is *Finanzgetriebener Kapitalismus. Entstehung – Krise – Entwicklungstendenzen* [Finance-Driven Capitalism: Origins – Crisis – Development Tendencies], Hamburg (forthcoming).

Lutz Brangsch was a researcher at the Academy of Social Sciences in Berlin and from 1990 to 1999 was on the staff of the National Executive of the PDS. Since 1999 he has been a researcher at the Rosa Luxembourg Foundation, and since 2009 Senior Research Fellow in the Institute for Critical Social Analysis of the Rosa Luxemburg Foundation where he specializes in economics, economic and social policy, and the theory of democracy.

Eric Canepa is a music historian. From 2001 to 2006 he was the Coordinator of the Socialist Scholars Conference/Left Forum in New York and from 2008 to 2012 Co-coordinator of the Rosa Luxemburg Foundation's project North-Atlantic Left Dialogue.

Patrice Cohen-Séat is a lawyer and President of Espaces Marx. From 1997 to 2013 he was a leader of the French Communist Party (PCF). In 2001 he was elected city councilor in the ninth district of Paris. In the 2007 presidential elections he was campaign manager for Marie-George Buffet. He is a member of the PCF's National Council. Among his many books is *Communisme: l'avenir d'une espérance* [Communist: The Future of a Hope] (Paris 2007).

Gabriel Colletis is Professor of Economics at the University of Toulouse (France) where he works on economic crisis, industrial economics, industrial policies, regional development, and the knowledge economy. He was Scientific Adviser for Industrial and Technological Development at the Commissariat Général du Plan (a commission serving the Prime Minister) and is today a member of the Economic Analysis Committee of the Regional Council of Midi-Pyrénées.

Marc Delepouve, facilitator of the transform! Akademia working group 'Science, Society and Democracy', teaches mathematics and is a member of the research team Scité at Lille University. A General Secretary of Attac France from 2006 to 2009, he has worked on international issues for the higher-education union SNESUP-FSU. He is the author of *Une société intoxiquée par les chiffres: propositions pour sortir de la crise globale* (2011) and is co-author of *Science pour qui?* (2013).

Frank Deppe was until 2006 professor of Political Science at the University of Marburg. He has written on Marxist theory, the history of working class movements, and European integration. A co-editor of the journals *Sozialismus* and *Z. Zeitschrift Marxistische Erneuerung*, he is a member of Die LINKE in Germany. From 2012 to 2014 he was a member of the executive board of the Rosa Luxemburg Foundation.

Fabien Escalona is lecturer in political science at the Grenoble Institute of Political Studies (IEP). His research focuses on the fate of European social democratic and radical left party families. He is the co-editor of two recent collective books: *The Palgrave Handbook of Social Democracy in the European Union* (2013) and *European Social Democracy and the Global Economic Crisis* (2014). He has worked with several think tanks and websites.

Elisabeth Gauthier is director of Espaces Marx (France), member of the Managing Board of transform! europe and member of the National Council of the French Communist Party. Her latest publication (with Marie-Christine Vergiat and Louis Weber) is *Changer d'Europe,* (Paris 2013).

Alfonso Gianni was a member of Italy's Chamber of Deputies from 1979 to 1986, first in the PdUP, then as an independent in the Communist Party list. Subsequently, he was a trade-union official (CGIL), chief of staff for Fausto Bertinotti (Party of Communist Refoundation), and a deputy again in 2001. In 2006 he became Under-Secretary for Economic Development in the second Prodi government. He directs the foundation Cercare Ancora and is part of the National Steering Committee of L'Altra Europa con Tsipras.

Sandra Gobet is an illustrator and art teacher. She studied engraving at the Real Casa de la Moneda (Madrid) and illustration at Arte10 (Madrid) and collaborated on different publications and media as illustrator, including *Malamag, Rumba Magazine, Peruste, Pez Globo,* Aache publications, *Concepto Radio* and *Ensemble*. She lives and teaches in Santiago, Chile, where she developed the crowdfunding project 'Caribú, Taller Itinerante', giving free art classes to children and adults of Chiloe Island. <www.sangobet.es>.

Haris Golemis is an economist, Director of the Nicos Poulantzas Institute (Greece), and member of the Central Committee of Syriza. He is the legal representative of the transform! europe network.

Cornelia Hildebrandt is Vice Director of the Institute for Critical Social Analysis of the Rosa Luxemburg Foundation (RLS) and its consultant on parties and social movements. She is responsible for the structuring of party research within the foundation as well as the development of the 'Left Politics' project as part of transform! europe. She is the RLS's specialist on issues regarding ideological dialogue.

Eva Himmelstoss is a historian and philologist active in science and arts management. From 2005 to 2013 she was General Manager of the International Conference of Labour and Social History (ITH). Since 2014 she has been in charge of transform! europe's communication and publication activities. Her latest publication is *Create One World. Practices of 'International Solidarity' and 'International Development'*, edited with Berthold Unfried (Leipzig 2012).

Thilo Janssen is a political scientist specialising in European studies. His research focuses on right-wing parties at the European level, left-wing parties in Europe, and social policy in the EU. Since 2008 he has been a political advisor to Die LINKE's MEP Gabriele Zimmer. He is the author of the studies *What is the Political Right-Wing Doing in the European Parliament?* (2012) and *The Parties of the Left in Europe – A Comparison of Their Positions on European Policy* (2013), both published by the Rosa Luxemburg Foundation.

Inger V. Johansen is a member of the European Affairs Committee and International Committee of the Red-Green Alliance, Denmark. She is on the Executive Board of the Party of the European Left and its Secretariat, and on the Board of transform!danmark.

Anej Korsika is a PhD. candidate at the Faculty of Arts of the University of Ljubljana. He has been active in various student struggles. From 2007 to 2009 he was the president of Polituss, an association of political science students. He is a member of the editorial board of the magazine *Borec* [Fighter], a member of the Institute for Labour Studies, and a secretary for international affairs of the Slovenian parliamentary party Initiative for Democratic Socialism in the United Left coalition.

Steffen Lehndorff is an economist and research fellow at the Institut Arbeit und Qualifikation [Institute for Work, Skills, and Training] at the University of Duisburg/Essen, Germany. His research focuses on employment relations and working time at organisational, national, and international levels, as well as comparative research into European employment models and industrial relations systems < http://www.iaq.uni-due.de/personal/maseite.php?mid=005>.

Jiří Málek graduated from The Institute of Chemical Technology in Prague. He was active in the youth movement and in the Communist Party and was in charge of education, universities, and academic science for the municipality of Prague. After 1990 he was active in private business and then in the Party of Democratic Socialism. He is a chairman of the managing board of the Society for European Dialogue (SPED).

Bernhard Müller is a German sociologist and Co-editor of the monthly *Sozialismus* in Hamburg. His latest book is *Erosion der gesellschaftlichen Mitte: Mythen über die Mittelschicht, Zerklüftung der Lohnarbeit, Prekarisierung und Armut, Abstiegsängste* [Erosion of the Societal Middle: Myths About the Middle Stratum, the Fragmenting of Wage Labour, Precarisation and Poverty, and Fear of Downward Mobility] (Hamburg 2013).

Krzysztof Pilawski has been a journalist in Poland since the mid-1980s. From 1992 to 2002 he worked as a correspondent for the Polish newspaper *Trybuna* in Moscow, before becoming its editor, which he remained until

2006. He is now working as a freelance publicist and journalist, dealing mainly with issues of political history in Poland and other countries in the region. He has authored and edited numerous books, including the 2005 publication *Skąd się biorą komuniści* [Where Do Communists Come From?].

Holger Politt has been collaborating with the Rosa Luxemburg Foundation since 2002 and heading the foundation's Warsaw office from 2002 to 2009. Since 2010 his main focus has been Rosa Luxemburg's work concerning Poland, culminating in publications such as *Autonomy and the Question of Nationality* (2012) and various texts on anti-Semitism as well as on the 1905/06 revolution (2014).

Luís Ramiro, Department of Politics and International Relations, University of Leicester, UK, studies political behaviour, organisations, and parties. He has published extensively on these topics, including three books on Spanish and European parties. His articles have appeared in journals such as *The Journal of Communist and Post-Communist Studies*, *South European Society and Politics*, *Mobilization,* and *Party Politics*.

Alexis Tsipras is the leader of the opposition in Greece and of the Coalition of the Radical Left (Syriza). He is also Vice President of the Party of the European Left and was its candidate for the Presidency of the European Commission in the 2014 European Parliament election.

Mathieu Vieira is a PhD. candidate in political science at Grenoble and the Brussels Free University. He is co-author of *European Social Democracy During the Global Economic Crisis: Renovation or Resignation?* (2014), and Co-editor of *The Palgrave Handbook of Social Democracy in the European Union* (2013) and of *Une droitisation de la classe ouvrière en Europe?* (Paris 2012).

transform! european network for alternative thinking and political dialogue

www.transform-network.net
email: office@transform-network.net

transform!europe ASBL
No 0890.414.864
Square de Meeûs 25
1000 Brussels, Belgium

Working address:
Gusshausstraße 14/3
1040 Wien, Austria

Members and observers

Austria
transform!at
www.transform.or.at
email: office@transform.or.at

Belgium
Cultural Association Joseph Jacquemotte (ACJJ)
www.acjj.be
email: acjj@skynet.be

Catalonia
Alternative Foundation
www.fundacioalternativa.cat
email: info@fundacioalternativa.cat

Cyprus

Research Institute PROMITHEAS★
www.inep.org.cy
email: info@inep.org.cy

Czech Republic

Society for European Dialogue (SPED)
email: malek_j@cbox.cz

Denmark

transform!danmark
www.transformdanmark.dk
email: kontakt@transformdanmark.dk

Finland

Left Forum
www.vasemmistofoorumi.fi
email: ruurik.holm@vasemmistofoorumi.fi

Democratic Civic Association (DCA / DSL)★
www.desili.fi
email: dsl@kolumbus.fi

France

Espaces Marx
www.espaces-marx.net
email: espaces_marx@internatif.org

Foundation Copernic★
www.fondation-copernic.org
email: fondation.copernic@fondation-copernic.org

Foundation Gabriel Péri★
www.gabrielperi.fr
email: fondation@gabrielperi.fr

Germany

Journal *Sozialismus*
www.sozialismus.de
email: redaktion@sozialismus.de

Rosa Luxemburg Foundation
www.rosalux.de
email: info@rosalux.de

Institute for Social, Ecological and Economic Studies (ISW)
www.isw-muenchen.de
email: isw_muenchen@t-online.de

Greece

Nicos Poulantzas Institute (NPI)
www.poulantzas.gr
email: info@poulantzas.gr

Italy

transform! italia
transformitalia.wordpress.com
email: roberto.morea@gmail.com

Cultural Association Punto Rosso★
www.puntorosso.it
email: info@puntorosso.it

Luxembourg

Transform! Luxembourg
www.transform.lu
email: info@transform.lu

Moldova

Transform! Moldova★
email: transformmoldova@gmail.com

Norway

Manifesto Foundation★
manifestanalyse.no
email: post@manifestanalyse.no

Portugal

Cultures of Labour and Socialism CUL:TRA
cultra.pt
email: info@cultra.pt

Romania

Association for the Development of the Romanian Social Forum★
www.forumulsocialroman.ro
email: pedroxma@yahoo.com

Slovenia

Institute for Labour Studies★
www.dpu.si
email: info@delavske-studije.si

Spain

Foundation for Marxist Studies
www.fim.org.es
email: info@fim.org.es

Europe of Citizens Foundation (FEC)
www.fundacioneuropadelosciudadanos.eu
email: tecnicodeproyectos@fundacioneuropadelosciudadanos.eu

Sweden

Center for Marxist Social Studies
www.cmsmarx.org
email: cms@cmsmarx.org

Turkey

Social Investigations and Cultural Development Foundation (TAKSAV)★
www.taksav.org
email: istanbul@taksav.org

★ *Observers*